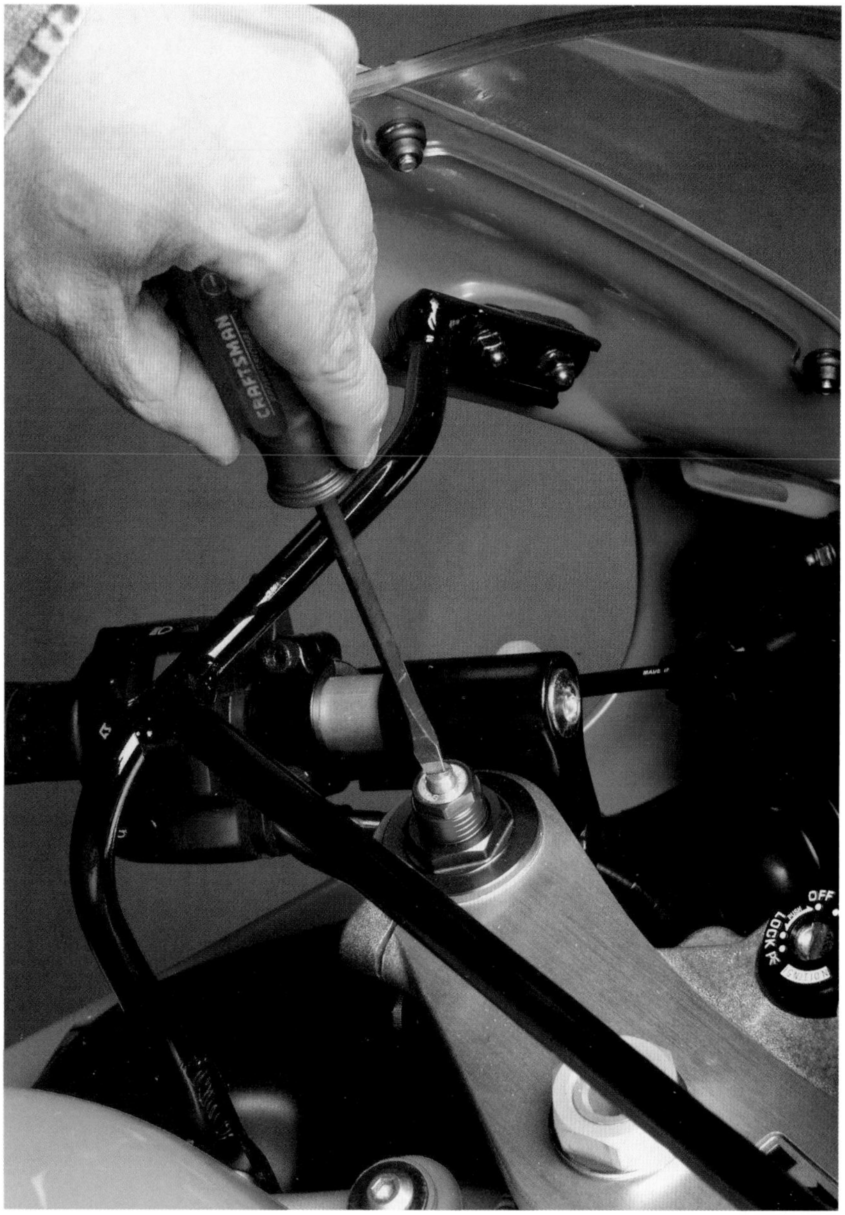
CRAFTSMAN
OFF
LOCK

How To Repair Your
Motorcycle

Charles Everitt

First published in 2007 by Motorbooks, an imprint of MBI Publishing Company, 400 First Avenue North, Suite 300, Minneapolis, MN 55401 USA

Motorbooks titles are also available at discounts in bulk quantity for industrial or sales-promotional use. For details write to Special Sales Manager at MBI Publishing Company, 400 First Avenue North, Suite 300, Minneapolis, MN 55401 USA.

To find out more about our books, join us online at www.motorbooks.com.

ISBN: 978-0-7603-3137-8

Editor: Lee Klancher
Designer: Sara Holle

Printed in China

Library of Congress Cataloging-in-Publication Data

Everitt, Charles.
  How to repair your motorcycle / by Charles Everitt.
    p. cm.
  Includes index.
  ISBN: 978-0-7603-3137-8 (softbound)
  1. Motorcycles—Maintenance and repair. I. Title.
TL444.E94 2007
629.28'775—dc22
                2007030874

Photo courtesy of Motorcyclist *magazine/Kevin Wing*

About the author
Charles Everitt has been riding and working on motorcycles for nearly four decades. His first bike, a 1969 Bultaco, provided an excellent apprenticeship in all the things that could go wrong on a motorcycle.

While getting his journalism degree, Everitt worked as a line mechanic in a variety of motorcycle shops. After graduating, he spent 25 years, on staff or as a contributor, writing tech articles, road tests, features, and other stories for virtually every major street-bike magazine in the United States, including *Cycle Guide*, *Cycle World*, *Cycle*, *Motorcyclist*, *Rider*, and others.

Although Everitt currently shares a hovel in Beverly Hills, California, with his wife, Kathryn, he hastens to point out he most definitely is not rich.

On the front cover
Main image: Replacing your bike's original rubber brake lines with stainless steel lines is a simple and highly effective improvement. *Evans Brasfield*
Small image: Any chain-drive motorcycle will eventually need to have the front and rear sprockets replaced. *Evans Brasfield*

All illustrations copyright © Hector Cademartori, 2007

Photography contributed by Evans Brasfield, Jeff Hackett, Lee Klancher, and Kenna Love

Project text contributed by Evans Brasfield, Kip Woodring, and Mark Zimmerman

Contents

Introduction

When it comes to learning how to repair or maintain your motorcycle, everybody has to start somewhere. No one is born with a complete working knowledge of a motorcycle's seemingly infinite complexities and peculiarities, no more than they're born with a similar knowledge of all algorithms, the final digit of pi, or how cats purr.

For the first quandary, *How to Repair Your Motorcycle* is a good place to start. Why? Largely because it was written as a ground-level entry into how a motorcycle's various systems work. Selfishly, I also hoped that by writing this book it might also foster a deeper connection between you and your motorcycle, whether it was an intellectual one because of your greater understanding of how things work, or an emotional one because the book provided you with a measure of self-sufficiency.

You'll find far more technical, scholarly tomes available, and if after reading *How to Repair Your Motorcycle* they pique your interest, I heartily recommend them. They'll further your understanding of what is, to many of us, a life's work in progress. Of course, if there's simply no connection, intellectual or emotional, between you and your motorcycle, then by all means save your money.

However you connect with your machine, this book will be of value to you because it offers a multitude of ways to keep your scoot in absolute A-1 running order and condition. Perhaps, in lieu of emotional or intellectual rewards, simply saving money will do.

Whatever your reasons for picking up this book, it will function best as a companion to your bike's service manual. *How to Repair Your Motorcycle* covers the generalities of procedure; the service manual covers the specifics. It's not that all motorcycles are so terribly different. It's just that each manufacturer has its own way of doing things (such as building motorcycles) and of wanting them done (such as maintenance and repair).

As I mentioned earlier, my fondest hope for this book is that it helps make your motorcycle riding and ownership more complete and more enjoyable through better understanding. I also hope it helps you see that your motorcycle is an incredible technological marvel—compared to a family sedan, your bike is pure Space Shuttle tech. And, lastly, I hope this book makes owning, riding, and caring for your bike—essentially, the journey of *really* becoming a motorcyclist—as rich and rewarding as it has been for me.

Chapter 1

Basics and Troubleshooting

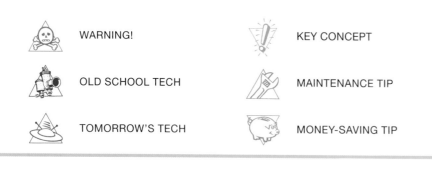

WARNING!

OLD SCHOOL TECH

TOMORROW'S TECH

KEY CONCEPT

MAINTENANCE TIP

MONEY-SAVING TIP

Modern motorcycles' sheer sophistication has given them near-telepathic handling, phenomenal speed, and mind-bending acceleration that enthralls riders with the merest whiff of throttle. Such sophistication and capabilities can intimidate new riders when it comes to the simplest of maintenance procedures.

The fundamental purpose of this book is to assist such riders, as well as those returning to motorcycling, to learn how to maintain their bikes with a measure of confidence, rather than regard their two-wheeled rocket with the same uncomprehending gaze of a seagull staring at a Saturn V.

As high-tech as today's motorcycles are, they still have two wheels and tires, an engine and transmission, plus suspension, brake, and steering systems. If you can invest roughly half as much time as your nephew spends playing on his Wii, you'll learn how each of your bike's systems work, as well as how to diagnose and troubleshoot problems with each of those systems. No, this book won't make you a master mechanic, but you'll be able to communicate with two-wheel professionals and not sound like a rookie. Plus—should you choose to—you'll be able to maintain, service, and repair many of these systems.

Each chapter deals with a major system in depth, and the troubleshooting guides help you identify and confirm specific problems. If your motorcycle starts to behave differently, recognize that could be the start of something big—as in expensive to repair. Use your eyes, ears, nose, and hands to identify what's happening, whether it's

potentially serious, what might be the cause, how to confirm the diagnosis, how to fix the problem—and whether to fix it yourself or take it to a pro.

Hopefully this book will take the question marks out of motorcycle ownership. By using this book as a dynamic reference, you'll know how to identify what might be wrong, what needs to be done to fix it, and how much it will cost.

It might help to view this book as you would a savings account: Invest your time and energy toward understanding your motorcycle, and the return on that investment will not only be significant savings, but potentially far more fun.

And in today's world, we can certainly all use more of that.

THE ICONS

This book uses six different icons to call attention to important parts of the text and to make it easier for you to find the information you need to get your motorcycle back on the road.

The icons are as follows:

Warning!

This is to alert you to dangerous chemicals or practices that you need to know about while doing a procedure.

Old School Tech

Technical information that concerns older bikes is flagged with this icon. If you are a bottom-line person, you can probably skip past this. If you are interested in history or have an older motorcycle, this information is for you.

Tomorrow's Tech

There is also information on emerging technologies. This probably won't apply to your bike today, but it might down the road.

Key Concept

Bottom-line explanations of how things work or how to fix things. If you want to quickly understand a system or process, turn to these.

Maintenance Tip

Tips on maintaining your bike's systems are marked with this icon. But you probably already figured that out.

Money-Saving Tip

These tips deal with shifting your money from motorcycle maintenance to more worthy causes.

The Projects

This book contains 50 projects that most mechanically minded people can do at home. Some are very simple and can be done by most anyone, while others are a little more complex. You'll find step-by-step photographs of each, along with a chart that tells you how hard the task

is to perform (Talent), what tools and parts you'll need, the benefit, and a relative cost rating, with one dollar sign roughly equaling $100.

Note that a few of the projects are Harley-Davidson-specific, as they apply particularly well to those motorcycles.

The Troubleshooting Charts

These simple charts will give you some basic guidelines to follow if you have trouble with your motorcycle. These were put together to give you enough information to maybe try some simple fixes at home and, once you've done what most people can do at home, you can take it to your mechanic and have an idea what's going wrong.

KNOW YOUR MOTORCYCLE

Before you get to start twirling wrenches around your bike, you might want to expend a little time and energy to get to know your bike—how it operates, what it needs in terms of maintenance, and how to deal with any problems that arise. The easiest way to find all this information is in the owner's manual that comes with every new bike.

Truth is, reading the owner's manual is one of the most important things you can bring to the bike ownership experience. And it's one of the best ways to throw a rope around the expenses associated with owning and maintaining a motorcycle.

What's more, the getting-to-know-you procedure is worthwhile, whether it's your first motorcycle or your 101st. Almost every manufacturer has its own design conventions—or idiosyncratic quirks—such as Honda's insistence on using a dipstick to check engine oil level after other makers had gone to the arguably more convenient sight glass.

Overall, though, for the most basic information—tire pressures; maximum weight capacity; location of important items, such as fluid reservoirs, suspension adjustments, the toolkit, etc.; how to fix a flat—the owner's manual provides you with almost every piece of information you'll need to be a happy owner.

In addition to all the useful operating tips to help you get the most from your motorcycle, this little bible also covers all the maintenance requirements and intervals, identifies other owner-accessible components, and explains the myriad warning lights and what you should do if they come on while you're riding.

What's more, the manual can give you crucial detail information into many of the procedures presented here,

preventive maintenance—not a particularly Western concept, but one that's far cheaper than fixing things after they've failed. In fact, preventive maintenance will all but eliminate such unexpected breakdowns, and will give you a far better understanding of how your motorcycle—all motorcycles—work.

To start with, you'll need to come up with a workspace of some sort. It needs to be indoors, clean, and dry. It ought to be at least big enough to swing a cat, and have good light and ventilation, a concrete or tarmac floor, electricity, and a work bench. It should be sufficiently secure so you can stop in the middle of a task and take a break, get some more parts or advice (both inevitabilities), or—heaven forbid—return to your day job. If at all possible, make it *inviting*. Put in a space heater for winter, tack up some posters if you like, tile the floor if you're particularly bucks-up. You're going to spend what should be enjoyable time there; it's your workspace, and it shouldn't resemble a Turkish prison cell.

Then you'll want to get an official service manual from your bike's manufacturer. Yes, times have changed for the better. Third-party service manuals are not the two-wheel equivalent of *The Necronomicon* they once were. Still, you're better off with the manufacturer's version; they built the bike, after all.

Every motorcycle is slightly different, and the service manual will provide invaluable specifics, such as how to actually **get** to parts on your particular bike that need service, as well as tolerances, gaps, thicknesses, runouts, and so on. Perhaps one of the most useful things it will have, apart from specialized service procedures, is torque values for almost every fastener on your motorcycle. The importance of this information will become clearer as you get further along with the projects herein.

Once you've got your space and your service manual, you're ready for a great rite of passage for every motorcyclist; the acquisition of tools. While other primates have opposing thumbs and lower-order animals have learned to use tools, surely one of the highest expressions of humanity is the hand holding a Snap-on wrench.

such as the correct amount of slack you want when adjusting the chain. It can even provide you with insight into how expensive your bike will be to maintain and own, based on the required maintenance schedule.

Lastly, your simple owner's manual used to be the source of some unexpected linguistic gems. For instance, a Spanish motorcycle's owner's manual from the late 1960s contained a warning that went, roughly, "If you are a person of unusual strength, do not engage in a test of will with the nuts and bolts on this motorcycle." In other words, don't go stripping the fasteners left and right, you dummy.

A 1962 Honda manual allegedly contained these words of wisdom: "Give big space to the festive dog that makes sport in roadway. Avoid entanglement of dog with wheel spokes." There was also: "Go soothingly on the grease mud, as there lurks the skid demon."

Sadly, in these modern, PC times, such gems are all but impossible to find. But if you don't read the owner's manual, you'll never know.

WHAT YOU NEED IN A HOME SHOP

You've probably already figured out one of the best ways to save money servicing your motorcycle is the DIY—do it yourself—method. Dealerships and independent shops charge up to $100 per hour or more for service labor. Replace that with your own labor and you'll make a considerable saving. This book has 50 projects most people can do at home, showing you step-by-step ways to save time and money on your bike. A good portion of them are

While many consider Snap-on Tools the gold standard, several reputable brands offer equal service, if not equal status. One of Snap-on's greatest claims to fame has been that its tools are guaranteed for life, and replaced virtually without question. However, several other manufacturers, including Cornwell, Craftsman, Kobalt, Husky, Mac, Pittsburgh, and Northern can make the same claim.

> 🐷 The single most important piece of tool-buying advice you'll get is to buy the best tools you can afford. Their fit, function, and feel will be superior, and they'll make tasks far easier and enjoyable than low-ball tools. This doesn't mean you should even consider selling your offspring into slavery just to buy tools. But definitely do not Scrooge out on tools either. Purchasing a 100-piece tool kit from the same place you buy your groceries will almost certainly provide you with a crystal-clear alternate definition of the word *cheesy*.

Recommended tools are broken down here into three groups:

- First group should be considered the absolute bare minimum, a.k.a. tier one, for being able to perform most of the projects in this book. Also included will be additional alternate tools that would be beneficial but not crucial.
- You can consider the alternates to be semi-pro, or Tier Two tools. If you're flush or dedicated, or both, you'll acquire these tools as you come to realize how much they'll aid your work.
- Lastly are the pro, or tier three tools, which you'll see in shops of motorcycling friends or dealership service departments. They're expensive, perhaps of limited or overly specialized usefulness, but pure gold when it comes to saving time and stress.

Tier One (The Absolute Minimum)
Yes, you can get by with fewer tools than those listed here. Many have. But doing so means almost every task will take longer, and possibly become exponentially more frustrating, maybe even dangerous.

Combination Wrenches
These have an open and a closed end on each wrench, and come in only one size. For most bikes you'll want them in 8-mm, 10-mm, 12-mm, 14-mm, 17-mm and 19-mm sizes; for Harley-Davidsons, 1/4-inch through 13/16-inch. Smaller or larger sizes should be acquired as needed or as funds permit. Do not—repeat, do not—give

in to the temptation to buy the cheaper double-open-end wrenches with different sizes on each end; it's false economy. Proper combination wrenches' closed ends are the same shape as a 12-point socket, a boon when working in tight confines. Tier Two wrenches include shorter versions of the same items, as well as ratcheting-end combination wrenches. The latter's closed ends function similarly to a ratchet wrench.

Ratchet Handle and Sockets
A ratchet handle has a gear drive with a positive stop; you can tighten or loosen a fastener, reverse the handle however many degrees are available, then rotate it again to tighten/loosen further. A 3/8-inch-drive handle is the most useful, with sockets in the same range as the combination wrenches, metric- or inch-size. Similarly, smaller- or larger-size sockets should be acquired as needed or as funds permit. Tier Two ratchets will come in 1/4-inch- and 1/2-inch-drives, for more delicate- or heavier-duty work respectively. Pros have a full selection of both 12-point and 6-point sockets (6-pointers are better for removing recalcitrant fasteners because they put more force on their flanks rather than their points, as with the 12-pointers). Breaker bars are specifically designed to break loose those same troublesome nuts and bolts, thanks to their simplicity (no ratchet mechanism) and length.

Screwdrivers
To begin with, just get three flat-blade and three Phillips-head screwdrivers. The small, medium, large flat-blade drivers and the No. 1, No. 2, and No. 3 Phillips will fit virtually everything on your bike. As you get further into the projects, you'll doubtless find a need for Tier Two specialty drivers, such as extra-long, extra-short, and right-angle versions. Likewise, flat-blade and Phillips-head bits to fit on your ratchet handle will also become useful.

Allen Wrenches
Again, to start, a simple, relatively inexpensive collection of Allen keys; almost every tool manufacturer sells them in the necessary range of metric and inch sizes. As you step up to Tier Two, you'll find you'll want Allen bits, just as with the screwdriver bits, or T-handles with Allens on the ends. T-handles are longer tools, again useful in certain situations, and always faster than their key or bit counterparts.

Pliers
You can make do with the crude battery-style pliers in your bike's toolkit; you'd be better off, though, getting a higher-quality item from a reputable manufacturer, plus a pair of needle-nose pliers for finer, tighter work. Pliers

come in a dizzying variety of shapes and types, spanning Tiers Two and Three: Channellocks, Vise-Grips, duckbills, diagonal cutters, wire cutters/strippers, and so on.

Impact Wrench/Hammer

Sometimes, especially with older bikes that use Phillips screws in the engine cases, the only way to get those fasteners to budge is with an impact wrench. A dead-blow hammer is a good partner to the impact wrench, as all of its force goes into the target; the blow forces the Phillips bit into the screw head. Believe it or not, there are actually Tier Two hammers: soft-face (rubber or plastic), and hard-face (malleable brass, ball peen, etc.).

Torque Wrench

Invaluable for finer work, especially on the engine, suspension parts, and so on, a torque wrench indicates the amount of force used to tighten a fastener. The cheapest and simplest is a beam-type with a pointer to indicate the force (in inch-pounds, foot-pounds, Newton-meters, etc.). It is possible to do decent work with a beam-type torque wrench. Better still, though, are the Tier Two click-stop (the wrench makes an audible "click" when the selected torque setting is reached) and dial-gauge wrenches. If you're rich as Midas, you'll have at least the latter two, one in inch-pounds, the other in foot-pounds.

Oil Filter Wrench

This should be self-explanatory, and comes in either a universal strap-type to go around the filter body, or a specific shallow sort of socket that goes on the filter end.

Paddock Stand

Once upon a time, almost every motorcycle had a centerstand, an integral device which held the bike upright so the chain could be lubed, wheels cleaned, and other simple tasks completed. The race for sportbike supremacy, though, led to the centerstand's demise in order to make the bike lighter. So, those previously simple tasks are exceedingly difficult without a proper paddock stand, which lifts the rear of the bike via the swingarm. For Tier Two you can add a similar stand for the front end. Best of both situations is the Abba Superbike Stand from the United Kingdom, which hoists the bike via a rod placed through the (usually) hollow swingarm pivot shaft, which can then allow either wheel to be lifted off the ground.

Tire Gauge

Another tool that should be obvious in its need and its usage. Proper tire pressures are crucial to your bike's performance.

Measuring Tools

At the very least you'll want a meter-long steel scale, useful for setting suspension sag; a tape measure, preferably metric scaled, can also be used. Valve adjustments require thin metal feeler gauges, while current fine-wire spark plug electrodes prefer wire-type gauges. Tier Two devices include a dial-gauge vernier caliper and/or a 0–2-centimeter micrometer, either of which can be used to measure valve adjustment shims.

Lastly, you'll want a wide variety of aerosol- spray lubricants, cleaners, nostrums, potions, and lotions: chain lube for obvious reasons, grease for axles and suspension linkage bolts, brake and/or electrical parts cleaners, thread-locking compounds, and polishes. And you'll need duct tape, which can repair virtually anything or at least disguise it. In addition, you'll need a few funnels; latex gloves, or an alternative for those with an allergy to latex; nylon Cordura work gloves; and safety glasses. You don't want to put your eye out, now, do you?

Tier Two (Semi-Pro)

Along with the tools mentioned in the previous section, these include:

Manometers, a.k.a. Vacuum Gauges

Used to synchronize carburetors or throttle bodies, these take the form of dial gauges or tubes of mercury, usually a pair or a group of four. They measure vacuum, or suction, in the intake manifold or throttle body, making each cylinder read the same results in smoother running and better throttle response.

Electrical Items—Drill, Multimeter, Battery Charger

Drills come in handy for certain fabrication jobs, or just to drill out a ruined bolt; a multimeter will assist you in curing certain electrical maladies; and a battery charger is for those inevitable occasions when your motorcycle's battery has gone dead.

Tire Irons, Rim Protectors, Flat Kit

Another inevitability of motorcycling is the flat tire, and these tools will make the repair process far less painful. Similarly, you'll need to replace tires, wherein the first two items come into play.

Cutting Tools, i.e. a Hacksaw, Knife, Gasket Scraper

These won't see a great deal of use, but when you need them, nothing else will do.

Tier Three and Beyond

We still haven't hit the top end of useful items for your garage—the tool parts catalogs are full of goodies ranging from air compressors and air-powered tools to welders and lift stands. This stuff is expensive, but extremely useful if you do extensive service work—or if perhaps you're starting to like working on motorcycles as much or more than merely riding them. You will find high-quality taps and dies or Easy-Out invaluable kits for repairing stripped threaded holes, parts washers, and the like invaluable when you need them. There's no real point in describing each one, because by the time you're contemplating buying something in this tier, you *know* what it's for and exactly why you want or need it.

Of course, if you have this entire armada of tools both simple and sophisticated at your disposal, you need not fear any procedure you'll find in this book—or precious few others, for that matter.

RECOMMENDED MAINTENANCE SCHEDULE

The manufacturer who designed, engineered, and built your sophisticated motorcycle has already provided a detailed schedule of required maintenance to keep your bike running strong for quite some time. It's all outlined in your owner's manual.

But how much of that is really essential to overall reliability and durability? How much of

the work can you do versus how much needs to be done by a professional? Can the professional service be done by an independent shop, or does it have to be done by the dealer?

Based on considerable experience, the following is a basic maintenance schedule for the essentials—those maintenance services that really are necessary for your bike to provide a full service-life. Will it break or fail if you do not follow this schedule and/or perform these services? Not necessarily. There are tens of thousands of very lucky owners who live in blissful ignorance and continue to ride their motorcycles far beyond the recommended maintenance intervals . . . at least until something finally fails and leaves them stranded on the side of the road, frustrated and very angry at the bike for failing them.

Is the reverse also true? Yes, at times. Even with the most meticulous maintenance program, motorcycles fail. Engines expire, gearboxes frag, and radiators lose their coolant—that's part of the risk of owning a motorized vehicle.

But there is absolutely no doubt that if you do, or have done, the basic maintenance necessary for your motorcycle's survival, the percentages are well and truly on your side. It will make the difference between a bike that delivers substantial miles without a major failure, and one that leaves you standing by the curb, stranded, with a massive repair bill. Like the old saying goes, pay your money and take your choice.

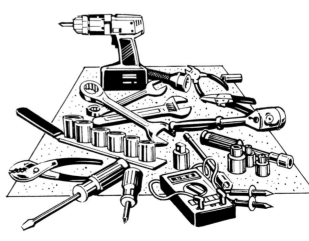

MAINTENANCE SCHEDULE

TASK	INTERVAL	SHOP COST	DIY COST	REASON TO DO	PROJECT NO.
Lubricate and adjust final drive chain	500 miles	$25–45	$5–12	Prolong chain life	Project 6: Adjust your chain
Change engine oil and filter	3,000 miles	$35–50	$10–60	Engine longevity	Project 17: Change Your oil and filter
Remove spark plug(s); inspect or replace with anti-seize	12,000 miles	$15–150	$5–60	Monitor engine performance; improve fuel mileage and performance	Project 22: Spark plug check and replacement
Change air filter	8,000–10,000 miles	$25–90	$10–40	Engine longevity; improve fuel mileage and performance	Project 12: Clean/replace your air filter
Adjust valves	Follow manufacturer's recommendation	$150–500	$5–90	Engine longevity	Project 19: Adjust intake and exhaust valves
Change brake pads	As needed	$60–100 per caliper	$25–40 per caliper	Maintain safe braking performance; avoid costly damage to rotors and drums	Project 43: Brake pad change
Change engine coolant	8,000–10,000 miles	$50–75	$5–15	Maintain proper engine temperature; avoid overheating, corrosion	Project 23: Check your coolant
Change brake (or clutch) fluid	8,000–10,000 miles	$45 (each system)	$5–10 (each system)	Maintain proper function; avoid corrosion, frozen/rusted parts	Project 44: Changing hydraulic fluid
Change fork oil	8,000–10,000 miles	$100–300	$10–50	Maintain proper function; improve handling	Project 31: Change your fork oil

Project 1
Adjust Controls to Fit You

TIME: 1 hour

TOOLS: Basic mechanical tools
           and rear stand

TALENT: 1

COST: None*

PARTS: *Possibly aftermarket
           replacements for the
           controls

TIP: When you alter the con-
           trols, make sure the new
           position doesn't interfere
           with the operation of the
           motorcycle

BENEFIT: A more comfortable rider
           and, therefore, better
           control of the motorcycle

Bikers come in a variety of body types, weights, and sizes. Building mass-produced bikes to suit each rider is not possible. Instead, manufacturers design for an "average" rider, whose height, weight, arm-, torso- and leg-length may vary from yours.

To find the most comfortable setup for your bike, put it on a rear stand and get into your riding position. If shifting or braking could be made easier or more comfortable by adjusting any hand or foot control, let's do it now. (For drawings and details specific to your bike, acquire a repair manual for your make and model and refer to it as necessary as we improve your bike throughout this book.)

Put your right hand on the brake lever. If your wrist is tilted back awkwardly, you'll need to lower the lever. Loosen the two bolts on the master cylinder clamp and rotate the lever downward slightly. Find the spot that feels best and snug up the bolts. It will take a ride or two to feel whether you have it just right.

Some older bikes and less-exotic sporty bikes (GS500 and Ninja 250, for example) don't have adjustable brake levers. If you find your reach to the lever

Your ability to brake and control the throttle simultaneously can be dramatically affected by the brake lever position. If it's too high (left), your wrist is bent into an awkward position. If it's too low, the lever could make it difficult to fully close the throttle while applying the brake. Note the difference between the wrist positions when the brake lever is too high versus the proper height (right).

is longer than you'd like, an adjustable lever from a later year or a different model may fit—enthusiast websites and shops specializing in your bike may know a good swap. Another approach is to buy aftermarket items from companies such as Lockhart Phillips or Flanders.

Clutch levers are a little bit easier to adjust. If your bike doesn't have an adjustable clutch lever, try loosening the thumbscrew locknut where the cable enters the lever housing. Then simply screw the adjuster in, increasing the clutch lever's free play. Be forewarned that excessive free play can keep the clutch plates from fully disengaging and contribute to premature clutch wear—not to mention clunky gear changes.

Another way to alter ride position on many bikes is to rotate the handlebars. On older bikes, you can often simply loosen the pinch bolts and shift the bars to the new position. While most of the clip-on handlebars on current sportbikes are affixed to both the fork legs and the triple clamps, some clip-ons can have their angle adjusted by simply loosening the pinch bolts and rotating the bar into its new position. If you find that the inward angle of the clip-ons makes you uncomfortable or strains your wrists, you may want to try altering the clip-on orientation outward to allow straighter access to the grips. (This is not possible on some bikes.) When changing the bar location or angle, be sure to consider tank, fairing, and instrument cluster clearance to ensure you don't limit maneuverability or put your fingers in a place where they'll get pinched. Make sure you firmly secure the bars—and any control you adjust—before riding.

The brake pedal needs to be low enough that you can cover it comfortably while you ride. If your ankle feels kinked after just a few minutes, try lowering the pedal. Hydraulic brakes usually allow the pedal to be adjusted on the master cylinder. Loosen the locknut and turn the bolt to lower the pedal—try small increments rather than a major position change. If the pedal is too low, you may find controlling brake pressure is easier with the pedal raised slightly. On bikes with drum brakes pedal height can be adjusted with a bolt, but don't forget to reset the pedal free play by turning the nut at the end of the brake rod and drum. Check brake light operation and adjust the switch if necessary.

The adjustments listed here are just the beginning. You can also find adjustable foot pegs, fairings to reduce wind fatigue, different seats or padding changes to alter seating height, harder or softer grips, different mirrors to alter rearward visibility, etc.

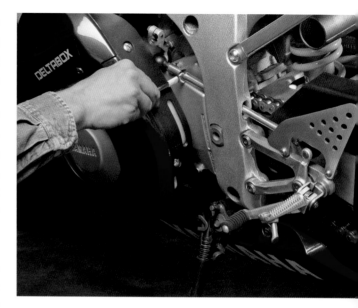

You should be able to shift up or down without lifting your foot off the peg. Be careful when preparing to adjust the rod length of the shifter. Look closely at the threads above the locknut. One end of the rod is reverse threaded. Why? Well, you'll see once both locknuts are loosened. Raising or lowering the shifter is as easy as rotating the rod with a wrench or a pair of pliers. The reverse threads are what make this possible. Once you're happy with the position, check to make sure that plenty of threads remain engaged in the ball joints, and be sure to tighten the locknuts. Little adjustments make big changes, so try moving the shifter a bit at a time, testing its position in the garage. Once you think it's right, go for a ride and take notes on how the changes improved the shifting. Or, better yet, toss a couple of wrenches in your tank bag and play with the position on a longer ride.

Notice how the rider's boot is in a comfortable position covering the brake pedal. Now, imagine commuting for 40 minutes with the brake covered. Would you rather have your foot in this position or bent upward?

Project 2
Preride Check

TIME:	2 minutes
TOOLS:	Tire pressure gauge
TALENT:	1
COST:	None
PARTS:	None
TIP:	Make this part of your routine, and you'll minimize surprises
BENEFIT:	A fully functional motor-cycle ready for whatever modifications you have in mind

Motorcycles go fast among solid, heavy, abrasive objects, and they offer little protection. They also carry us far from home. Taking just a moment to look over your ride before climbing aboard to face cars, trucks, trees, rocks, and endless miles of pavement is common sense. It's better to discover that damaged tire on your own, in your driveway, than for a sharp-eyed cop or EMT to spot it from the point where your bike left the road.

Start with the simple stuff as you approach your motorcycle. Do you see any fluid drips on the pavement? Does the fork look free of any leakage? Are there

A quick visual check of your tires every time you park or get on your bike will help you spot that piece of metal in the tread before it has a chance to puncture the carcass.

You'd be surprised how many bikes are out on the road with improper tire pressure. Having the right amount of air in your tires will improve your bike's handling and help you get the maximum life out of your tires. Improper pressure can lead to excessive wear or, in the worst-case scenario, tire failure.

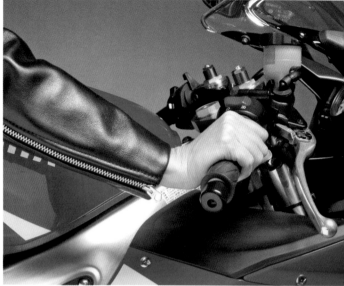

Without brakes, you're dead. All it takes is a couple of test squeezes every time you mount your bike.

Roll the throttle on and off before starting the engine. After the second roll-on, release the grip to see if the throttle snaps closed. If not, don't ride until the problem is remedied.

any gouges or cracks in the tires, or any foreign object lodged in them? Do they look properly inflated? Motorcycles ridden regularly only need to have tire pressure checked twice a week or so—as long as they get a visual inspection of the tread condition before every ride. Bikes that sit for several days should have their tire pressure checked before hitting the streets. Finally, check your tires with a quick glance every time you park your bike. Not only do you get to see how far you cranked it over on that canyon run, but you may also notice the nail you picked up riding past a construction site. Keep a tire pressure gauge in your jacket pocket or with your bike.

Look at your chain. Are you lubing it regularly, according to the manufacturer's instructions? There should be no rust on it, and it should not sag. Check the sprocket teeth for wear. When the chain and sprocket start to wear out, they will often click briefly on slow acceleration from a stop as they snug into place. If your bike has belt drive, when is the last time your replaced it? OK, now what is the replacement interval recommended by the manufacturer?

You should check your oil once a week. Why? Because your engine is toast if it gets too low or too dirty. If your bike's engine has a sight glass, stand your bike so that it is level—but don't put it on the rear stand because this added height can give an inaccurate reading.

Before starting the engine, test any controls operated by cables. A cable will rarely fail all at once. Instead, cables usually fray progressively until a complete breakage occurs. By operating the controls with the engine off, you will notice the subtle but telltale grinding feel of torn strands. Another sign is a more difficult-to-operate throttle or one that must be closed manually instead of by the return spring. By slowly rolling on the throttle a couple of times and squeezing the clutch lever, you can, in a matter of seconds, ascertain that the cables are in good working condition.

As you throw your leg over the seat, give the front brake lever a healthy squeeze. Is the pressure the same as yesterday? Does the lever come down to the grip? Give the rear brake pedal a press to see how it's doing.

Now you're ready to start the engine. While it warms up, check all your lights. If you do this after dark, the job is easy. Just look in front and behind you as you cycle through the high beam, low beam, front running lights, left and right turn signals, rear running light, and the brake light. In daylight, hold a hand in front of the various lights to see if they work. (Make sure the bike is in neutral when you get off and release the clutch—people have done it otherwise!) Check the brake lever and pedal individually to see that both trigger the stop lamp.

This process takes almost no time to complete and the latter portion can be done while the bike is warming up. Do it regularly and you'll save yourself time and headaches—such as knowing you're on reserve before heading out for a ride.

Project 3
General Lubrication

TIME:	30 minutes
TOOLS:	Assorted wrenches, cable lubrication tool, cable lube, chain cleaner, molybdenum-based grease, WD-40, small paintbrush
TALENT:	1
COST:	$
PARTS:	None
TIP:	Apply a thin coating of grease to cables where they attach to the controls
BENEFIT:	Silky-smooth control operation

Lubing your bike three times a season (the beginning, middle, and end) should suffice. If you ride the wheels off your motorcycle, give it a quick lube job every 7,500 miles. By performing this simple maintenance on a regular basis, you can prolong the life of the bike's components, ensure that everything works the way it should, and maybe even catch a problem as it starts.

Lubing your motorcycle's cables should take no more than 15 minutes, and it pays dividends every time you operate a control. For the throttle cables, unscrew the throttle housing on the grip and adjust the cables for maximum slack. After you release one of the cables, the other will slip right off. For the clutch cable, screw the adjuster all the way in for maximum slack, but line up the slot in the adjuster with the slot of the lever holder. You should be able to pull the end of the cable free of the adjuster and release the cable. Some bikes require that the clutch lever be removed from the mount before you can free the clutch cable.

The cable luber forces the lubricant through the cable, making sure the entire length of the cable is protected. Do not use chain lube on cables.

Apply a protective coat of grease to all exposed sections of cables. Don't forget to lube the fittings so they will move freely within their mounts.

Before lubing pivot points, wipe them clean of any dirt or grit. Keep the threads clean and dry. Retorque the fasteners to the proper spec to keep them from vibrating loose.

All moving parts, such as peg pivots and side stands, will benefit from a shot of WD-40 or a few drops of oil to keep them working freely. If you're particularly fastidious, you can disassemble the parts and grease them.

For quick work on the cables, nothing beats a pressure cable luber from accessory companies such as Motion Pro or Lockhart Phillips. Basically, you clamp a rubber stopper over one end of the cable, insert a tube from a can of silicon-based cable lubricant into a little hole, and give the nozzle a squeeze. The can's pressure forces the lubricant through the cable. Apply the lubricant in short bursts until the bottom end of the cable begins to bubble or drip. A well-placed rag can catch the drips before they make a mess of the engine.

Before you reassemble each cable, apply a dab of grease to all the places the cable might rub. The fittings at the cable ends need grease, and any exposed sections of the cable should receive a protective coating, too. A small paintbrush will help you grease parts in tight places.

Don't forget the choke and speedometer cables. Lubricate the choke cable like all the others. Mechanical speedometer cables (a dying breed but still around on many bikes) should be unhooked from the speedometer. Pull out the inner cable and pack the cable top with molybdenum grease. Slide the cable back into place. Any time the front wheel is removed, pack some moly grease into the drive mechanism.

Now go over your bike and lubricate every part that moves. Unscrew the handlebar lever pivots and brush on some grease. Apply a couple drops of oil to the side stand pivot. Give the rider and passenger pegs a quick squirt of WD-40 or oil. Don't forget to spritz floorboard mounts. Remove the shifter pivot and clean any grit out of the works. Apply grease to the pivot, but be sure to keep the pivot's threads clean and dry. Some manufacturers recommend a drop of nonpermanent thread-locking agent, such as Loctite, on the threads to make sure the pivot bolt doesn't back out after

reassembly. Be sure to torque it to the proper spec. Follow the same precautions for the brake pedal.

Before you lube the chain, spray a clean rag with WD-40 and wipe it clean. If your chain is really grungy, Motorex makes a chain cleaner that will strip the gunk without harming the O-rings. Never touch the chain with the bike's engine running. Clean it with the engine off, rotating the wheel by hand.

Once you've cleaned the chain, apply a coat of quality chain lube to the space between the links where the O-rings reside, spraying from the inside run of the chain to allow centrifugal force to push it through to the other side. If you spray on too much, take another clean rag dampened with WD-40 and wipe off the excess lube before your next ride. Lubricate your chain every 500 miles or so, or promptly after exposure to rain or other water.

Lubricate the chain when it is warm, but then let it sit until it cools off and the lube sets. To help keep your wheels clean, wipe off the excess lube before your next ride.

Project 4
Checking Vital Fluids

TIME:	5 minutes
TOOLS:	Eyes, a rag
TALENT:	1
COST:	None, unless replacement fluids needed
PARTS:	Vital fluids, if needed
TIP:	Make this part of your weekly routine and you'll minimize surprises
BENEFIT:	A well-hydrated, fully functional motorcycle

When things usually work the way they are supposed to, we don't worry so much about checking for signs of impending failure. Still, if you consider the potential consequences of a major mechanical failure, you'll see the importance of spending a few minutes every week or so to make sure that all your bike's precious bodily fluids are in satisfactory condition and available in enough quantity to do their job.

Motor oil can give you important information about your engine's internal condition. If you check it each week, you are more likely to notice symptoms of little problems before they get bigger.

Before checking the oil level, warm the engine to operating temperature. Shut off the engine and allow the oil to drain down from the top end for a few minutes. If your bike has a sight glass, hold the bike level—either from the saddle or beside the bike—and look at the window on the bottom of the engine to make sure the oil level is between the two marks on the case. For engines with a dipstick, check your owner's manual to make certain how the stick is to be inserted for an accurate reading. Usually, you will wipe the stick and insert it into the case until it makes contact with the filler plug's threads. Be sure the plug is straight or you may get an inaccurate reading. Oil darkens with use, but it should not be coal black and gritty. Keep track of mileage between changes and swap out the oil and filter according to your bike manufacturer's suggestions. If your bike has sat without running for more than a year,

change it regardless of miles. You may notice other problems—if the oil is milky white, it's polluted with coolant (in a water-cooled bike); if it smells like gas, fuel is getting past the rings. Both of these conditions require immediate attention.

Coolant is almost as vital. Run your water-cooled engine without some kind of coolant and you risk extensive damage. You want the level in your coolant overflow tank to lie between the high and low marks when the engine is cold. The color should be a lovely fluorescent green. If oil or a rust-colored hue appears in the coolant, your engine or radiator needs attention.

Similarly, your hydraulic fluid reservoirs need to be checked periodically. With the bike sitting level, the fluid should fall between the factory markings. Brake and clutch master cylinders with integrated reservoirs have sight glasses allowing you to view the contents. While checking the fluid levels also note their color—usually clear with a slight yellowish tint. If you see any other color, flush the system before contaminants damage the hydraulic internals. The white plastic remote reservoirs should not be opened to check the color of the contents—hydraulic fluid absorbs moisture from the air. You can get a good idea of the brake fluid color through the plastic. Don't forget to check the rear brake system, which usually has the reservoir tucked away behind the bodywork.

Regular fluid checks will keep your motorcycle functioning properly and disclose any problems before they get costly or dangerous.

The secret to getting an accurate view of the fluid level from a master cylinder with an integrated reservoir is to turn the bar until the reservoir is as level as possible. Don't be concerned if the reading drops over time. The brake pads are wearing, which requires more hydraulic fluid in the calipers. However, if the reading gets below the recommended height, check the brake pads before topping off the reservoir from a fresh container.

Reading the fluid level on the rear brake of the R6 is easy. It's hanging out in the open on the subframe. Some bikes tuck the reservoir away behind bodywork, requiring you to look through a slot to view the reservoir.

The oil level on this bike is pretty obvious. Look a little closer to check the condition of the oil. To read the sight glass correctly, the bike must be held level on flat ground.

Although it is hard to read in this photo, the coolant level in the expansion tank is right where it should be. If you check your antifreeze frequently, you will notice when it starts to drop, signaling a leak somewhere in the system.

CHECKING VITAL FLUIDS

Project 5
Rolling Gear Checkup

TIME: 2 minutes

TOOLS: Flashlight and optional front/rear stands

TALENT: 1

COST: None

PARTS: None

TIP: Make this part of your weekly routine and you'll minimize surprises

BENEFIT: Knowing the exact condition of your brakes and tires can help keep you from getting in over your head

Your brakes, suspension, and tires keep you on the road and deserve extra attention. You should make a rolling-gear inspection at least once a week.

Begin your brake check by looking at all the pads. To view the pads, try using a flashlight to sight along the disc. Some people resort to removing the calipers or covers. You want to look at the pads on both sides of the caliper.

While you're down on your hands and knees, give the rubber brake and clutch lines a quick flex to see if they're beginning to crack. You can use this low-angle view of your bike to make a couple of other quick inspections. While manufacturers do a good job of protecting the delicate parts of the fork, the sliders occasionally get dinged. Over time, the rough part on the slider will eat away at the fork's seal, leading to fork oil seepage. In its most minor form, a weeping fork seal is nothing more than a messy nuisance, but it can quickly develop into a hazardous mess—particularly in the traditional fork arrangement, where the oil can contaminate the brake disc surface and brake pads. The shock can also develop its own leaks. A quick glance at the shock shaft with a flashlight will reveal whether it's time for a rebuild.

The final stop in the tour of your bike's rolling gear is the tires. You can make a complete inspection by rolling the bike forward a couple of feet at a time. You're looking for any foreign objects that may be lodged in the tire. If you

If you're going to get a glimpse of the brake pads, don't be afraid to get personal with your tires. You need a minimum pad material of 2 to 3 mm. If you've let the pads get down to 1 mm, you're skating on dangerously thin ice. Once they arrive at the bitter end, brake pads have difficulty shedding heat and may fade on you when you need them most. Have the pads worn evenly? If not, you may have a problem with the caliper. If you see any fluid seepage around the calipers, one of the pistons may need its seals replaced. Don't forget to check the rear brake pads, too.

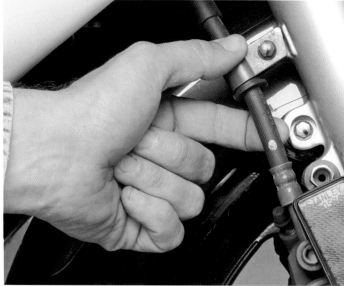

Wide rear wheels make the task of checking the pads a bit difficult. Get creative with your viewing angle.

Give the rubber portions of the hydraulic lines a bend to see if they're still flexible. If you notice any cracks, consider replacing them with shiny new braided stainless-steel ones.

find something, carefully pull it out. Check to see if the hole is leaking by rubbing a little saliva or soapy water over the opening. If it bubbles, repair or replace the tire. If it doesn't bubble, check the tire before each ride to see if it's losing air. You may also find cuts in the tread caused by running over road debris. Closely inspect the depth of the slice to make sure it doesn't go deep enough to expose the cords. Slices on the sidewall are particularly dangerous. If you have any, have a professional look at the tire.

Finally, look inside the tread grooves, or sipes, at the "wear bars" crossing through them. The tread depth is acceptable only when the wear bars lie below the tread surface. As soon as the bars start to wear, the tread is too shallow to provide adequate traction and channel water out from under the bike to avoid hydroplaning.

A new, just-scuffed-in tire will look like this. Note how deep into the sipe the wear bar lives.

While you try to find the wear bar, consider why this tire was on an F3 in a salvage yard. The center of the tread is worn down to the bottom of the sipes, giving the tire a square profile that could unsettle the bike when leaned over. Even a tire with adequate tread may have diminished grip if the tire is many years old, such that the rubber has hardened. Dry rot—small cracks—can also weaken a tire, particularly when combined with underinflation. If you ride two-up, be even more critical of wear and damage and err on the side of caution. Extra weight means extra stress—and that's two lives the tires are supporting.

Project 6
Adjust Your Chain

TIME:	20 minutes
TOOLS:	Assorted wrenches, socket for rear axle, torque wrench, tape measure, rubber mallet, rags for cleanup, rear stand (optional), string, an assistant
TALENT:	1
COST:	Minimal
PARTS:	New cotter pin
TIP:	Make sure the chain is properly aligned or you can prematurely wear out both the chain and the sprockets
BENEFIT:	Less driveline lash when modulating the throttle

To function properly without wearing out quickly or falling off or breaking, your chain needs to have a small amount of slack. As it wears, you will need to make

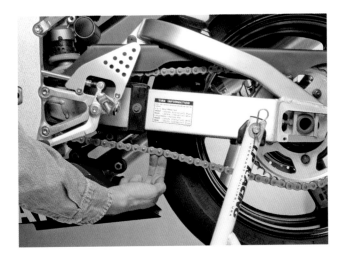

Find the link roughly centered between the front and rear sprocket on the lower run of the chain. Press down at this point until the chain is at its lowest point. Holding a tape measure in front of and perpendicular to the chain ("perpendicular" isn't quite the right term here since the chain is not a straight line as you push on it), align your tape with the tops of the inner and outer sides of this middle link. Now, press the chain up until it is tight and sight this measurement the same way. The difference between the two points on your tape is the amount of slack in your chain. If this figure is larger than what your manufacturer prescribes, you need to move the rear wheel back with the adjusters until you hit the recommended slack.

periodic adjustments (moving the wheel back) to maintain this setting.

Assuming your chain and sprockets check out, place the bike on the centerstand or a rear stand to make it level. With the chain cold, measure the slack halfway between the sprockets. If the slack is within spec, lube the chain and you're done. Otherwise, you'll need to move the rear wheel back slightly with the adjusters to take up any excess slack.

For bikes with locknuts on their chain adjusters, hold the adjuster in place with a wrench while loosening the locknut. Loosen the axle nut just enough to enable the chain adjusters to move it—otherwise the rear wheel can get out of alignment. For now, assume that your wheel is properly aligned, and make the same adjustments to both chain adjusters.

When the chain has the proper amount of slack, torque the axle nut. Next, tighten each adjuster about one-eighth turn against the axle. Hold the adjuster in position and set the locknuts.

The last step in any chain adjustment is making sure the rear wheel is properly aligned. The least expensive way to do this is the "string method." A simpler, but less precise, method for checking rear wheel alignment is to spin the rear wheel a few times and watch that the sprocket stays aligned in the center of the chain. If it rubs against one side or the other, the wheel is out of alignment—time for the string method.

Once you've adjusted your chain a few times, you'll get the feel for when it is loose, but the only way to be certain is to use a tape measure.

Chain adjusters come in many shapes and sizes (above/below). Small adjustments of a quarter-turn (or less if your chain is only slightly loose) are the safest bet. Measure the slack after every change. When the chain is within factory specifications (usually around 1.2–1.5 inches), tighten the axle nut to keep it from slipping. If you go too far and the chain becomes too tight, loosen the chain adjusters two full turns and use a rubber mallet or dead-blow hammer to knock the rear wheel forward against the adjusters and begin again.

The eccentric adjuster is found on many bikes, particularly those with a single-sided swingarm.

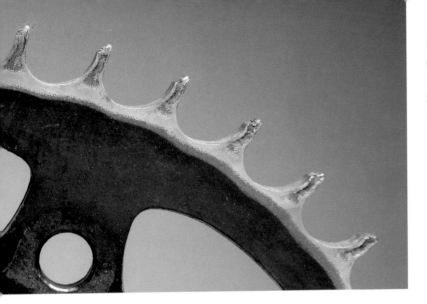

Before you adjust the slack, look closely at the sprockets. Are the sides of the teeth worn? If so, expect to find a matching wear pattern on the inside of the chain. Do the teeth look like cresting waves? When the sprockets show obvious wear, it's time to replace them and the chain. Don't replace just one or the other because looseness on either side will create misalignment and eat up the new part.

If you can pull the chain away to expose half of the sprocket's tooth, it's ready for replacement.

With an assistant's help, take a piece of string a little more than twice the length of the bike, find the center, and wrap it once around the forward edge of the front tire just below the front discs. Take each end of the string down opposite sides of the bike. Lie down on your stomach, pulling the strings taut so that they both lightly touch the leading edge of the rear tire. Since the rear wheel is wider than the front, there will be a slight gap on either side of the rear edge of the front tire where the string on each side goes past. Your assistant should make sure that the front wheel is straight by making that gap equal on both sides. Now, keeping your hands steady with the string only lightly touching the rear tire, compare the gaps between the strings and the rear edge of the rear tire. If they are not equal, tighten the adjuster slightly on the side that has the smaller gap. Finally, measure the slack one last time. Put a new cotter pin through the axle nut if it requires one.

Project 7

Checking and Tensioning Your Drive Belt

TIME:	30 minutes
TOOLS:	Belt tension tool (or fish scale), possibly a pair of needle-nose pliers or an awl—depending on whether or not there's debris in the belt
TALENT:	2
COST:	$
PARTS:	None
TIP:	A shot of Armor-All will quiet a squeaky belt
BENEFIT:	Longer belt life

If your bike suffers leakage in the primary drive area, the first thing to check is belt tension. What is proper tension? Assuming you have a Harley, use factory tool No. H-D 35381, hook the belt like a fish in between the pulleys and check that 10 pounds of force results in 5/16–3/8 inch of deflection in the belt, as seen through the little window in the bottom belt guard.

A belt that's too tight can cause problems far worse than oil leaks, including pulley splines stripping out. Also, belts don't like being bent into a radius of less than 3 inches or having their direction of rotation reversed once they've gotten used to it. If you can keep from cutting them or poking gaping holes in them with road debris, they will last for years. But belts aren't immortal. Checking the belt

regularly for damage and wear is a necessary part of getting the best out of them.

If you were to look at a cross-section of the belt's tooth pattern, relative to its counterpart in the pulley, you'd see that, when new, the belt tooth doesn't bottom out. When broken in, it might, slightly. When worn out, it will—excessively! Once this stage is reached, the teeth on the belt begin to get pulled out by their roots, where they attach to the cords.

Sometimes you can spot this early on by looking for a series of hairline cracks or wrinkles on the tips of the teeth running parallel to the run of the belt. Belts with just a few wrinkles can be considered sort of, well, middle-aged. But if the wrinkles extend from the top to the bottom of the teeth clear to the outside edge of the belt, it's all over. Keep riding on that one, and you're gonna wind up toothless.

If you don't have the factory tool or just can't figure out how to use a fish scale to adjust your belt's tension, try this instead. Grasp the belt with your thumb and two forefingers at about 1 1/2 inches back from where it exits the bottom of the primary case. Now twist the belt back and forth on its axis. You should feel serious resistance to this twisting at about a 45-degree angle from flat. If you can twist your belt more like 90 degrees with just a thumb and two fingers, it's too loose. If it feels tighter than a bowstring at only 25 to 30 degrees of twist, it's too tight. This may not be the rocket science method, but it's pretty accurate, just the same.

Look closely now. Aside from the familiar belt damage, like punctures, splits, cuts, and so on, there's this one, caused by a plastic lower belt guard getting cockeyed and going unnoticed. This belt died in less than 4,000 miles. It looks OK from the edges, but it has no teeth in the load-bearing middle. There's more than one way to wear out a belt!

Project 8
Adjust Clutch and Throttle Free Play

TIME:	30 minutes
TOOLS:	Phillips screwdriver, open-end wrenches, and (maybe) needle-nose pliers
TALENT:	1
COST:	None
PARTS:	None
TIP:	If you run out of adjustment range up at the lever, try adjusting the cables down by the engine
BENEFIT:	Precise throttle control gives you maximum flexibility in the on/off/on throttle scenarios you encounter when entering a corner, or riding a series of them.

One hallmark of a skilled rider is the ability to deliver the right amount of throttle at the right time. Smooth transitions on and off the throttle play a vital role in keeping the chassis stable in a corner. Whether you're trying for a smooth launch from a stoplight or flawless downshifts with a passenger on the back, you want your inputs to be seamless.

If the free play needs adjustment, loosen the locking nut(s) near the throttle grip. Some bikes will only have one adjuster. For two-adjuster models, loosen the nuts until there is plenty of slack in the system. Next, tighten the deceleration adjuster (the cable that pulls the grip into the throttle-closed position) so that there is no slack when the throttle is held closed. Tighten the deceleration locking nut. Now, adjust the acceleration cable's adjuster until the desired amount of free play is present in the grip, and tighten its locking nut. Ensure that there are plenty of threads (at least three) engaged in the adjuster body.

If you can't get the proper amount of free play with the adjuster(s), set the adjuster(s) to the middle of its/their range and adjust the cables down by the carburetors/throttle bodies. Begin by removing the tank and any bodywork that will interfere with your access to cables. On some bikes you may need to remove or disassemble the air box to reach the bell crank.

A word of warning about using less free play than the factory specifies: If the throttle cables are too tight, they can cause the throttle to stick, close very slowly, or not close completely, so check thoroughly by rolling the

throttle open and releasing it from a variety of settings. Finally, run the engine at idle speed and turn the handlebar to both the right and left to make sure that the engine speed does not change. If it does, check the cable routing and free play again.

Clutch Free Play

For bikes with hydraulic clutches, you can skip this section, because hydraulic systems are self-adjusting. Cable-actuated clutches should be checked regularly, though. Also, the clutch-lever free play adjustment can

To check throttle free play, hold the grip between your fingers and roll it back and forth until you begin to feel the pull of the cable. Pick a spot on the grip and watch it to measure free play. If you have trouble visualizing the measurement, hold a tape measure up to the grip. Most factory service manuals suggest that 2 to 3 mm is the correct amount of throttle free play.

accommodate various rider preferences and hand sizes. (If you have hand size problems with a hydraulic clutch, try buying an adjustable lever.) To measure the free play, pull in the clutch lever to take up the slack in the cable. Now measure the gap between the clutch lever holder and the lever itself. Again, most manufacturers recommend 2 to 3 mm of free play.

Sometimes cable stretch makes it impossible for you to get the proper clutch free play. If this happens, turn the adjuster on the lever holder so that 5 to 6 mm of the thread is visible. Next, adjust the slack at the lower end of the cable. Slide the cable dust cover out of the way, if there is one. Loosen the nuts as far as they will go. Now, pull the cable tight by sliding it inside the bracket. Tighten the nuts firmly enough so they will not vibrate loose, and return the dust cover to its proper position. The free play can now be adjusted by the screw at the lever. You've just officially outsmarted your motorcycle.

Space is usually pretty tight, so take your time as you adjust the cables on the bell crank. Food for thought: While 2 to 3 mm of free play may be the factory spec, many riders prefer even less free play, giving them the feeling of a seamless connection to the carburetors or injector housings. Experiment with different free-play amounts to find the setting that suits your riding style.

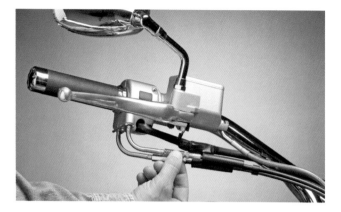

Set the free play with the cable adjusters on the throttle cables. If the bike has two adjusters, set the deceleration cable first. Locate the adjuster nuts for the throttle cables where they attach to the throttle body. Loosen the locknut on the deceleration cable and adjust the cable until there is no slack with the grip in the closed position. Now, adjust the free play of the acceleration cable to spec in the same manner. Any final fine-tuning to get the free play to your personal preferences can be done at the throttle grip end. Adjusting the throttle free play using this method is time consuming, but it pays off when you need to correct the free play in the future. When you are satisfied with the cable settings, tighten the locknuts firmly to prevent them from vibrating loose.

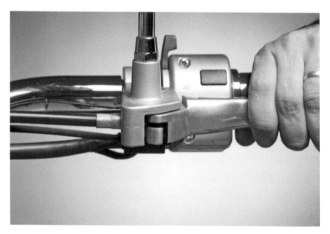

Take up the slack in the clutch cable and measure the gap between the lever holder and the lever.

Left: To adjust the free play, loosen the knurled lock screw on the clutch-lever holder. If your bike doesn't have one, look for an inline adjuster like this somewhere in the middle of the cable. Now, unscrew the adjuster for less slack or screw it in for more slack. Riders with smaller hands will probably want to have a bit more slack than those with larger hands. Also, depending on where the clutch engages in the lever travel, you may want to adjust it to engage at a different point. If you give the lever extra free play, make sure that the clutch releases fully when the lever is pulled all the way in. If it doesn't, your ability to shift smoothly will be compromised, and the transmission will undergo unnecessary stress when you downshift. If the free play is less than the recommended amount, the clutch may not fully engage, causing clutch slip and premature clutch wear.

Project 9
Replacing Throttle Cables

TIME: 1 hour

TOOLS: Phillips screwdrivers, open-end wrenches, pick, grease, rear stand

TALENT: 1

COST: $

PARTS: Throttle cables

TIP: Replace the cables one at a time, so you don't have to remember the exact path they take through the frame and other hardware

BENEFIT: Smooth throttle operation

A smooth hand and smooth operation of the throttle cables themselves are vital. If your throttle shows any signs of notchiness or if it becomes difficult to twist, you probably need new cables. Also, if you've lowered your clip-ons significantly, you may want to install shorter cables to keep them from rubbing against other components.

Begin by placing your bike securely on a rear stand to prevent accidentally knocking it off the side stand. Remove the tank and any bodywork that will interfere with your access to cables. On some bikes you may need to remove or disassemble the air box to reach the bell crank. Other components, such as the radiator on this R6, may need to be loosened to allow the cables' adjusters to fit through the tight space.

Before disassembling the throttle, loosen all of the cables' adjusters to gain maximum free play. Unscrew the throttle's plastic cover and fold it back out of the way, being careful not to pinch the wires or stress any of the connectors for the kill switch and starter button. If you don't have enough free play, use a pick or small screwdriver to lift the cable into position to allow the fitting to slide out of the throttle grip body. Once one cable is free, the second one will be simple.

Resist the urge to remove both cables at once. While you may have a photographic memory, something may

Even with the cable adjusters loosened all the way, you may need to use a pick to help get the fitting free of the grip.

Space is tight, so exercise a little patience to get the cables free of the carburetors.

Sometimes you can use the idle speed adjuster (right) to move the bell crank into a position that makes removing the fitting a little easier.

pull you away from this job, leaving you to decipher the line drawings in the service manual. If you do not run the cables in the proper path, they may bind when you turn the bars or, worse, they may cause the bike to rev. Removing the cables one at a time will leave a path for you to follow while inserting the new ones.

When sliding the fittings into their positions, lube them as described in Project 3. Giving the cables a quick squirt of lubricant wouldn't be a bad idea. Remove the throttle grip and give the clip-on a wipe and a spritz of WD-40 for lubricant. Once you have the cables run in the proper path, both ends secured, and the throttle body reassembled, set the adjuster near the throttle to the middle of its range. Now, adjust the free play to your

liking with the locknuts down by the carburetor. Any final fine-tuning to get the free play to your personal preferences can be done at the throttle grip end. Using this method is time consuming, but it pays dividends when you need to correct the free play in the future. When you are satisfied with the cable settings, tighten the locknuts firmly to prevent them from vibrating loose.

Check the cable routing one last time, and turn the bars from lock to lock to make sure nothing binds. Once you have the bike back together, warm up the engine and set the idle speed to the factory specification. One last time, turn the bars from lock to lock with the engine running to make sure that the idle speed doesn't change.

Even if you didn't change the idle speed while swapping cables, you'll need to set the idle to the operating temperature spec.

Project 10
Winterize Your Motorcycle

TIME:	2 hours
TOOLS:	Front and rear stands, intelligent battery charger, plug wrench, oil filter wrench, sockets, torque wrench
TALENT:	1
COST:	$–$$
PARTS:	Fuel stabilizer, fogging oil for cylinders, covers for intakes and exhaust openings, oil and filter, corrosion protectant, bike cover, coolant, fresh spark plugs (for next season)
TIP:	Winter is a great time to undertake a bunch of the other projects in this book, as well
BENEFIT:	You'll be riding while folks who don't winterize will be waiting for their bikes to get out of the shop

Riding a well-maintained motorcycle is a pleasure enjoyed worldwide. But in those regions that know winter a few months each year are less than amenable to two-wheeled pleasures. Putting your bike away right will get you back on the road sooner, save you money, and extend the life of your favorite possession. This project is organized so that the longer your bike will be stored, the further you should delve into the preparation for it.

Carburetors

Carburetors have many small parts with tiny orifices that clog easily and resist cleaning. When gasoline sits a while in your carbs, its volatile components evaporate, leaving behind among these small parts and passageways a sticky substance called varnish. That blockage accounts for the majority of coughing and sputtering your bike exhibits when you start it in the spring. If this stuff accumulates much, you're looking at a thorough disassembly and cleaning to get your engine running properly. To prevent varnish buildup, drain the float bowls any time you let your bike sit for more than a week or so without running it.

Battery

Left unused, batteries will discharge. Both high and low temperatures accelerate this loss of charge, and if it's allowed to continue, the battery will reach a deeply discharged state that can dramatically shorten its life. Add a constant drain from an alarm system, and your bike's battery can be stone dead in only two weeks.

The only way to maintain a motorcycle battery is to charge it periodically. Fortunately, "smart" charger technology has advanced to the point that buying one can pay for itself in a year or two of ownership. You don't even need to remove the battery from your bike. Just plug it in and forget about it. A fused cable tucked safely out of sight will work fine. However, if your bike will be stored in a subfreezing environment, you should let the battery spend the winter in a less stressful locale.

Gas Tank

If you're going to park your bike for more than a week, completely fill the tank. Otherwise, as the temperature rises and falls, any moisture in the air will condense on the bare metal inside the tank and can cause rust.

Engine

Once the engine stops running, combustion by-products settle out of the oil and can sink their teeth into unprotected metal. However, a quick oil change prior to parking your bike for the winter will remove most of them. After the change, ride your bike for a couple of miles to displace the old oil with the fresh.

The best way to drain the float bowls is to attach a hose to the nipple at the bottom of each float bowl. Then loosen the drain screw and let the fuel pour into a clean container. Examine the contents for water, rust, or any other contaminants. The second-best way to drain the carburetors is to close the petcock with the engine running. Once the engine has run dry, the carbs are safe against fouling from evaporation. Remember, though, you haven't cleared the float bowls of other forms of contamination, and you should drain the carbs properly at least once a year.

Although many bikes' cylinder walls are now coated with alloys rather than lined with iron, you'll still want to protect them from moisture contained in the air trapped in the chambers. Some people prefer to remove the spark plugs and squirt some 50W oil into the spark plug holes. Crank the engine over a few times to coat things before reinstalling the plugs. Another method is to spray fogging oil into the throttle bodies with the engine running, which may give the cylinders a more thorough protective coating. Fogging oil can be found at many auto parts stores.

If your water-cooled bike will be stored in an unheated garage that may see temperatures below

Intelligent chargers constantly monitor the state of a battery, and when the voltage drops, the charging feature kicks in. Once the voltage rises up to the proper level, the charger enters "float" mode, where a neutral charge keeps the voltage from dropping. The difference between these chargers and the trickle chargers that can be bought for less than $10 is the float mode. Trickle chargers just keep trickling away regardless of the battery's condition, which can do as much damage as not charging the battery at all.

Although a smart charger, such as a Battery Minder or Battery Tender, or Yuasa charger, costs considerably less than a new battery, some folks still want to use a trickle charger. If you're that type of person, plug it into a light timer that is set to run for about 15–20 minutes a day. Also, any nonsealed battery should be topped off with distilled water every month or so, if necessary.

freezing, you'll want to check to see that the antifreeze is up to snuff. Coolant is cheaper than a replacement engine block. Riders who take their bikes to track days should keep in mind that; if they swapped the glycol coolant for Water Wetter, their cooling systems will freeze at 32 degrees. Completely draining the system will prevent this. Just be sure to stick a big note on the triple clamp or speedometer, warning that the radiator is empty.

Tires

Bike and tire manufacturers generally agree that it's preferable to store a bike on stands, to prevent the tires from sitting on the same spot for several months. When storing on stands, reduce the tire pressure by 20 percent. If you leave your bike sitting on its tires, fill them up to their maximum recommended pressure and check the pressure every month.

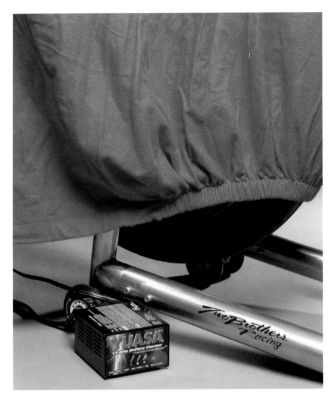

This soft Roadgear cover will protect your bike from dust and will keep the light from fading your paint. Elevating the tires off the ground keeps them from developing flat spots on the tread.

Chassis and Finish

Brake and clutch hydraulic fluid replacement and chassis lubrication is highly recommended. Pay particular attention to the cables and the chain. They will benefit from a protective layer of grease or other lubricant. Similarly, washing and waxing your bike prior to storage will help protect the finish. Apply a heavy coat of wax and don't buff it off until spring. Some people even go as far as waxing the inside of the bodywork and the frame. Finally, cover the bike (with an indoor or outdoor cover, as appropriate) to protect it from dust and grit—and salt from cars that may share the space.

Fuel stored for long periods can stratify into its components unless a fuel stabilizer is used. Be sure the tank is completely full, or the moisture in the air trapped in the tank can cause it to rust. If you're storing your bike for the winter, you have two choices for how to prepare the tank. Both methods of tank winterization require that you begin by draining the tank. This is a good maintenance procedure, anyway, since any crud or moisture that has collected during the riding season will be carried out with the fuel. The easiest option is to then pour a fuel stabilizer, like Sta-Bil, into the tank and then fill it completely with fresh gas. The alternative for people who can't or don't want to store their bike with a full tank is to pour a few ounces of heavy oil—50W at a minimum—into the empty tank. Close the tank and spend a few minutes rotating it until the oil has coated the tank internals and washed away any fuel remnants. Pour the remainder into your oil-recycling container. Next spring, empty out the oil that collected in the bottom of the tank before filling it with fresh gas. Always store your bike with the petcock turned off to prevent any accidental leakage. Cylinder walls, like the inside of gas tanks, need to be protected from moisture or they may rust. Spraying fogging oil into the cylinders can prevent this.

How to Wash Your Hands

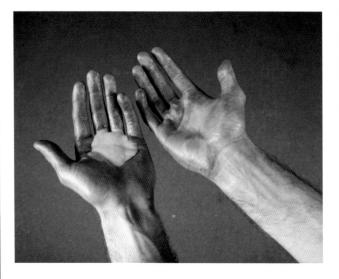

Some people steer clear of auto repairs just because of the dirt and grease. Fortunately, new auto-specific hand cleaners remove all the grease, grime, and oil. Apply a good dollop of an auto-grade hand cleaner in the palm of your hand.

Work it in well, not just to the front and back but in the knuckles and fingertips, too.

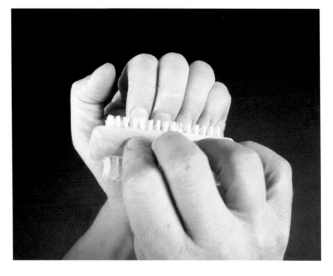

A stiff fingernail brush will get that grease out so none of your office-mates know you've been productive in the garage over the weekend.

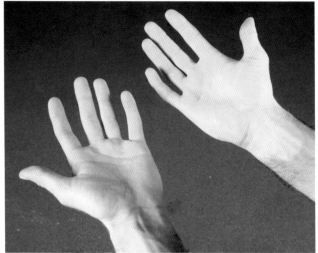

These are the same hands after the hand cleaner. Look near the wrists where the cleaner wasn't applied. Hands perfectly clean and ready for paperwork or a nice restaurant.

Chapter 2
Fuel System

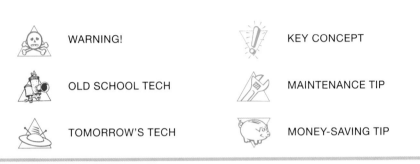

WARNING!

KEY CONCEPT

OLD SCHOOL TECH

MAINTENANCE TIP

TOMORROW'S TECH

MONEY-SAVING TIP

Depending on whose conversion formula you prefer to believe, a single gallon of gasoline is roughly equal to 50 pounds of TNT, almost five dozen Big Macs, or two brontosaurs, two triceratops, *and* two tyrannosaurs.

Admittedly, trying to get any of those into your motorcycle's gas tank, let alone get them to burn evenly (if at all), would be problematic at best. Unlike those fossil fuel equivalents, gasoline can be atomized, and then vaporized and mixed with air, so it can burned to produce power.

So how is the fuel processed so that it's ready to burn in the engine? That's the definition of your bike's fuel system. Perhaps the simplest way to understand the fuel system in your motorcycle is to identify its three main functions: storage, transportation, and delivery.

When you stop by the self-service gas station, stick the automatic dispensing nozzle into the fuel filler opening of your bike's gas tank, and squeeze the handle, you are starting the fuel on the last leg of its long journey. From oil fields somewhere in the world—Saudi Arabia, Kuwait, Mexico, Venezuela—it takes a trip across one of the two big ponds in a huge tanker, piped underground to a refining plant, trucked to the gas station, stored in an underground tank, and finally pumped into your fuel tank—whew! And all this for a product that still costs less than most designer bottled waters!

When you fill your tank, you're safely storing enough fuel to ride your motorcycle some 100–250 miles. The tank itself is a steel or plastic container affixed to the chassis, and is sometimes fitted with internal baffles to prevent sloshing and spillage. It delivers fuel to the engine either via gravity, or (more commonly, these days) is plumbed to deliver the fuel to the engine via a fuel pump and fuel lines. The tank is effectively sealed once the filler cap is properly tightened, not just to prevent spillage but to prevent fuel vapors from escaping into the atmosphere.

On California-only motorcycles, the vapors generated by the gasoline in the tank are collected in a charcoal canister secured somewhere on the motorcycle, which stores them until the engine is started. A purge valve opens another valve to apply engine manifold vacuum to the canister to draw these vapors into the induction system and burn them as the engine gets up to operating temperature. The idea is to completely consume the fuel vapors to prevent them from escaping into the atmosphere.

All right, the tank's full, the filler cap is secure, and you're ready to start the engine. In the decades before fuel injection, motorcycle fuel systems almost universally used simple, reliable, and always available gravity to move fuel from the tank to the engine.

Many modern motorcycles use electric fuel pumps built into the gas tank (more on those pumps can be found under the heading Fuel Injection).

CARBURETORS

From their primitive, earliest days (when they were little more than glorified wicks) carburetors became relatively sophisticated instruments that altered fuel's physical state from a liquid to a vapor, which mixed with the incoming air drawn into the engine by the downward motion of the pistons. It is this vaporized air/fuel mixture that the engine then burns to make power.

Carburetors feature a number of different circuits to help them complete the job. As the fuel enters the carburetor from the fuel line, it fills a float chamber or bowl—a small reservoir of fuel in the carburetor body. The flow of fuel into this chamber is metered by a simple needle and seat valve operated by a mechanical float arm. As the fuel level in the chamber rises or falls, it progressively closes or opens the valve, regulating the level of fuel in the chamber and available to the engine.

Early in carburetor's development, they utilized a manually operated mechanical choke to aid cold starts. The choke is nothing more than a round plate that rotates to restrict airflow through the carb body, thus increasing the percentage of fuel that mixes with the air and providing a richer air/fuel mixture to help the engine start and warm up. The next step was a dedicated enrichener circuit. Less crude than the hand-over-the-mouth approach of the choke plate, the enrichener circuit accomplishes the same task for more easily starting a cold engine, and it remains manually operated.

The most remarkable feature of a carburetor is its venturi, based on the aerodynamic principle of the venturi effect. When atmospheric air is drawn through an opening into a chamber of increasing volume, its pressure decreases. The throttle valve—a cylindrical or flat slide, or butterfly-type—which is connected to and opened/closed by the throttle grip on the right end of the bike's handlebar(s)—varies the venturi opening, which controls the volume of air being drawn into the engine. At idle the throttle is almost closed, restricting airflow into the engine. At full throttle, such as when you're trying to safely enter a freeway before some semi cuts you off, airflow into the engine is maximized.

Remember the fuel waiting in the float bowl/chamber? It is under normal atmospheric pressure. Main jets are small tubes, or orifices, that connect the bottom of the float chamber to the venturi. As the throttle is opened and closed, the pressure differential between the float chamber and venturi meters the amount of fuel pushed from the chamber through the jets into the air stream drawn through the venturi. By varying the volume of air and amount of fuel drawn into the engine from the carburetor, you regulate the power your motorcycle produces.

Many carburetors also feature an accelerator pump, which mechanically squirts a little extra fuel into the venturi as you open the throttle. Throttle movement activates this little pump, which helps the engine begin accelerating cleanly.

For the first six decades of the motorcycle, carburetors were the device of choice to regulate and mix fuel with the incoming air. And carburetors did a fine job in most cases. They were relatively easy to tune by varying the size of the main jets, for example, and when tuned well, they provided good performance and fuel economy.

Carburetor Drawbacks
As good and highly developed as carburetors have gotten, even their most ardent devotees have had to admit, to paraphrase Clint Eastwood, "Every man's got to realize his carburetor's limitations." One of those limitations is the carb's inability to recognize and accommodate changes in atmospheric air pressure. For example, a carburetor tuned properly for operation at sea level along the coast won't perform very well in the mountains. The higher the altitude, the lower the ambient air pressure, the fewer molecules of air per cubic foot. But the carburetor only knows how many cubic feet of air flows through it. Consequently, the sea-level-tuned carb delivers too much fuel for the amount of air pulled through it in the mountains, meaning the engine will run too rich.

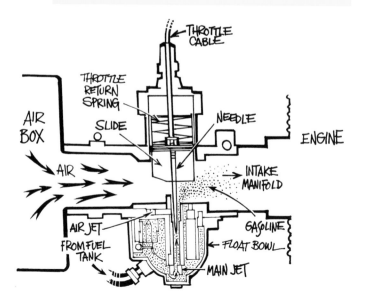

Carburetors have other drawbacks as well, particularly in controlling emissions of unburned hydrocarbons. External emissions systems were added to the last generations of carburetors in an attempt to help them conform to the first generation of emissions requirements in the 1970s and early 1980s. These add-on devices were somewhat successful, but overly complex, extremely annoying, and often caused rideability issues.

Moreover, carbs can behave erratically when subjected to the particular demands of high-performance engines—which includes virtually every motorcycle powerplant of the last couple of decades. Higher stages of tuning rely increasingly on pressure waves from the exhaust system to generate more horsepower. But at certain rpm, a wave can blow a portion of the entering charge *back* through the carburetor. The next wave pulls that same charge—now triple-enriched—back into the cylinder. Loaded with too much fuel to burn properly, it makes the torque curve sag, which the rider feels as a nagging flat-spot in the carburetion.

ELECTRONIC FUEL INJECTION (EFI)

Kawasaki built the first mass-produced fuel-injected motorcycle, the 1980 Z1000 Z-1 Classic. Other manufacturers eventually followed suit, but it wasn't until well into the new millennium that the majority of street bikes sold were equipped with electronic fuel injection (EFI). The manufacturers' desire to improve performance while meeting increasingly tighter emissions regulations made the switch to EFI inevitable.

Compared to a carburetor, fuel injection provides improved performance and fuel economy, and reduces emissions. Why does fuel injection do a better job? In simple terms, modern EFI systems do a better job of controlling *precisely* how much fuel is metered into the engine, and a much better job of atomizing the fuel, making it easier to vaporize and burn.

Fuel injection works by pushing fuel under significant mechanical pressure into the airstream drawn into the engine. This higher pressure atomizes the fuel into smaller droplets, which then vaporize better in the low-pressure air (vacuum) flowing into the engine. This helps the fuel vapor mix with the air and burn more efficiently.

EFI systems offer a number of practical advantages over carburetors. EFI is simpler, requires fewer components, and as such is more reliable and durable. But, more importantly, electronic fuel injection systems are completely controlled by computers. That means the computer can be programmed, or mapped, to provide exactly the correct amount of fuel to each cylinder in virtually every conceivable situation. The increase in efficiency,

performance, rideability, and fuel mileage, coupled with the reduction in emissions, means EFI has long outperformed carbs, due to the system's superior fuel delivery.

> Electronic fuel injection is deceptively simple. The fuel pump for these systems is now mounted near or inside the fuel tank for two reasons: first, to deliver fuel at much higher pressures, often 40 to 80 psi (it's mechanically easier to push rather than pull the fuel), and second, the tank-mounted pump is far less prone to engine heat and subsequent possible vapor lock.

The pump draws fuel through a fine screen, and then pushes the fuel under significant pressure through a large filter (generally) and on to the fuel rail to be distributed to each injector. In a throttle-body injection system, fuel is delivered to one or more fuel injectors mounted in a venturi-shaped throttle body, which somewhat resembles a carburetor. The engine management computer (also known as the electronic control unit or ECU), regulates the precise amount of time the injector is open—its pulse width or the amount of time it spews high-test—thus accurately controlling how much well-atomized fuel is sprayed into the venturi, where it mixes with the incoming air and is delivered via the intake manifold to each cylinder.

A typical injector is a simple electromagnetic solenoid, which when energized by a pulse-width signal from the ECU, opens the injector for a specific period of time (measured in milliseconds) to deliver an extremely precise and finely atomized spray of fuel.

One primary advantage of throttle-body injection is an injector (or two) for every cylinder, which provides extremely accurate fuel metering. In addition, racing experience has shown the benefit of so-called showerhead injectors, usually another complete set mounted in the airbox. These come into play at higher rpm for better throttle response, and subsequent higher peak power.

ENGINE MANAGEMENT SYSTEM

Modern motorcycles feature incredibly sophisticated computer-controlled engine management systems with far more computing power than the systems on early spacecraft. Sensors located in several places on the bike provide information to the computer—such as coolant temperature, engine speed, crankshaft position, throttle position, manifold pressure, and incoming air temperature—so it can calculate the amount of fuel necessary for that instant in time, then command the injectors to open for a specific duration, or pulse width, delivering precisely the

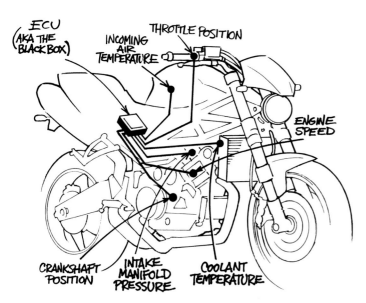

ECU (AKA THE BLACK BOX)

INCOMING AIR TEMPERATURE

THROTTLE POSITION

ENGINE SPEED

CRANKSHAFT POSITION

INTAKE MANIFOLD PRESSURE

COOLANT TEMPERATURE

correct amount of fuel. The ECU repeats this process hundreds of times per second. By comparison, carburetors start to look a bit Stone Age.

Once the engine is warmed up, the pulse width is finely tuned by a signal from an oxygen sensor (also known as a lambda sensor) in the exhaust's head pipes. This crucial sensor compares the percentage of oxygen in the exhaust gases coming from the engine with the percentage of oxygen in the atmosphere. It then generates an electrical voltage signal based on this difference to the computer many times per second, which then adjusts the EFI system's air/fuel mixture as close to perfect—the ideal 14.7:1 ratio, otherwise known as stoichiometric—as possible.

By now, EFI systems' inherent efficiency should be making carburetors look decidedly Stone Age. Yet, despite fuel injection's inherent superiority, some bikes' EFI systems provide throttle response at certain rpm that will make you grind your teeth in frustration. Why? Because compromises have to be made to fuel delivery in order for motorcycles to pass increasingly tougher emissions standards. What a rider can end up with, though, are dips in the torque curve that are felt as flat spots in the engine's fueling, and/or annoyingly abrupt response directly off-idle.

Fortunately, there's a fairly simple solution. Several aftermarket companies sell electronic black boxes that can alter an injector's pulse width, richening or leaning the air/fuel mixture throughout the rpm band. Such devices are available from Yoshimura (Electronic Management System, or EMS), Cobra (FI2000R) and Techlusion (Fuel Injection Module). But perhaps the best known—and the best supported—is Dynojet's Power Commander.

Like the others, the Power Commander simply plugs into your bike's wiring harness. Where it differs from the others, though, is in its range of tuning abilities.

Each Power Commander comes loaded with a base map of new values for your engine's fuel curve, whether the engine is stock, has an aftermarket exhaust and/or air filter, or more extensive tuning. Or you can download maps from Dynojet's Web site; for Honda's CBR600RR, for instance, Dynojet offered 41 maps as this book was being written. Plus, you can have a custom map made at one of Dynojet's tuning centers, for the best possible fueling, power, and rideability.

TAKING CARE OF THE FUEL SYSTEM

Basic modern motorcycle fuel-system maintenance involves little more than two Fs: filters and fuel. Motorcycles equipped with gravity-fed carburetors rarely came with filtering any more elaborate than a tiny screen in the tank's on/off switch, or petcock. And, interestingly, most non-gravity-fed carbureted motorcycle engines didn't even have fuel filters between the fuel tank and fuel pump.

Fuel Filter Changes

Simply put, it's crucial to look after fuel injection system filters. Typically, FI filters are quite large in size and volume and mounted inside the fuel tank. They trap debris, crud, and even water from the fuel, and should be changed (if possible) according to your owner's manual instructions. Once the filter begins to clog, its resistance to fuel flow increases, which works the

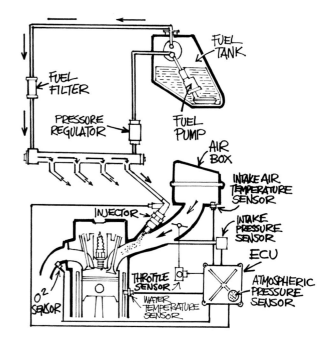

FUEL TANK

FUEL FILTER

PRESSURE REGULATOR

FUEL PUMP

AIR BOX

INTAKE AIR TEMPERATURE SENSOR

INTAKE PRESSURE SENSOR

ECU

INJECTOR

THROTTLE SENSOR

WATER TEMPERATURE SENSOR

ATMOSPHERIC PRESSURE SENSOR

O² SENSOR

electric fuel pump much harder; a $25 fuel filter is a far simpler and less expensive service than it would be to have the fuel pump replaced. And, of course, a clogged fuel filter or croaked fuel pump will leave you and your bike dead on the side of the road as surely as a dropped valve. You can't make a fuel-injected vehicle with a clogged fuel system limp home; the engine simply will not run.

> One extremely important service note when replacing fuel filters: On a carbureted engine, some minor fuel spillage might occur when the fuel line is disconnected to change the filter. Remember, though, fuel-injected engines operate at high fuel pressures. Consequently, opening or disconnecting any fuel system component without fully de-pressurizing the system is extremely dangerous. What's more, many fuel filters require a special tool to disconnect the fuel lines. That's why changing the fuel filter on modern EFI systems is a task best left to a pro at your dealership.

Air Filter Changes

> It is impossible to overestimate the importance of keeping your bike's air filter in top shape. The filter is designed to remove fine particles, dirt, and debris from the air before they are ingested by the engine. Any type of debris entering the engine acts like sandpaper, increasing the rate of wear on pistons, rings, and cylinder walls, and shortening their lives and the life of the engine. This is always a bad thing, so make sure the air induction system components are well sealed and change the air filter regularly.

There's widespread disagreement on what size contaminants are most likely to cause engine damage. But it is reasonable to assume anything 10 microns or larger is destructive enough. For comparison, the average human hair is 70 microns, particles of talcum powder measure around 10 microns, red blood cells are 8 microns, and bacteria are 2 microns.

The best advice you'll get is to keep it simple: Change the air filter once a year. If you ride in a dusty environment or on dirt roads, change the air filter more frequently, perhaps every six months. Any serious restriction of airflow through the air filter will significantly decrease the fuel mileage from your vehicle. This restriction will literally strangle your engine.

Choose the Proper Fuel

> The other F in fuel system maintenance is the fuel itself. For gasoline engines, your first concern is to use the correct octane fuel for your motorcycle, which you'll find in the . . . owner's manual! Here's the rule of thumb: Use the lowest octane fuel your bike's engine will operate on satisfactorily. The corollary: There is no advantage to using fuel with an octane rating higher than the engine requires—none. With the price of gasoline continuing to climb, that's worthwhile information.

The vast majority of motorcycles operate perfectly satisfactorily on regular unleaded, which carries an average octane rating of 86–88. Some higher-performance, higher-power, and/or higher-priced motorcycles require premium octane fuels, typically in the 91–93 octane range. Many, if not most, of these can operate satisfactorily on 89–90 octane midgrade fuels, if not on 87 octane regular. Why? Knock sensors.

A knock sensor—literally a small microphone that's tuned to hear the unique sounds of engine knock or ping caused by inadequate-octane fuel—provides another input to the engine management computer to help it determine the precise air/fuel mixture and spark timing for the engine.

In most cases, pinging sounds like a handful of small pebbles in a tin can and is most often heard under light to moderate acceleration. If and when the knock sensor hears this, the computer richens the mixture and/or retards ignition timing, both of which will lower combustion temperatures to prevent knock and potential engine damage.

FUEL SYSTEM TROUBLESHOOTING

PROBLEM	PROBABLE CAUSES	ACTION TO REPAIR
ENGINE CRANKS BUT WON'T START	No fuel pressure because the bike is out of gas; fuel pump malfunctioning	Start with Fuel Pump Hum/Sound Test
	Fuel Pump Hum/Sound Test	Turn on key, listen for fuel pump operation (a whine or hum that lasts for about 2 seconds). Fuel pump should run for 2 seconds, then stop
	If you hear fuel pump hum, fuel pump is working	Go to **Check Ignition Switch**
	If you don't hear hum, fuel pump might not be working	Go to **Check Ignition Switch**
NO FUEL PUMP OPERATION	**Check Ignition Switch**	Do instrument panel warning lights illuminate when key is turned to "On"?
	Ignition switch tests bad	Replace ignition switch
	Ignition switch tests OK	Go to **Check Fuel Pump/Fuse**
	Check Fuel Pump/Fuse	Find fuse box (see your owner's manual); slots should be labeled. Remove fuse from fuel pump/ECU slot. Replace with new fuse and turn ignition switch on and listen for fuel pump hum
	Failed/open fuse	Replace fuse
	Fuse is OK	Take to dealership
LONG CRANK TIME BEFORE ENGINE STARTS	Blocked fuel tank vent creating vacuum	Remove fuel filler cap, try starting engine again
	Loss of fuel pressure preventing engine from starting	Check fuel pump: Disconnect fuel line from carburetor or injector. Place open end in an empty container. Turn key on/push engine start switch—fuel should gush from line. If not . . .
	Plugged fuel filter	Replace fuel filter
	Still no fuel flow? Go back to **Check Fuel Pump/Fuse**	

Project 12
Clean/Replace Your Air Filter

TIME: 30 minutes or overnight if air-drying a filter

TOOLS: Wrenches, sockets, ratchet, No. 2 Phillips screwdriver, rear stand, clean rags, compressed air

TALENT: 1

COST: $

PARTS: OE or aftermarket air filter, air filter cleaner, air filter oil

TIP: Buying a washable aftermarket filter will pay for itself in a couple of cleanings

BENEFIT: Consistent fuel mixture, better airflow

For your engine to operate at peak efficiencies, the air filter needs to be clean to allow maximum airflow. Let your filter get dirty, and you'll experience power loss, reduced gas mileage, and possible plug fouling. Regular—at least annual—cleaning of your bike's air filter is a simple way to promote good performance.

Gaining access to your air filter may be as simple as removing the cover on the side of the engine, or you may have to remove the tank. Consult your owner's or factory service manual to see if the seat or any bodywork needs to be removed prior to unbolting the tank. If you have to remove the tank, be sure to turn the petcock off and place a rag below the fuel line you'll be disconnecting. Remove the bolts securing the tank and make sure you disconnect all the hoses and wires. Label any hoses that aren't already color coded to ease reassembly. Some bikes with tank-top instrumentation require that the housing be removed before lifting off the tank, while others can be left in place. Check that factory service manual!

Remove the tank and place it out of harm's way. Give the top of the air box a quick blast with compressed air to clear out any dirt that may have accumulated in the screw holes. Remove the Phillips-head screws on the air box cover, making sure that you don't drop any into the depths of the engine compartment, never to be seen again. (Sometimes a dropped part can be retrieved with a magnetic pickup tool—if you're lucky.) Once all the screws are removed, remove the lid and inspect the air box to determine the path of airflow in from the outside. Carefully, remove the air filter, making sure you don't knock any grit into the clean side of the air box. If the top of the air box is going to be off for more than a minute or so, cover the throttle intakes with clean rags or paper towels.

Air filters vary by manufacturer. Generally, you clean foam filters in a solvent. Paper filters can be blown out with compressed air from the back side of the filter. The best idea, though, is to buy an aftermarket filter such as BMC or K&N. These pleated cotton filters are reusable and should last the life of your motorcycle.

Although this is not as crucial with a V-twin with the filter hanging off the side as with a V-four with a more traditional airbox, you should keep the dirty side of the filter away from the throttle intakes.

Rinsing from the clean side out, use cold water to flush out the dirt, oil, and solvent. Let the filter air dry. Don't use compressed air or a hair dryer.

Oil the filter one pleat at a time. Let it sit for 20 minutes, then reoil any white spots in the cotton.

Cleaning a reusable filter is a four-part operation. First, spray or pour on solvent to cut the oil used to trap the dirt and let it soak for a few minutes. Rinse out the oil from the back side (the clean side) of the filter with cold water until the cotton fibers are clean. Dry the filter in the sun for a few hours or hang it in your garage overnight. Do not use compressed air or a hair dryer or you will shrink the cotton and render the filter useless. When it's dry, you want to coat the cotton with filter oil. (Never use any other kind of oil but filter oil.) If you are using a spray, one pass per pleat will suffice. For squeeze bottles, make one pass per pleat in the bottom of the pleat. Don't saturate the filter. Let it sit for 20 minutes and reoil any white spots on the cotton.

Installing a fresh or cleaned filter is as easy as its removal. However, you should make sure that you have the filter facing the correct direction. For example, paper filters will generally have a screen to support the back of the filter to keep it from flexing or tearing during operation. If your air box has an O-ring to seal the filter access, ascertain that it is in position.

After you close the air box, take a moment to make sure that it sealed properly. Screw the cover in place in an alternating pattern (rather than going around the circumference) to make sure that the pressure is evenly applied. Reinstall the tank, bodywork, and seat as necessary—and breathe easy.

With paper filters, you should tap the filter on a table or trash can to knock the big chunks of crud free. Remove the rest of the dirt by blowing from the back side of the filter.

Chapter 3
Engine

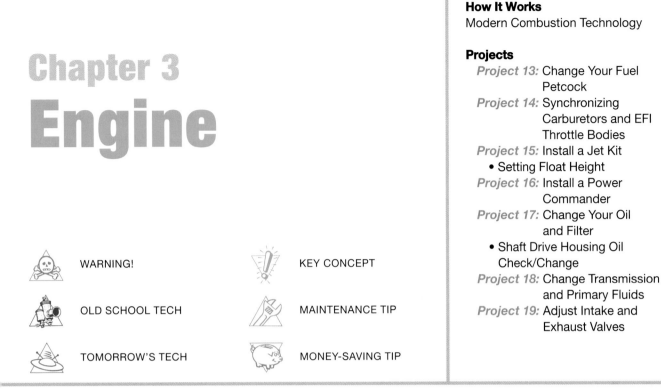

WARNING!

KEY CONCEPT

OLD SCHOOL TECH

MAINTENANCE TIP

TOMORROW'S TECH

MONEY-SAVING TIP

Fireworks. Jerry Bruckheimer movies. Countless Darwin award winners. Such things should make it self-evident that guys *really* like explosions. And, as if by divine design, the internal combustion engine is all about explosions, too—lots of them. It's how they roll.

Your motorcycle's powerplant is an internal combustion engine, and almost certainly a four-stroke (virtually all bikes on the road in the United States these days are four-strokes). It's also a direct descendant of the original, the Otto cycle engine, created by one Nikolaus Otto in 1876. To understand how an internal combustion engine works, let's focus on a single-cylinder four-stroke, like the ones that power some manufacturers' entry-level bikes, or their dual-sport machines.

Fuel gets metered to the engine through the carburetor, where it is atomized (broken into tiny little droplets), then mixed with air, and drawn through the intake valve(s) into the cylinder. Now, a camshaft closes the intake valve(s) as the piston starts up toward the top of the cylinder. The air/fuel mixture—ideally 14.7 parts air to 1 part fuel—gets compressed as the piston approaches the top of the cylinder, squeezing the mixture into the combustion chamber.

At precisely the right instant, a set of ignition contact points, usually operated off the camshaft, opens. That action causes the collapse of a magnetic field in the ignition coil, creating a high-voltage spark; the spark jumps across the spark plug's electrodes, which protrude into the combustion chamber. The spark lights a fire and starts the combustion process. The air/fuel mixture burns progressively but extremely quickly, generating a tremendous amount of heat and pressure in the cylinder.

Substitute electronic fuel injection and electronic spark control for the carburetor and ignition points, and you've got the basics of a modern motorcycle engine.

How does the engine convert this burning process into work? To begin with, work is defined as when a force moves a mass (your motorcycle, for instance) over a distance (such as a road). In this case, your bike's engine performs work by converting the chemical energy of fuel into an energy applied to the rear wheel, thereby putting the motorcycle into motion.

And it's (internal) combustion that does the initial job of converting fuel's chemical energy, as the resultant 1,600-degree Fahrenheit heat and the tremendous pressure of rapidly expanding gases apply massive pressure to the piston's crown, driving the piston downward in the cylinder. The piston, joined to the connecting rod, transmits this force to an offset pin on the crankshaft, which in turn translates the combustion pressure into a rotational force at the crankshaft.

Now, multiply this process by the number of cylinders in the engine and by the rotational speed of the crankshaft,

45

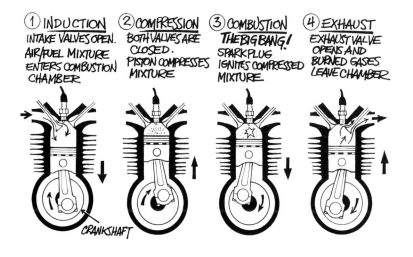

① **INDUCTION**
INTAKE VALVES OPEN.
AIR/FUEL MIXTURE
ENTERS COMBUSTION
CHAMBER

② **COMPRESSION**
BOTH VALVES ARE
CLOSED.
PISTON COMPRESSES
MIXTURE

③ **COMBUSTION**
THE BIG BANG!
SPARK PLUG
IGNITES COMPRESSED
MIXTURE

④ **EXHAUST**
EXHAUST VALVE
OPENS AND
BURNED GASES
LEAVE CHAMBER

CRANKSHAFT

and presto, you've got useable power with which to ride your motorcycle. Is physics cool or what?

Modern gasoline motorcycle engines are almost universally four-stroke; that is, four separate piston movements are necessary to fully complete one power cycle. The four strokes are (again, using a single-cylinder engine as an example):

• **Intake**—intake valve(s) open(s) as the piston moves downward, drawing air/fuel mix into the combustion chamber; exhaust valve(s) closed

• **Compression**—intake valve(s) close(s), as the piston moves upward in the cylinder, compressing the mixture; exhaust valve(s) close(d)

• **Combustion**—a spark ignites the mixture near the top of piston stroke (top dead center, or TDC), generating heat and pressure that forces the piston back down the cylinder; intake and exhaust valves closed

• **Exhaust**—exhaust valve(s) open(s) as the piston starts back up the cylinder, forcing burned gases out of combustion chamber; intake valve(s) close(d)

MODERN COMBUSTION TECHNOLOGY

With well over 100 years of development, modern gasoline engines are remarkably refined and efficient. Lots of new technology has been applied to improve performance and efficiency, and reduce emissions. None of it is new in the sense of just being discovered, but modern technology, design, engineering, and manufacturing have made these following items mainstays of motorcycling's mainstream.

Overhead camshaft(s): By mounting the cam, or camshafts, on top of the cylinder head and operating the valves either directly or by rocker arms, fewer parts and lighter weight benefit the valvetrain's efficiency. Lighter weight also allows higher rpm, and more horsepower as a result.

Four valves: Instead of a single intake and exhaust valve for each cylinder, a pair of intake and exhaust valves each per cylinder allows better gas flow at higher valve lifts and higher rpm. Four-valve setups are also generally lighter than equivalent two-valve designs, permitting higher rpm and, thus, more power as well. In fact, Yamaha pioneered and produced five-valve engines— three intake and two exhaust— starting with the 1985 FZ750, until the tuning-fork firm abandoned the concept with the 2007 model-year.

Electronic fuel injection (EFI): EFI revolutionized fuel delivery, allowing more power and performance, plus greater efficiency and lower emissions than possible with carburetors, along with incredible durability and reliability of the EFI components

Electronic ignition: Like EFI, electronic ignitions have eliminated most of the mechanical/moving parts in ignition systems; increased accuracy and control of ignition timing; and improved performance, efficiency, rideability, and durability.

Direct ignition (DI) or Coil-on-plug ignition (COP): (See Chapter 4) Both DI and COP systems eliminate spark plug wires entirely, and utilize multiple ignition coils; COP ignitions generally have one coil per cylinder, mounted

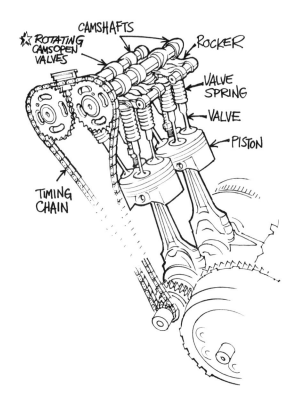

CAMSHAFTS

ROTATING CAMS OPEN VALVES

ROCKER

VALVE SPRING

VALVE

PISTON

TIMING CHAIN

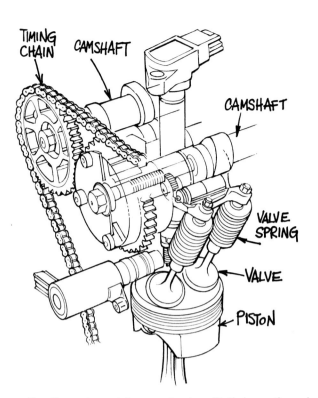

directly on top of the spark plug. Both have the advantages of longer coil life, and of working well at elevated rpm (10,000 rpm or higher).

Variable valve timing: This provides electro-hydraulic control of valve timing (when the intake/exhaust valves open/close) by varying the timing relationship between the crankshaft, camshaft, and valves. It improves efficiency by allowing optimal valve timing at any rpm. Although it can be particularly useful in helping smaller engines deliver good power at low rpm, the application has not yet found widespread use in motorcycles largely because of the increased weight and complexity of such systems.

Historically, two-stroke gasoline engines enjoyed the benefit of light weight and high power-to-weight ratios. But emissions regulations have sidelined two-strokes for street-bike use for now. Off-road motorcycles are mostly four-strokes these days, as the four-stroke race bikes are incredibly powerful and California laws restrict the use of two-stroke off-road bikes to closed race courses only.

Just so you understand, though, here's how a two-stroke engine operates. Ports or openings in the cylinder wall are uncovered and covered by the piston's movement, which allows the air/fuel mixture into, and exhaust gases out of, the engine. Because the piston can do this with each up/down movement, the engine can fire the mixture each cycle rather than every other cycle as with a four-stroke.

Don't write off two-strokes quite yet. Several manufacturers are working on high-tech two-stroke engines that produce minimal emissions and sound. Honda's direct injection system is just one of these being tested and developed. If these systems are perfected, we may see two-strokes return to the market, both on and off the highway.

TURBOCHARGING

When an exhaust-driven air pump is powered by hot, rapidly expanding exhaust gases, the engine is turbocharged. Turbos take a moment to spool up to 20,000–30,000 rpm as the throttle is open, thus creating just a bit of throttle lag. But they work very well with small engines, helping them produce big power at higher rpm, yet still delivering the fuel mileage of a small engine. Motorcycling went through its turbo age in the early 1980s, but, again, the extra weight and complexity, plus turbo lag, made them unsuitable for further use.

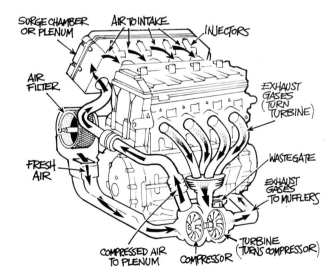

ENGINE TROUBLESHOOTING

PROBLEM	PROBABLE CAUSES	ACTION TO REPAIR	RELEVANT PROJECTS
ENGINE LOCKED UP (WON'T TURN OVER EVEN WITH FUNCTIONING BATTERY AND STARTER)	Hydraulic lock with fuel, water, or coolant	Remove spark plugs, pull fuse(s) to disable ignition/fuel injection. Try starter/try to turn engine with socket on end of crank (if accessible)	
	Mechanical failure—seized bearing/broken rod/piston/valve	Replace or rebuild engine	
EXCESSIVE BLUE SMOKE FROM EXHAUST	Oil smoke from worn piston rings/valve guides/seals	Replace valve seals—might reduce oil smoke/consumption	
ENGINE STOPS ENTIRELY	ECU/ignition/fuel delivery problem	See Electrical System Troubleshooting	
EXCESSIVE WHITE SMOKE FROM EXHAUST	Coolant leaking into combustion chambers; possible cylinder head gasket failure	Presure-test cooling system; chemically test for hydrocarbons in coolant. DIY—remove spark plugs right after shutting down engine. Look for white vapor emitting from plug holes	
BLUE SMOKE FROM EXHAUST WHEN ENGINE FIRST STARTED, THEN EXHAUST EMISSIONS APPEAR NORMAL	Worn valve guides/seals. Oil leaks into combustion chamber after engine is shut off	Replace valve seals—might reduce smoke	
LOUD BANGING, CLANKING, KNOCKING, RATTLE FROM ENGINE	Mechanical noise from worn engine bearing/broken valvetrain component, worn/loose timing chain	Do not operate engine until checked by a professional. DIY—Use mechanical stethoscope to locate source of noise	
ENGINE SPRAYS OIL	Loose oil-fill cap	Tighten or replace cap	
LOW OIL-PRESSURE LIGHT ILLUMINATES OR GAUGE SHOWS LOW OIL PRESSURE	Oil leak from valve cover/cylinder head/main oil seal	Identify and repair leak	

ENGINE TROUBLESHOOTING

PROBLEM	PROBABLE CAUSES	ACTION TO REPAIR	RELEVANT PROJECTS
LOW OIL-PRESSURE LIGHT ILLUMINATES OR GAUGE SHOWS LOW OIL PRESSURE	Oil level low	Check oil and fill to (owner's-manual-) recommended level	Project 4: Checking vital fluids and Project 17: Change oil and filter
	Oil pump failing, worn engine bearings	Have engine/bearings/oil pump checked at dealership	
SMOKE EMANATES FROM ENGINE	Oil leak onto hot exhaust	Identify and repair oil leak	
	Hot coolant leaking from engine/radiator	Identify and repair coolant leak	

ENGINE

3

Project 13
Change Your Fuel Petcock

TIME:	1 hour
TOOLS:	Sidecutter, screwdriver, WD-40, razor, fuel-proof thread sealant, open-end wrenches/wrench for the petcock, clamps for the fuel line, a funnel
TALENT:	1
COST:	$–$$
PARTS:	The fuel valve of choice, new factory pinch clamps and the special tool required or quality conventional hose clamps, drain container for the fuel, new fuel filter (now's the time)
TIP:	Make sure the gas cap is venting properly or the fuel won't drop—a vapor lock sort of thing
BENEFIT:	Harder pull at high rpm

Harley-Davidson introduced the vacuum-operated petcock (fuel valve) on its 1995 models. Harley thought they were doing us a favor, because most of us forget to turn the manual petcocks off, which can lead to a puddle of gas leaking from your carb. The company figured this foolproof, fail-safe design that prevents fuel from leaking past the carburetor's needle seat when the bike's motor is not running was safer and smarter. Then reformulated MTBE gasoline hit the tanks in the summer of 1995. A tank or two of that stuff and riders were "running out of gas" on full tanks, even though the lever on the vacuum petcock hadn't been touched. To correct this problem, Harley introduced a revised vacuum petcock with a different rubber compound on the internal diaphragm and a new filter screen. It's identified by the letter "M" stamped on the right side. The new filter screen can be identified by its orange color.

Another problem the redesign may or may not have fixed is the fuel diaphragm unsnapping itself from the vacuum diaphragm inside of the petcock, which immediately stops gas flow. Amusingly, this problem seems to happen mostly to the old timers, who were used to manual fuel valves. They turn the gas off at the lever and then forget to turn it on again before they start the engine. The tremendous initial suction from the engine firing with the lever in the off position just rips up the diaphragm. This is absolutely no problem if you leave the petcock on.

For decades, Harley riders have had to train themselves to turn off their manual petcock (the one on the left). Then, in 1995, Harley decided it was time to relieve us of that chore by fitting an automatic petcock, only to have this nifty convenience cause more trouble than it was worth because the rubber parts couldn't stand up to the new reformulated gasohols that were mandated in some cities. The problem has been solved with stouter rubber internals on new machines and by a recall on the older automatic petcocks.

The simplest fix for this is to convert to a manual petcock, available from Harley-Davidson and aftermarket petcock suppliers such as Pingel, Accel, EMS, and others. Pay attention to which direction the outlet nipple faces and the thread size on the petcock body. Harleys of the relevant years use 22-mm threads. Pingel valves and

Pingel is not the only game in town for high-flow petcocks, as this Accel valve clearly demonstrates. EMS is another company trying to carve out a niche, with features that improve on or solve certain deficiencies in design, like the frequent need to rebuild. Accel and EMS are both less prone to this, and they have positive stops for lever position. It pays to shop around for the features you want, as well as the performance you need.

For those afflicted prior to the recall, the only fix was to swap petcocks. Most opted to return to the good old manual version. Others, knowing that the stocker only passes about one-third the fuel volume of some high-performance aftermarket petcocks, opted to upgrade to a high-flow unit like this Pingel. Not that all problems go away with the change. You still need to remember to manually shut off the valve, and most hot rod petcocks have very little reserve capacity. The average Pingel gives you about 0.2 gallon (5 to 10 miles) of reserve fuel, so you'll need to learn to run off of the top half of your fuel supply or never get too far from a gas station.

This is the part of a gas cap that needs to be beautiful, as in work beautifully. The cap on the left is the unvented one, if you have two. The cap on the right must vent properly to perform well, and that says nothing about the general need to reengineer some late-model one-way tank venting. If need be, one can simply put a hole in the black one-way valve built into that belly button–looking gray area, using a deft touch, a hammer, and a punch.

some others require an adapter nut to suit your stock tank—get it when you buy the valve. You will also need a vacuum-line cap to plug the unused nipple extending from the carburetor to the petcock. As for the direction the outlet nipple faces, that depends on the fuel tank you have. Some tanks need to have the nipple facing the front of the machine, some the rear, and others straight down. Make sure the replacement valve faces the same way as the original, or find one that has a rotating nipple.

To change the fuel valve, drain the fuel, remove the fuel line, unscrew the nut holding the petcock to the tank, and let everything quit dripping. Use some Teflon tape or TSP in a tube on the petcock nut threads and screw it on the valve. Once it's hand tight, snug it up a bit with a wrench; as long as it doesn't leak and can't be moved by hand, you're good to go.

A fringe benefit from switching petcocks is increased fuel flow, which is sometimes necessary for high-performance Harleys. Yet most people would do themselves more good by ensuring a properly vented gas cap than by swapping to a higher flow petcock. You can slap on the nicest high-flow petcock on the planet and not do your motor a bit of good if there's a partial vacuum forming inside the tank. This sort of so-called vapor lock isn't really that uncommon in stock Harleys, particularly when your tank is closer to empty than full. Sometimes you notice this problem even while cruising in the form of a sort of hunting or surging after an hour or so of running at 70-plus on a hot day. Motors making much more power than stock can have even worse issues.

Project 14

Synchronizing Carburetors and EFI Throttle Bodies

TIME:	1 hour
TOOLS:	Wrenches, sockets, ratchet, No. 2 Phillips screwdriver, clean rags, carb balancer, box fan, auxiliary fuel tank
TALENT:	2
COST:	$
PARTS:	None
TIP:	Make sure all vacuum leaks are plugged or you will get false readings
BENEFIT:	Smoother power delivery

Most (but not all) motorcycle engines use multiple carburetors or throttle bodies. If these induction devices are not in synch and delivering the same amount of fuel to each cylinder, your bike will run poorly or not at all. The symptoms can be as mild as rough idling or an uneven engine sound at partial throttle. Severe cases can cause surging while at any constant throttle setting.

The reward for spending an hour synching your carbs is a smoother-idling, quicker-revving engine. The only tools required other than typical home mechanic's sockets and wrenches are a vacuum gauge and an auxiliary fuel tank (for bikes that don't have a fuel pump).

Since your bike will be running, make sure your work area for this project has good ventilation. Start by removing the seat, gas tank, and anything that gets in the way of the carbs. Be careful when disconnecting the fuel line from the petcock, particularly if the engine is hot. Hold a rag under the open line until all the gas has drained out. To avoid damage to the petcock and possible fuel spillage, place the fuel tank on an old tire to keep it from tipping over. Label the various hoses as you disconnect them from the air box and tank.

Some manufacturers fit hoses to the carbs or throttle bodies to allow for easy synchronization. Your factory service manual will help you find them.

Locate and uncover the ports into the intake tract. You will find either bolt plugs or capped nipples. Your carb balancer should include threaded adapters to fit the port. While most port threads will be 5 mm, some bikes use 6-mm threads.

While the engine warms up, listen for any vacuum leaks you may have forgotten to seal. After your engine reaches operating temperature, make sure you have a fan blowing across the radiator (or engine in air-cooled configurations) to help keep your bike from overheating. If you let it get too hot, the carb synching may not be accurate. Finally, make sure the idle speed is set to factory specs.

You can synchronize most bikes by adjusting the linkage connecting the butterfly valves. However, some fuel-injected bikes simply require that you adjust an air screw in each throttle body to get it to match the one body that doesn't have an air screw. Check your factory service manual.

Multis, be they inline-four sporty bikes or V-four cruisers, must be done in steps—as must EFI systems that use the butterfly valves (rather than air screws) to synchronize the throttle bodies. Begin by finding the adjuster screw between the number 1 and 2 cylinders. Turn it until you have the two carb-balancer readings identical. Blip the throttle slightly and let the engine return to idle. Make an adjustment if necessary. Once you're happy with the results, switch to the adjustment of the number 3 and 4 cylinders. Again, once the two sets of two carburetors are set, find the adjuster screw between the number 2 and 3 cylinders to balance the two pairs of butterfly valves.

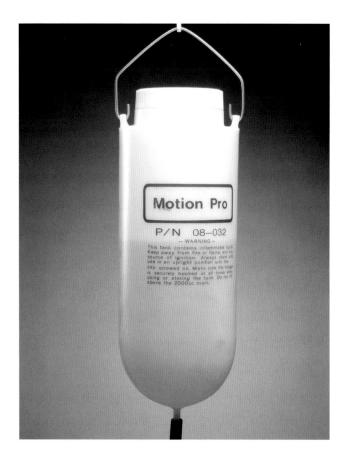

Motion Pro sells two reasonably priced versions of their carb tuner through distributors and motorcycle dealerships. Because you'll be running your engine for a while, you need a supply of gas for your carburetors. A purpose-built auxiliary tank supplies fuel to your engine while keeping any gas from dripping on the engine's hot parts. Hang the auxiliary tank above the level of the carbs, but out of the way of your wrenching. If your bike uses a fuel pump that is built into the gas tank, you will need to find a way to keep the fuel line, return line, wiring harness, and tank mounted to feed the carbs/throttle bodies—a tricky operation.

Even liquid-cooled bikes need to have air moving around them to maintain proper operating temperature. A box fan will work nicely.

Now that the carbs are in sync, raise the rpm to 3,000 and hold it steady. The columns of mercury should settle at a consistent height. If one or more of the columns rises less than the others, there is a vacuum leak or some other fault. Common problems are a worn slide that is sticking or something failing in the linkage. Finally, adjust the engine's idle speed back to the factory specs if it changed. Carefully remove the carb tool and reposition all vacuum hoses and plugs. Start the engine again to see if there are air leaks—the idle speed should stay the same. Replace the tank, paying special attention to the fuel and vacuum lines connected to the petcock. Your bike's engine should now idle smoother and rev cleaner.

Your bike will either have a capped nipple or a threaded plug. Some manufacturers make your job easier by routing hoses out from under the throttle bodies. If you don't have those hoses and can't access the nipples on the throttle bodies with the airbox in place, disassemble and remove it. You'll need to attach your carb balancer either to the nipple or hose.

SYNCHRONIZING CARBURETORS
AND EFI THROTTLE BODIES

After, and possibly while, adjusting the linkage to improve throttle synchronization, you will need to adjust the idle speed back to factory spec. Either way you adjust the synchronization, the carb balancer displays the same information. The vacuum created in the intake tract will draw the mercury up from the reservoir in the bottom of the carb tool. There will always be some variance between the columns, but most manufacturers say that a 1/2- to 1-inch difference of mercury level is fine. However, adjusting the columns of mercury so that they are as close to identical as possible is worth the minimal effort it requires. Twins will have only one screw to adjust the synchronization. So, you're done at this point.

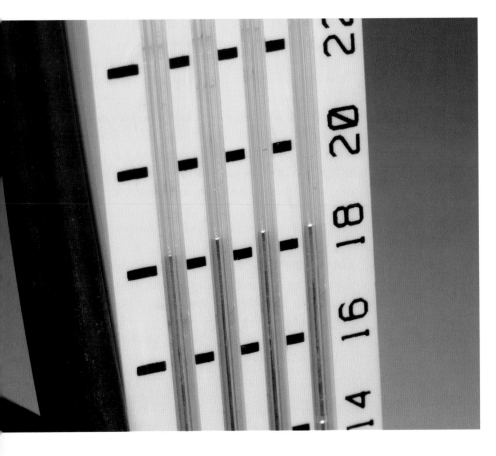

Once you have the adapters screwed in, attach the hoses to the nipples. Starting at the No. 1 cylinder (the front cylinder on V-twins or the front left on other multicylinder configurations), connect the first hose and move across the front cylinders (if the bike has them) left to right before the rear cylinder(s) making sure to keep the hoses in order. Find a convenient place to hang the carb balancer so that you can see it while the engine is running. Before you start the engine, make sure that the hoses do not interfere with the throttle linkage. Also, make a thorough visual check to see that all possible vacuum leaks have been sealed. When you start the engine, don't blip the throttle too energetically, or you'll suck the mercury out of the carb stick into the engine. You want your columns of mercury to look like this when you're finished with your adjustments. Be sure to test the synchronization at cruising rpm to make sure that they maintain their relative closeness.

Project 15
Install a Jet Kit

TIME:	2 hours
TOOLS:	Wrenches, sockets, ratchet, Phillips screwdriver, flathead screwdriver, drill with screw attachment (optional), Allen keys, float height tool (if required), pliers, drill, rags
TALENT:	2
COST:	$
PARTS:	Jet kit
TIP:	Installing a jet kit is more than just tossing in a new main jet—take your time and work carefully
BENEFIT:	A bike that carburets cleanly throughout the entire rev range

Many bikes come from the factory with extremely lean jetting to meet EPA requirements, and sometimes something as simple as raising the needle with a shim can produce a night-and-day difference in your bike's performance, particularly off-throttle to on-throttle transitions. When you order a jet kit for your bike, be sure to order one based on your bike's current state of tune. Don't get a Stage III kit just because you plan to make big changes later on.

With the correct kit in hand, place the bike in gear on its side stand or on a bike lift. If the carburetors are tucked under the tank, you'll also need to remove the gas tank, air box, and any other obstructions. Label all hoses and wire connections. ("Carburetor" will also apply to multiple carbs in the following discussion.)

Loosen all the clamps securing the carburetor mouth to the rubber and the intake manifold. Gently wiggle the carb up and down until it pops free of the boot. Don't put it down just yet. Hold the carb over a suitable container and drain the float bowl. Before you do anything else, place clean rags or paper towels in the intake manifold to keep any nasties out.

Turn the carburetor upside down. Remove the float bowl with either a Phillips screwdriver or Allen key. (A drill with a screw attachment really speeds things up—particularly for bikes with four mixers.) Clean out any gunk that may have collected in the bottom of the float bowl. Also check to be sure that the float bowl gasket is not cracked, dried, or ripped. Replace it if you suspect it is deteriorating.

In order to access the idle jet, you need to remove the EPA-mandated cover. Prior to exposing the carb's innards, you might as well remove the brass plug covering the idle screw. Most jet kits will include a drill bit and self-tapping screw to remove the plug. If you don't have one, use a 1/8-inch drill bit and any wood or drywall screw you have sitting around. To keep from drilling too deeply past the plug and possibly damaging the idle jet, wrap a piece of tape around it about 1/8-inch above the tip. Don't drill any deeper than the tape. Insert the screw far enough to have a solid grip on the plug with the threads. Using a pair of pliers (locking pliers if you like), pull the plug free of the carburetor body. Before you go any further, insert a flathead screwdriver and count the number of turns as you screw the idle jet's needle valve into the carburetor until it touches bottom. Do not tighten the valve against the jet, or you may damage both the needle and the jet itself. Write down the number of turns you counted in case you someday decide to return to stock jetting. Now, unscrew the needle valve the number of turns specified by your jet kit.

If you don't have a large flathead screwdriver, use an 8-mm socket to remove the main jet and emulsion tube together. You'll still need to remove the main jet, though. Install the new one and snug it into place. Save the old jet in case you decide to go back to stock jetting.

When working on the main jet, make sure you don't put any pressure on the float, or you could bend the tab responsible for the fuel height. While most jet kits don't have you fiddle with the float height, some do. See the sidebar "Setting Float Height," for the lowdown on how to check and set float height.

The brass main jet is located in the center of the carb body. You can identify it by the flathead screwdriver slot in the base of the jet. Make sure your screwdriver fits snugly into the jet or you may mangle it as you attempt to remove it.

Flip the carb to access the top cover and unscrew the retaining screws/bolts. Under the cover is the top of a diaphragm. Constant velocity (CV) carburetors use the vacuum created as air flows through the carb's throat to lift a slide. The slide performs two duties. First, by restricting the size of the throat opening at lower air speeds (usually during lower rpm), the slide keeps the air speed high as it passes over the nozzle (or emulsion tube), thus atomizing the fuel more effectively. Second, it helps keep the engine from stumbling when you whack the carb open, since the slide will only rise as quickly as the airflow requires.

Some jet kits include an emulsion tube. If the emulsion tube (the brass part into which the main jet is screwed) turns with the jet, hold it in position with an 8-mm wrench. Jet kits without a new emulsion tube simply require that you screw in the new jet in place of the old one. If your jet kit includes a new pilot jet, you'll want to replace it the same way you did the main jet. The pilot jet is near the main jet but significantly smaller. Simply unscrew it and replace it with the new one. Before you reinstall the float bowl, make sure the gasket surfaces are clear of any dirt or grit. One grain of sand can cause a leak that forces you to tunnel back down to the carbs. When screwing the float bowl back onto the carb, make sure the screws are tight, but not overly tight.

The OE needle (top) has no adjustability, unless you want to shim it up slightly with a washer. The Factory Pro Tuning needle (bottom) allows you to richen or lean out the mixture as your engine setup requires. When affixing the circlip to the appropriate slot in the needle, always count from the top slot. If your jet kit instructions specify installing a washer, make sure it is on the needle below the circlip to raise the needle halfway between two circlip notches. If the jet kit requires the slide vacuum hole to be drilled, make sure you deburr the new hole. Slip the new needle and washer (if required) into the slide assembly. Place the spring holder in with its prongs down toward the needle.

Carefully, lift out the slide and examine the rubber diaphragm. If you find any cracks or pinholes, the diaphragm must be replaced. Notice how the needle hangs out of the bottom of the slide. Press up from the tip of the needle to remove it from the slide—but be sure you remember the order in which parts come out of the slide. You will find a spacer that holds the slide spring in place above the needle. You may also find a small washer below the needle. Carefully set these parts aside for use later.

Since carburetors with factory jetting usually have nonadjustable needles, most jet kits include an adjustable needle with instructions on how to correctly set the needle height.

Once you have replaced the jet, installed the needle, and adjusted the idle screw, you need to reinstall the carburetor. A little WD-40 on the carb mouth will ease its reinsertion into the boot. Tighten the clamp to secure the carb. Reinstall the throttle cables and adjust the throttle free play. When the engine has warmed up, adjust the idle speed to factory specifications. If the jet kit you installed was designed for your bike's exact engine/pipe configuration, you should now go out and enjoy your new power. However, if you've made other modifications to the engine, you may have some debugging to do in order to make it perfect.

Carefully check the diaphragm on top of the vacuum slide. When reinstalling the slide, make sure that the needle fits into the top of the emulsion tube. Carefully place the lip of the diaphragm in the groove at the top of the carb body. Any folds or buckles will lessen the vacuum inside the top of the carburetor and prevent proper slide function. If the diaphragm has any cracks or pinholes, it will need to be replaced.

SETTING FLOAT HEIGHT

If your jet kit recommends a specific float bowl height, perform the height adjustment after you've installed the other parts of the jet kit. With the carb standing on end (resting the end on your work bench will make it easier to steady the assembly while you're measuring the float height), tilt it until the float shifts toward the carburetor body. The idea is to have the float move the valve pin to a closed position—and no farther. You don't want the valve spring to compress.

While holding the carb in position, measure the float height with Factory Pro Tuning's float-height tool. The two arms of the tool should rest on the float-bowl gasket surface while the measuring bar gets slid into position so that it just barely touches the highest point on the float (when measured from the gasket surface). You may have to perform several adjustments of the measuring bar to keep it from compressing the float spring slightly.

To change the height, you need to bend the tang over the valve's spring

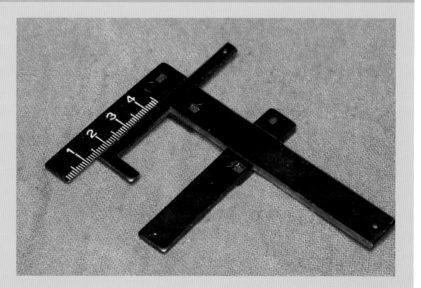

loops. A little bend goes a long way, so be careful. You'll find that it's better to move in little steps rather than trying to make large corrections. Your goal is to get the measurements as close as possible to the desired height with a maximum of 0.5-mm difference among all the carburetors if you have more than one.

Although it may not look like much, Factory Pro's float-height tool is precision-machined to allow accurate measurement of float height. It's worth every penny when you're tuning carburetors.

Project 16

Install a Power Commander

TIME:	1 hour (installation), many hours developing maps
TOOLS:	Basic mechanics tools, (laptop) computer and assorted cables for Power Commander, dyno
TALENT:	3
COST:	$$$$
PARTS:	Power Commander, Cobra Fi2000, or Dynatek F.I. Controller
TIP:	For a good starting point, use fuel maps created for your exhaust system, if available
BENEFIT:	The best possible fuel mixture and power at any rpm

The switch from carburetors to fuel injection has opened a whole new door to controlling mixture throughout the rpm range. Companies such as Dynojet and Cobra have created electronic control boxes that can share engine management duties with your factory electronics to improve performance throughout the rpm range. The manufacturer can guide you to the unit appropriate for your bike. Installing an aftermarket fuel injection controller is about the easiest bolt-on improvement you can make. For illustration, we'll discuss the Power Commander first, then follow with details on a Cobra and Dynatek model. With the ignition off, remove the seat to gain access to both the battery and the wiring harness. You may also need to remove the battery cover. Unbolt and remove the tank. Locate the main wiring harness on the frame. Follow the wires from the injector rail to the connector on the main harness. This is where you will attach the Power Commander.

Now that you know where the unit will go on your bike, clean the mounting location with alcohol to remove any grease. Place the controller in a position that will give you access to the accessory and USB

Different bikes will have different mounting locations for the aftermarket controller. For example, on the Vulcan 2000 featured in the photos, it will rest on top of the battery between the shock and the tank support. Snugly tucked away, the Power Commander leaves plenty of room for access to its USB port without compromising your storage.

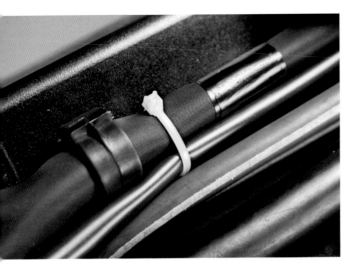 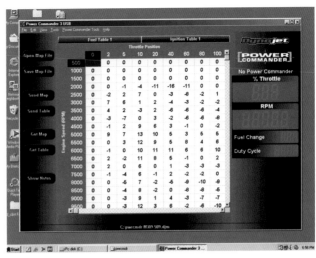

Zip-tie the Power Commander's wires to your bikes harness. Keep wires out of the way, making sure not to place them where they can get pinched and damaged by the gas tank, seat, or any of the parts you removed.

Detail-oriented folks will be in heaven with the Power Commander software. You can twiddle with the fuel and ignition maps to your heart's content. If you're of a Mac persuasion, the application runs fine under Virtual PC. If you're on the road (or don't have access to a computer), you can make mixture changes with the three buttons on top of the Power Commander unit.

ports. If your bike requires that you slip a protective cover over the unit, do so now.

Reassemble your bike. Because you bought the controller with the base map already installed, your bike is ready to ride. If you want to modify the base map, you have two choices. First (and most flexible), hook your new controller up to your computer and either manually tweak the maps or download a map from the controller's or your exhaust pipe manufacturer's website.

If you're not comfortable making changes, many bike shops that have dynos also have computers and all the appropriate cables to help you map your controller. As you modify your bike further, you can create new maps to fit your engine's needs. Also, if you don't like the changes you made to one map, with the push of a button, you can revert to your previous one.

Cobra Fi2000 and Dynatek F.I. Controller (SB16-1)

Cobra and Dynatek took a slightly different—but still effective—approach. Both modules utilize three small knobs (called pots—for potentiometers) to adjust the fuel mixture. Consequently, no computer or maps are required to adjust your cruiser's tuning. Instead, the three

pots control different aspects of the mixture. The primary difference between these modules is that the Dynatek unit can enrich or lean the fuel mixture, clipping on with factory connectors, while the Cobra unit uses wire taps and can only enrich the mixture.

Installation varies depending on your bike model. On the Cobra unit, you essentially connect four wires (two control wires, one power, and one ground), which will be the same colors as those on the corresponding bike. Using wire taps that splice into the stock harness without actually severing any wires, you create a link to the Fi2000 that then modifies the fuel mixture based on rpm. The Dynatek simply hooks into the stock connectors, plus positive and negative leads.

You can adjust either on a dyno or the street—without a tether to a computer. Start from the manufacturer's recommended bike-specific settings found in the instruction manuals and focus on the various rpm ranges one at a time. Spending a little time on the dyno will yield the best results.

TIME:	1 hour
TOOLS:	Oil filter wrench, oil catch pan, wrench for drain plug, contact cleaner, rags for cleanup
TALENT:	1
COST:	$
PARTS:	Oil filer, drain plug gasket, several quarts oil (check your factory service manual)
TIP:	Never dump used oil, a ground-water pollutant, down a drain; find your local oil recycling center at www.earth911.org or service stations in many areas take used oil
BENEFIT:	Better engine operation and longevity

Project 17
Change Your Oil and Filter

Regardless of debates you may encounter, use motorcycle oil in your bike, not regular motor oil. Oils have changed more in the last 10 years than they did in the previous 50, and today even air-cooled V-twins are machined to tolerances much tighter than previous generations of engines. Moreover, motorcycle engines share oil with the transmission and clutch. The shearing forces applied by the transmission and clutch will wear out cheap automobile oil much faster than motorcycle oil. Also, the newer low-friction or "energy-conserving" automobile oils use friction modifiers that may have a negative effect on your clutch's ability to engage properly. If you're willing to perform projects, maintenance, and upgrades costing far more, don't try to save a couple bucks here by buying oil less than perfect for your ride.

Whether to use petroleum-based or synthetic oil is another point of debate. On this question, you can't go wrong with what your bike manufacturer recommends. Synthetics generally perform better, but either type that is compatible with your engine will work fine. Maintaining clean oil and filter and proper oil level is more important than this decision, if both are approved for your engine.

The limited space on some cruisers often leaves little room for removing a filter by hand.

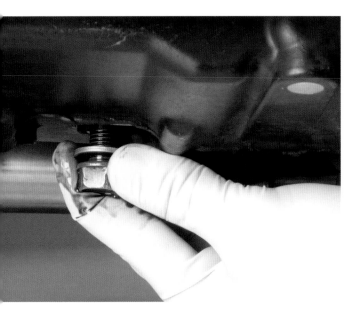

You can't remove a drain plug without getting oil on your hand. Be smart and wear a latex glove, which is cheap, disposable, and doesn't leave your hand filthy and raw.

Lube the filter's O-ring with fresh oil to help it get a good seal with the engine. Make sure the contact surface is clean, too.

Most resources recommend warming up the engine before you drain the oil. Before doing that, make sure you can loosen your oil filter so you don't burn your fingers fighting with it once the pipes are hot. If you can't get to it, buy an appropriately sized filter wrench. Novice mechanics shouldn't worry about violating a new bike's warranty. Just save your receipts and keep a record of the date and mileage of each change. Take your time and follow these steps.

Park your bike on a level surface. Wear latex gloves during the messy part of the oil change because used motor oil is a carcinogen. It also promotes unwanted fingerprints and stains. Locate the drain plug on the bottom of the oil pan and carefully loosen it. If the plug gives you trouble, brace the bike so it doesn't roll off the stand before you give the wrench a yank or resort to a breaker bar. Use a socket or box-end wrench for a tight bolt so you don't strip it.

Either use a funnel to drain the oil directly into a container for transport—like a gallon jug—or find a drain pan with a pour spout for the same transfer later. Once the oil has drained completely, move your drain pan beneath the filter and remove it. Don't forget to pour out the remaining oil from the filter into the catch pan. If your engine has an oil screen separate from the oil filter, you may need to clean it in solvent. Check your factory service manual to make sure.

Using your finger, wipe a film of fresh oil on the filter's O-ring. Prior to screwing the filter into place, wipe down

Oil pans are expensive and difficult to replace or rethread. Use a torque wrench to make the drain plug stay put without risking stripped threads.

the gasket's contact surface on the engine and make sure there is no grit anywhere that might break the O-ring's seal. Follow the filter manufacturer's specifications for tightening the filter. Use a new drain plug washer, and torque it to the factory specification.

Fill the engine with the amount and type of oil recommended in the owner's manual. Wipe down all the engine's oily surfaces so they don't smoke.

Now it's time to take the bike back out of gear and start it up. When you first start your engine, don't be alarmed if the oil light stays on a little longer than usual. The filter needs to fill with oil. Some fussy riders crank the starter and kill the engine when it fires, repeating the process until the oil light shuts off, in an effort to avoid running the engine while dry. Others crank the engine with the kill switch off until the light disappears. Once the engine reaches operating temperature, shut it down and wait a minute or so before checking the oil level. You may need to add or subtract oil as necessary, since the filter holds a few ounces of oil. Check for leaks, and you're done. Now, go for a ride.

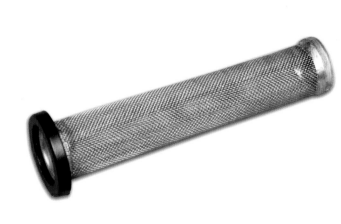

If your bike has an oil screen, don't forget to check the screen for metal shavings that might signal engine problems before you clean it with a high-flash-point solvent.

SHAFT DRIVE HOUSING OIL CHECK/CHANGE

Unlike chain or belt drives, which require occasional adjustment, shaft drives just need their lubricant changed as part of your bike's long-term maintenance. For example, after the initial 600-mile fluid change, the periodic maintenance schedule for the Mean Streak shown here recommends the next change be at 24,000 miles. That doesn't mean you should forget the shaft drive until the next change. You should still inspect the housing for leaks and check the oil level at the bare minimum of every other engine oil change.

Checking the gear case oil level is pretty simple. Make sure your bike is straight up and down. Using a really big flathead screwdriver, remove the oil filler cap. The oil level should be at the bottom of the opening. If not, double check for leaks before topping off the hypoid-gear oil with the manufacturer's recommended viscosity.

If you're going to change the oil, take your bike for a ride to heat up the oil. Once your bike is level on a stand, remove

the filler cap and drain plug. (You can store the used oil in the same container as your engine oil.) Clean up any oil spills that could end up on your tire to prevent bad things from happening. Install a fresh drain plug gasket and torque the plug to spec. Fill the gear case to the bottom of the filler with the manufacturer's recommended viscosity oil. Close the filler. After your next ride, check for leaks.

This gear case is ready to go until the next inspection.

Project 18

Change Transmission and Primary Fluids in Your Harley-Davidson

TIME: 1/2 to 1 hour

TOOLS: See the specific items listed below

TALENT: 1

COST: $

PARTS: Primary inspection gasket, drain plug washer or O-ring, and Teflon sealant (as required)

TIP: Some Big Twins have an exhaust pipe right in the way of the tranny drain plug; you may be able to work around it by modifying the drain plug removal tool so that you needn't remove the exhaust; just loosen it a bit and sneak in

BENEFIT: Added longevity for the primary chain and the gears in the box; clean fluid actually adds to the shift quality. Changing often is the best way to get another 100,000 miles out of a tranny that already had its first 100,000 when you bought it

COMPLEMENTARY MODIFICATION:
Convert to synthetic oil

Most foreign motorcycles use one oil for every-thing—multi-grade motorcycle oil for not only the engine but the transmission, clutch, and anything else they've got stuffed in there. Big Twins use three kinds of oil: (1) motorcycle engine oil specially formulated for roller-bearing engines; (2) gear oil with additives to bol-ster its film strength; and (3) primary lube, which has two jobs—keeping the clutch moist and happy and the pri-mary soaked and rust free. Sportsters get the motorcycle oil, same as the Big Twins, but since XLs are so-called unit construction (the same cases hold engine and gear bits), the trans and the clutch share oil.

Originally these three oils were different in spec as well as purpose. But Harley-Davidson changed that approach a few years ago. Now, H-D says it's OK to run one oil in everything—as long as it's their own, namely, Syn 3. Believing in the superiority of synthetics is not the same as believing in one fluid fits all. The factory's reversal on this issue seems a matter of marketing more than engineering. So, decide whether you'll stick with traditional oils, switch to synthetics for each purpose, or run the factory's cure-all. Then begin.

Changing Transmission Oil on a Big Twin

To begin, you'll need the following:
- 1/2 quart of transmission lube (check your manual)
- 3/8-inch Allen wrench (for removing the filler plug)
- 3/16-inch Allen wrench for the drain plug on early models
- No. T-40 Torx for drain plugs on late models
- Dump container
- Rags

Since there's little rocket science involved in this, use the procedures in your shop manual. One thing that's not covered there is exhaust pipe interference. On several models the stock pipe inhibits access to the drain plug. Aftermarket pipes can create this problem on any model. You can either loosen the pipe every time you change gearbox fluid, use a turkey baster or similar suction tool to suck the fluid out the filler hole, or braze the Allen/Torx bit you need for removal onto a small swivel socket, add an extension to the ratchet, and try to sneak past the pipe with that.

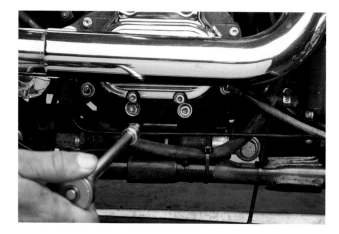

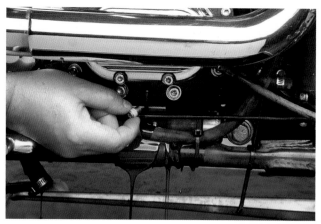

Sportsters use the same fluid for both transmission and primary lubrication. Changing, as per the manual, is pretty much a snap. Big Twins, all else equal, are not as easy. Softails and pre-1993 FLTs and FXRs often have an exhaust pipe right in front of the little drain plug at the bottom of the tranny end cover. You can loosen and swing the pipe away, or remove it, as shown in this photo, or make up a special tool to snake around the pipe. A wobbler extension, with the appropriate Allen or Torx bit brazed onto an old socket, will usually do the trick. Some folks also use a Mity-Vac with a small-diameter hose stuck down the filler hole to suck the gear oil out. This is not the most effective way to get the last drop, but since most contaminants in the gearbox wind up in the bottom of the box, this method will work once in awhile. Sooner or later, however, you'll have to do it right.

Big Twin Primary Lube Change

Begin with:

- 1–2 quarts of primary chaincase lube (check your manual)
- No. T-27 Torx to remove the inspection cover screws (late models)
- 5/32-inch Allen to remove the inspection cover screws (early models)
- Derby cover O-ring (No. 25416-84)—just in case
- 3/16-inch Allen wrench for early-model drain plugs
- No. T-40 Torx wrench, for late-model drain plugs
- Inspection gasket No. 60567-90A (long primary, oval-shaped) or No. 34906-85A (short primary, D-shaped). Long primary models include Softails and Dynas; short primary models are used on FLT/FXRs
- Dump container
- Rags

Some primary drain plugs are located in the inner primary housing (such as 1984–1985 FLTs), but most are identical to the tranny drain plug in appearance and are located in the lowest part of the outer primary cover. The shop manual tells you where yours is and how to drain the fluid but not what to do if the plug decides to strip out. If yours won't come out, try a heat gun on the surrounding

This is the infamous No. 739A drain plug. It's used for both the tranny drain and the primary drain on most Big Twins, and it's been through a couple of changes over the years. The early plug has an Allen head, and frankly, the magnetic tip had a tendency to come loose, sometimes falling into the motor. Second, the plug is a fine thread going into aluminum, therefore, a prime candidate for getting stuck in its hole or stripping out. It's a fine plan to have at least one new one of these on hand during fluid changes. The latest version is a Torx head, with a secure magnet and Teflon on the threads so finger-tight and half a twist will keep it secure and hassle-free.

Filling the transmission requires a small funnel and a little patience. Big Twins with five-speed boxes take exactly 1 pint (16 ounces) to fill (if completely drained). Four-speed Big Twins and Sportsters with four gears take 1 1/2 pints (24 ounces). Five-speed XLs use a full quart (32 ounces) of gear lube, but tradition has it that you simply hold a four-speed Sporty straight up and fill until oil runs out the check screw on the primary. (That's the one about a third of the way up, with a fiber washer under a Phillips head.)

aluminum first, then an Easy-Out; lastly remove the whole primary cover and back the plug out from the inside with a pair of Vise-Grips on the magnetic tip, or a drill. Go easy. Older drain plugs can have loose magnets as it is, so plan on replacing the whole plug once you've fought it out.

The factory has changed their mind a few times over the years as to exactly how much fluid you need in the

Primary fluid is easily drained on all models. Just keep that extra No. 739A plug handy and check for metallic fuzz on the original. Those magnets help prevent a lot of potential mischief in there, so the least you can do is help out with thorough cleaning during changes. Watching drain plug fuzz may not be an Olympic sport anytime soon, but it's the best early warning system on the engine. A certain amount of growth is normal, but if the plug goes from a little fuzz to long hair between routine changes, you need to unbutton the primary case for a close inspection.

primary. Keep in mind, however, that the object of the exercise is to keep the chain wet, not to see if your derby O-ring will leak. Long primaries typically use 1 1/2 quarts, short ones 1 quart. Check your manual or ask your dealer if in doubt.

Note: Early FXRs and FLTs may have a 7/8-inch tranny drain plug and a 13/16-inch oil drain plug. Double-check before you dig into it.

Sportster Transmission/Primary Fluid Change

Begin with:
- 1 quart of Sport-Trans Fluid
- No. T-27 Torx to remove the inspection cover screws on 1994 and later five-speed models
- Phillips screwdriver to remove the check screw on four-speed and early five-speed models
- 3/4-inch socket or wrench to remove the drain plug
- New O-ring (No. 11105) for the drain plug—just in case
- Dump container
- Rags

Until 1994, the correct level of transmission/primary fluid in Sportsters was determined by filling slowly until it ran out the level screw hole in the primary. Nice and simple if the bike was sitting straight up. When the Sportster finally got its first derby cover in 1994, the process suddenly resembled that used on Big Twins. For this setup, you

FLT's and Dyna's gear oil drains from a sump plug. The tip here is that once the plug is loosened with a socket, unscrew it by hand while keeping a slight upward pressure on this vertical plug. That way you don't get hot oil all over your hands as you snatch the plug away to drain the gear oil. Of course, you could always wear gloves.

The debate rages over exactly how much fluid goes into a Big Twin primary. Even your service manual might be in error on the subject. The factory has changed its mind a couple of times, and there are service bulletins to prove it. From 1990–on, long primaries (Dynas and Softails) are fine with 32 ounces (1 quart), while short primary models (FLTs and FXRs) call for 38 to 44 ounces. The 1984 to 1989 models typically use 1 1/2 quarts, regardless of primary length. The key is to keep the primary chain wet without drowning the clutch, and you can vary things as much as 6 to 8 ounces without making much difference. You can check with the dealer for any specific deviations peculiar to your bike. Clean fluid makes as much difference as the amount, so change it regularly, checking to ensure that the derby cover is flat and marked so it goes back on exactly as it came off. Even a new derby O-ring won't seal a warped cover.

need precisely a pint and a half in a four-speed and exactly a quart in a five-speed, no matter which way it's installed and checked (as long as it doesn't leak).

Project 19
Adjust Intake and Exhaust Valves

TIME:	6 hours
TOOLS:	Sockets, Allen sockets, ratchet, torque wrench (foot-pounds and inch-pounds), wrenches, contact cleaner, gasket sealer, rags, oil catch pan, feeler gauge, micrometer, magnet, heavy-gauge wire or large zip-tie, paper tape
TALENT:	3
COST:	$
PARTS:	Replacement shims (if needed), valve cover gasket, cam tensioner gasket (if removed), molybdenum disulfide grease
TIP:	Always recheck the clearance after installing new shims
BENEFIT:	Proper engine breathing
COMPLEMENTARY MODIFICATION:	Alter cam timing for more power, replace spark plugs, change coolant

Valve adjustment is one of the most time-consuming routine maintenance items. Fortunately, current sportbikes offer long adjustment intervals. For example, the valve adjustment maintenance interval for a 2000 ZX-6R is 12,000 miles. Other motorcycles can go as long as 26,000 miles. Older bikes with screw-and-locknut adjusters may need the work as often as every 6,000 miles.

Fortunately, most bikes now use some kind of shim-and-bucket arrangement, so that the cam lobe can act more or less directly on the valve itself, rather than using a pivoted finger that could exert side forces on the valve and wear it out. Of course, Ducati goes its own way by using the desmodromic system, which mechanically opens and closes the valves with rockers. Over time valves wear and need to be adjusted—properly. When clearances are too tight, they might not close completely; when they're too loose, the valve may not open completely. Either condition produces power loss, and excessive looseness can produce other damage.

Adjusting your valves will take the better part of a day. Begin with the engine cold. You need to gain access to the top of the cylinder head, so anything that could get in the way needs to be removed. On many bikes, you may need to remove the radiator. If the coolant is still good, store it in a place where it won't pick up any dirt, and reuse it. Since you must remove the spark plugs, check them too. Label all electrical connectors or take digital photos of the parts as they come off. Measure the clearance of each valve, and write it down. Then loosen and remove the valve cover bolts in a crisscross pattern and remove the cover. You will also probably have to remove the cover providing access to the crankshaft, and possibly one more to see timing marks.

Loosening the camshaft caps safely requires that you work in a crisscross pattern moving from the outside caps to those in the center of the engine. As a precaution, loosen the cap bolts in stages. (Loosen them all one turn and then repeat with one to two turns in sequence until the bolts come out.) Some of the cam lobes will be

With the gearbox in neutral, use a breaker bar to rotate the crank in the direction specified by your service manual. Always turn the engine in the proper direction to avoid potential internal damage. When you reach the timing mark indicated (there may be more than one) by your service manual, visually inspect the cam lobes on the cylinder you're measuring. Depending on your bike, you may be measuring the clearances for one cylinder, or multiple ones. Also, some manufacturers give you multiple timing marks to use for valve adjustment, while others will give you one and expect you to calculate crankshaft rotation for the remainder of the cylinders.

pressing against the valves, so the cam will tend to pop up as the caps are loosened. If you let one side get higher than another, you risk tweaking a cam or cap. To prevent having a cap bolt or retaining pin fall into the cam chain tunnel, stuff a clean rag into the tunnel. When you lift the caps free, the dowel pins may stay in either the head or the cap. Remove all the pins and set them aside with the bolts. Lay the caps on a clean rag in the same orientation as they were on the head for ease in reassembly. Temporarily remove the rag and lift the cams free. After you set the

cams aside, secure the chain with a piece of wire to keep it from falling inside the engine. Replace the rag so you don't accidentally drop a valve shim into the bottom end.

Once you've written down all the adjustments, take your sheet to your local shop to buy shims. Those who are particularly anal may want to take a micrometer to the shop to verify shim sizes before taking the parts home. Either way, don't believe the numbers on the shims. Always double-check the sizes before installing them in the engine.

When you're measuring the valve clearance, you'll want to do it on the compression stroke when the intake and exhaust cam lobes on the cylinder you're checking are pointing away from each other. However, some engines will have you measure more than one cylinder at a time for a given cam position. When checking clearance with a thickness gauge, you want to be able to feel the gauge contact both the bucket and cam at the same time. If you can't, try the next larger size until you do. What you want to feel is the metal of the feeler sliding between the parts as if you were sliding it in and out of a heavy book. If you feel more friction than that, or can't get the feeler in the space, try a smaller size until you do. Record the measurement even if it is within tolerances. Drawing a grid pattern that represents the valve and cylinder locations will make tracking which valve shims you need to change easier. Also, if you keep the chart, you'll have a record for the next time you adjust your valves. Once you've measured all of the clearances, you know whether you need to proceed. If even one valve measures out of spec, you've got some work ahead of you.

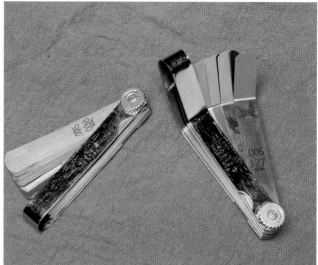

To ease reassembly of the top end, mark the cam sprockets and chain before you remove anything.

When all the new shims have been installed, you need to reinstall the cams. Using moly grease, lubricate all camshaft bearings, journals, and lobes. Verify that the crankshaft is still aligned with its timing mark. Install the exhaust cam first by pulling the timing chain on the exhaust side tight. Slip the exhaust cam sprocket into the chain so that the timing mark on the sprocket aligns with the edge of the cylinder head. While holding the chain taut from the exhaust cam to the intake side, install the intake cam with the timing mark properly aligned. Temporarily place a rag in the timing-chain tunnel. Insert all of the dowel pins in the head. When mounting the camshaft caps, make sure that you have them in the proper position and in correct orientation.

On bikes that use a shim-under-bucket arrangement, like most sport-bikes, you need to remove the cams to gain access to the shims. Just work slowly and methodically with your factory service manual outlining any specific tricks for your model bike. Generally, the manual will tell you to line up a timing mark to ease reinstalling the cams. If you're planning to replace or change the timing of the camshaft sprockets, you'll want to loosen their bolts prior to taking them out of the engine—it's a lot easier that way, because cams can be slippery and you can't put them in a vise. Otherwise, don't worry about those sprocket bolts. (If you have timed your cams and you loosen these bolts, you'll have to retime them. So, beware!) Next, remove the cam chain tensioner. Make sure the gasket comes off, because you'll be installing a new one—unless it uses an
O-ring. Some engines require that one or more chain guides be removed. If you can't access the gap between the cam and the bucket without bending a straight feeler, you may not be able to get an accurate reading. Try using an angled feeler.

To get a reading, slide the feeler gauge between the cam and the bucket. You want to feel about the amount of friction you would experience sliding the gauge in and out of a heavy book. Note how this feeler had to be trimmed to fit in the small space.

Removing the cams to access the buckets and shims requires close attention to detail. Working with one valve at a time, remove the bucket for each out-of-tolerance valve. Getting the shim out of its home may require a magnet. Next, measure the shim with a caliper. Now, return the parts to position to avoid mixing them up with other valves pieces. If the valve clearance is too tight, subtract the measured clearance from recommended clearance. Take this number and subtract it from the shim measurement to discover what shim size will be required to bring the clearance within tolerances. (For the too-loose scenario, reverse the first equation, then add the result to the shim measurement.) Write down this result in the appropriate box on the chart. If you're afraid of math or if you simply want to verify your calculations, most factory service manuals have a chart that allows you to determine what shim you need.

They will be labeled in a manner described in the service manual. Don't forget to install any chain guides you had to remove. Install the timing chain tensioner per the manufacturer's instructions. Again, tighten the cam cap bolts in steps, working from the center of the engine outward in a crisscross pattern. Finish by torquing the bolts down in the same pattern.

Rotate the crankshaft until its timing marks line up. Now verify that the marks on the cam sprockets are in alignment with the edge of the head. If they don't line up exactly, try skipping a tooth on the tensioner side. If that doesn't work, remove and reinstall the cam. Once you've checked the timing, you need to remeasure the valve clearance on the valves that have new shims. The clearance should be perfect. If not, disassemble the top end again and remeasure the shims to be certain you have the right size. When you have the clearances right, you can button up the engine, remount all the parts you had to remove, and go ride with confidence.

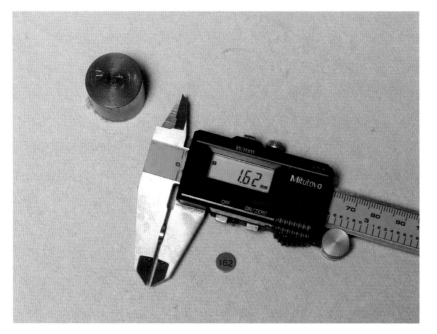

Don't trust the numbers printed on top of the shim. Always verify thickness by measuring it with a caliper. Kawasaki ZX-7 shims range from 2.50 to 3.50 mm in increments of 0.05 mm (approximately 0.002 inch). Yamaha's R6 shim sizes range from 1.20 to 2.40 mm in 0.05-mm increments. So, it is likely that no single shim will result in the optimum clearance. In those situations, choose the shim that will net the next-closest clearance. When installing the new shim in the bucket, put the side with the printed numbers on it facing up against the bucket. Lube the shim with molybdenum grease before inserting it. Coat the outside of the bucket with oil prior to reinstalling it in the head. The bucket should turn smoothly by hand once inserted. If not, remove it and add more lubricant.

Chapter 4
Electrical System

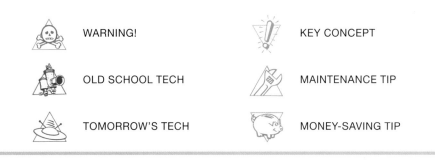

WARNING!

KEY CONCEPT

OLD SCHOOL TECH

MAINTENANCE TIP

TOMORROW'S TECH

MONEY-SAVING TIP

A wag once said, "Electricity is magic, and 'carburetor' is a French word for 'Don't mess with it!'" We dealt with the carburetor portion of that quip in Chapter 2. Now, let's see if we can make a motorcycle's electrical system seem a bit less like part of David Copperfield's routine.

THE BATTERY

Attempting to eschew all possible current puns, let's simply say that although motorcycle batteries are rated at a nominal 12 volts, in truth the voltage at the posts of a fully charged battery should be 12.66 volts at room temperature, the sum of six individual cells each rated at 2.11 volts.

This voltage is created chemically inside the battery when the liquid electrolyte—sulfuric acid and (distilled) water—washes over the lead plates in each cell. When it is new and fully charged, a battery can produce full voltage and maximum amperage—the current, or volume, of electricity the battery can deliver on demand. As the battery ages or is discharged, its fully charged voltage can fall, and its amperage output will drop until it will no longer start your motorcycle.

Battery Maintenance

Taking care of your battery isn't particularly difficult, but there is some danger. Remember, batteries are filled with (diluted) sulfuric acid—not something you ever want to come into physical contact with. So, remember the safety precautions of wearing gloves and eye protection, every time.

Check, clean, and retighten battery cables and connections twice a year. Wipe or brush off any dirt, grease, or corrosion from around the terminals, making sure none of the white crud ends up on something that can rust. And here's a quality tip: Remove the battery, then pour a small amount of sugar-free diet soft drink on each terminal. The carbonation and acidity of diet pop does a pretty good job of washing away the buildup of corrosion.

Physically check the tightness of the battery connections with your gloved hand. If they're at all loose, remove, clean, and reconnect securely. You might want to add a battery corrosion preventive to each terminal to prevent or slow any future corrosion.

If the battery has removable cell covers, pry them up or unscrew them and visually inspect the level of each cell's electrolyte. Gloves and eye protection are absolutely mandatory for this, as you're exposing the electrolyte/sulfuric acid. The battery should be as fully charged as possible when you make this inspection; otherwise the electrolyte level can be low due to the state of discharge. Filling the cells while the battery is significantly discharged can force excess electrolyte out of the vent tube as the battery is recharged.

If the top of the plates are exposed in any of the cells, add distilled water with a small turkey-baster tool, just enough to cover the tops of the plates. Replace the covers, and don't forget to wipe the battery clean to remove any acid that might have splashed or accumulated on the top of the battery. Use paper towels and throw them directly into the trash afterward.

The second important aspect of battery maintenance is to make sure the alternator, voltage regulator, and charging system are in good order. Motorcycle batteries are designed to spend most of their life fully charged, and don't like to be less than roughly 90 percent charged for any significant length of time. Proper function of the charging system ensures that. It keeps the battery topped up and ready to deliver full amperage the next time you start the engine.

If you are going to store the bike for a significant amount of time, or are one of the lucky motorcyclists with more machinery than you can ride, here's a hot tip. Buy a battery tender and hook it up to your inert motorcycles. This little device will regularly charge the battery and keep it fresh. If you store a motorcycle for months at a time and don't do this, you will be replacing batteries on a regular basis. You can find battery tenders at your local motorcycle dealer.

ALTERNATOR AND CHARGING SYSTEM

So, how does that battery stay charged? Heck, the battery naturally discharges (1/100 volt per day), and warm weather simply worsens that trait (the battery discharges twice as fast for every 18 degree Fahrenheit rise in temperature). Left untouched in warm weather, your battery would become 100 percent discharged in short order. There needs to be some way to recharge the battery with the engine running. And there is—the alternator.

Alternators are generally small, light, and quite efficient. However, they produce alternating current (AC) rather than direct current (DC)—and DC is what powers your bike's electrical system.

No problem. Diodes and rectifiers allow only DC current from the unit, and the voltage regulator turns the current on and off fast enough to keep the charging voltage in the proper 12- to 15-volt range for a 12-volt system. In order to actually recharge the battery (that is, chemically reverse the discharge process), the charging system must produce voltage about 2 volts higher than the battery's roughly 12.5 volts. Such higher voltage (or pressure) forces amperage back into the battery, so to speak, reversing the chemical reaction and recharging the battery.

The voltage regulator does exactly what its name describes. A voltage regulator failure can either allow the battery to progressively discharge as the vehicle is operated, or actually overcharge and kill the battery by supplying an overly high, unregulated voltage, due to a component failure in the regulator.

Easy Test for Your Charging System
Is there a quick DIY charging system test? You bet. Your handy digital voltmeter can check the battery voltage before the engine is even started, as described earlier. Then get the engine started if you can—replacement battery, recharged battery, or jump start—and recheck voltage at the battery. Your meter should read between about 13.5 and 15 volts, indicating that the charging system is trying to recharge the battery. If it stays in that 12-volt range and does not move as the engine starts, well, you better head for your local dealer while they're still open.

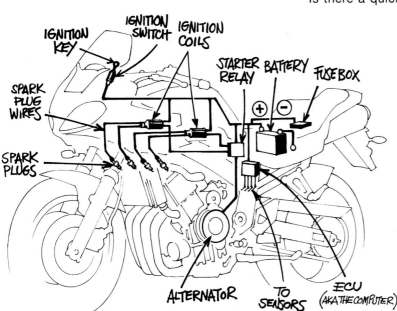

IGNITION KEY
IGNITION SWITCH
IGNITION COILS
SPARK PLUG WIRES
STARTER RELAY
BATTERY
FUSE BOX
+ −
SPARK PLUGS
ALTERNATOR
TO SENSORS
ECU (AKA THE COMPUTER)

STARTING SYSTEM

Your bike's starting system is perhaps its simplest electrical system, but the most important, of course. It consists of switches, wiring, and connections that operate a powerful starter motor that engages and spins the engine at 200 to 300 rpm to get it started.

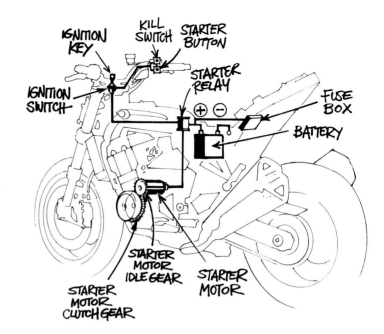

When the key is turned to the ON position, and you press the starter button, an electrical signal gets sent to the starter relay, and/or solenoid, which electrically switches on the starter motor and mechanically engages the starter drive gear. The starter relay, or solenoid, is basically a large electromagnetic switch that connects the battery to the starter motor. If the battery is strong, if the connections are clean and solid, if the engine is in tune, if the phases of the moon are aligned, then hopefully your engine will fire right up.

Let There Be Spark

A strong battery and solid starter motor can spin the engine over all day (well, not all day but plenty long enough), if the ignition system is supplying and distributing the proper spark to each cylinder at precisely the right time.

The simplest battery-powered ignitions feature a battery to supply the basic current, contact points (and condenser, to buffer the voltage so the points don't melt) to energize an electrical coil that produces a very high-voltage spark, individual spark plug wires, and spark plugs to deliver that spark into the combustion chamber to ignite the air/fuel mixture.

The Ignition Coil

The ignition coil is an elegantly simple device. Battery voltage is supplied to a tightly wound coil of wire that surrounds an iron core. This magnetizes the core. When the current running through the coil is stopped suddenly, the magnetic field around the core collapses and a surge of electrical energy is directed through the plug wire to the spark plug. This electrical energy jumps across an air gap between two electrodes at the tip of the spark plug to produce a bright blue arc, or spark, which lights the fire in the combustion chamber. It's the same basic principle as in direct ignition (DI) or coil-on-plug (COP) ignitions, where there are separate coils for each spark plug. For the engine to actually run, the coil must do its job hundreds of times a second—something uniquely suited to both DI and COP systems.

Can you see why a tune-up was so essential for so many years? Either a fresh set of points/condenser, or at least an adjustment of the air gap on the points to ensure the correct rise time—the amount of time current flowed into the coil to build the magnetic field—for the coil, helped make certain the engine ran smoothly, cleanly and efficiently.

Electronic Control Modules

In the 1980s motorcycle manufacturers almost universally replaced points-and-condenser ignitions with electronic components, such as magnetic pickup coils and electronic ignition modules. Ignition timing and control is now largely done by computer, and just as precisely mapped as is fuel injection. These systems still use coils to generate the spark, but now they're multiple coils. In some cases, there's an ignition coil for each cylinder, often mounted right on top of the spark plug (COP).

The first major advantage of such systems should be obvious: no moving parts. No points, no condenser, nothing to wear out, burn away, or break—not mechanically, anyway. And secondly, because of the

ELECTRICAL SYSTEM TROUBLESHOOTING

PROBLEM	PROBABLE CAUSES	ACTION TO REPAIR
ENGINE WON'T CRANK	Dead battery	Recharge/replace battery
	Poor electrical connections	Clean and tighten battery connections, look for loose wires
	Mechanical problem of hydraulic lock	See Engine Troubleshooting Chart
ENGINE CRANKS, BUT WON'T START	Out of gas	Add fuel
	Fuel pump fuse is bad	Check/replace fuse
	Fuel pump has failed	Check fuel pressure. Pull fuel line from fuel rail; turn key on/off and/or depress starter button. You should see strong jet of fuel from the fuel line. If not, and there's merely a dribble of fuel, there is no fuel pressure WARNING: Keep all open flames away from the area you do this test in as fuel will be released into the air
	Bad ignition switch, electronic control module, or fuse	Check ignition, electronic control module, and fuses. Replace any failed fuses
	No spark	Check for spark at spark plug while cranking engine. If you see healthy blue spark on spark plug, your engine is most likely not getting fuel. See Fuel System Troubleshooting Chart If no spark, check different spark plugs to ensure problem is not with one isolated spark plug. If only one plug lacks spark, check continuity of plug wires from coil(s) If several plugs are without spark, check all fuses (see your owner's manual). If fuses test OK, take to dealership for diagnosis
ONE OR BOTH HEADLIGHTS OUT	Headlight bulb burned out	Check headlight bulbs and replace bulb(s) that have broken filament(s)
BOTH HEADLIGHTS OUT	Headlight bulbs burned out, fuse failed	Replace failed bulbs and/or fuses

ELECTRICAL SYSTEM TROUBLESHOOTING

PROBLEM	PROBABLE CAUSES	ACTION TO REPAIR
NO HIGH/LOW BEAMS	Loose connection in wiring harness	Check high/low beam switch (if bike is so equipped) and connector/harness
NO BRAKE LIGHT	Faulty/misadjusted brake light switch	Check brake light switch connections
		Use jumper to connect wires together for test; brake light should illuminate
		Adjust brake light switch (at brake pedal). In most cases, push switch up toward pedal linkage, then step firmly on brake pedal
	Bad connection in harness	Check harness/connection to brake light
NO TURN SIGNALS OR EMERGENCY FLASHERS	Bad flasher unit	Check flasher unit; try replacement

microprocessor control of the ignition, electronic ignition systems deliver much more precise and accurate spark timing for each cylinder under all operating conditions. Today's ignition systems not only perform light-years better than their predecessors, but are far more durable and reliable, and require much less maintenance. Indeed, accurate spark timing and fuel control mean spark plugs live much longer, and 20,000 to 50,000 miles between replacements is not uncommon.

Although some of today's ignition components have complex names or duties, they are really simple devices that recognize and identify the specific rotational position of the engine in order to provide spark timing information to the ignition module—the little microprocessor that decides exactly when to supply a spark to each cylinder.

Project 20

Headlight/ Turn-Signal Replacement and Adjustment

TIME:	30 minutes
TOOLS:	Screwdrivers, possibly sockets, continuity tester, tape measure, dielectric grease, a willing assistant
TALENT:	1
COST:	$
PARTS:	Headlight or turn-signal bulb(s)
TIP:	Adjusting your headlight for the load you're carrying will enable you to actually see where you're going after dark
BENEFIT:	You will make yourself more visible to other road users

A motorcycle's headlight not only allows you to see, it helps others to see you—even in daylight. The Motorcycle Safety Foundation recommends that riders use the high beam during daylight riding.

If you discover that your headlight isn't working on high or low beam, check that the bulb is properly seated in its plug. On some bikes you may have to remove bodywork to get in there. With others you only need to peel off the detachable rubber dust seal. To check the bulb, you don't have to remove it completely unless you are con-

ducting a visual inspection. A bulb that appears to be normal may have an internal problem—which a continuity tester will reveal.

Remove the plug to expose the prongs on the back of the bulb. Using a continuity tester, press one electrode onto two of the prongs extending from the back of the bulb. Now, touch the other probe to one of the remaining prongs. Repeat with the two other possible pairings. If you don't get continuity on at least two pairs of the prongs, the bulb is bad. If you get continuity on both filaments, you

Inspect the bulb's connectors for signs of moisture or corrosion. The tabs sticking out of the side of this headlight bulb key it into the proper position in the housing.

Note how the tester's probe is being held against the side of this turn-signal bulb. This is where it makes the negative contact with the socket. The buttons on the bottom are the positive contacts for the filaments. If the bulb is OK, clean the contacts before reinstalling it.

Turn-signal bulbs either pop out easily or they take some elbow grease. If you find yourself exerting more than minimal effort, use a rag or a pair of gloves to protect yourself from accidental bulb breakage. If the socket is corroded, a dab of dielectric grease will prevent the parts from sticking in the future.

may have a blown headlight fuse or a short somewhere in the electrical system. Also check the plug for corrosion.

If you need a new headlight, be sure to replace a blown bulb with a similar type. The bulbs are keyed so that they will only fit in the housing in the proper orientation. Avoid touching the bulb itself with your bare fingers. Check to make sure the light works before completely assembling the housing. Make sure the rubber cover is snugly in place over the headlight housing.

The process of checking a dual-filament bulb, like a front-turn-signal or brake-light bulb, is almost identical to the headlight. Remove the bulb from the turn-signal stalk. If you have trouble removing the bulb, use a rag or gloves to get a safer grip on the glass. Bulbs that have corroded into position may break before you're able to remove them. If this happens, a little WD-40 and needle-nose pliers will help. Then clean up the corrosion to get good contacts before fitting the new bulb.

Hold one probe of the continuity tester on the outside metal edge of the bulb. Now, check the continuity on each of the two little buttons on the bottom of the bulb. Again, don't trust a visual inspection unless it shows an obviously blown filament. Before you screw the cover back on, check to be sure the new bulb works.

Many riders never consider the load a bike carries and its effect on the headlight aim. Yes, the headlight angle is set at the factory, but it is set based on some average—the age-old compromise. What if you're

Make small adjustments to the headlight. Sometimes the results are subtle, other times they're not.

heavier than average or you've changed your bike's ride height? What about the fact that you've just strapped 65 pounds of gear to your bike for the annual pilgrimage to Daytona? You owe it to yourself and those traveling in the opposite direction to make sure your headlight is properly adjusted. Your owner's manual will show you where the adjusters are and how to take the measurements. To accurately gauge your headlight's adjustment, make sure your bike has the same load and suspension settings under which it will be operating.

Motorcycles in the United States should have their headlight height measured at a distance of 25 feet. While shining the headlight on a wall, have your assistant measure from the center of the headlight beam to the ground while the bike is loaded. The brightest spot of the high beam on the wall should be 2 inches below the measured height of the headlight center. Of course, seeing this will be easier at dusk or after dark. Using a screwdriver or the headlight's adjuster knobs, center the beam on the appropriate spot. Adjust the second bulb on bikes with two headlights to match the first. If you notice that either beam aims to one side instead of straight ahead, adjust this too. Single headlights should also point straight ahead.

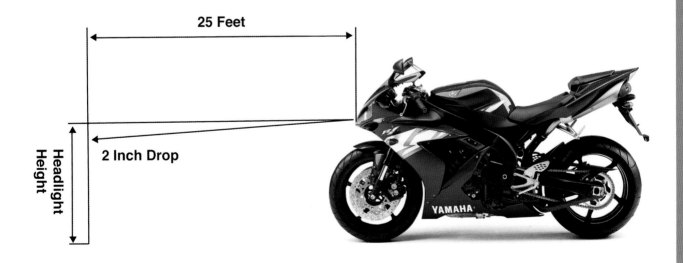

25 Feet

2 Inch Drop

Headlight Height

You should adjust the headlight based on the standard of a 2-inch drop in 25 feet. Remember: Load affects the headlight alignment, so set the height based on what you plan to carry.

Project 21
Service Your Battery

TIME:	1/2 to 1 hour
TOOLS:	10-mm wrench, multi-meter, small hydrometer, dielectric grease, distilled water, needle-nose pliers
TALENT:	1
COST:	$
PARTS:	Optional sealed battery upgrade stuff, if applicable
TIP:	Don't assume that a battery can't be the problem just because it's new or you recently checked it
BENEFIT:	Reliable starting
COMPLEMENTARY MODIFICATION:	Sealed batteries and gel-cell aftermarket batteries; voltmeter or ammeter

Here are three reasons to care about this project: Most failures that leave you stranded are electrical, most electrical failures are traceable to the battery, and most of these battery failures are preventable.

One of the keys to long battery life is proper initial service. A brand new wet-cell battery needs to be filled with electrolyte (battery acid) to the proper level in each cell before it's put into service. Once the battery's filled with fluid, it must be charged properly to ensure a long and happy life. For low-maintenance batteries, you should use a variable- or tapered-rate battery charger, rated at 4, 6, 8, or 10 amps. These tapered-rate chargers might stuff anywhere between 2 and 8 amps into a new battery when you hook it up, but after an hour or so, the meter may read close to zero. At this point, the battery may make its full voltage, but you should charge a minimum of 12 hours to "set" the plates. A trickle charger of 1 amp or less of charging current may take 24 hours, at least.

Follow-up is just as important as the initial charge. Batteries, like plants and humans, need watering. Use only distilled water to top up your battery—never use battery acid or plain tap water. The first time you look into a cell and its level is low enough to expose the plates, start budgeting for a new battery.

The hardest thing on a motorcycle battery is just letting the motorcycle sit. Inactivity of the battery causes sulfation,

which can create a discharge of 1/2 to 1 percent per day (more in warm weather). Charge your battery at least once a month when you're not using it. Better yet, buy a Battery Tender (a sophisticated smart charger) and keep it hooked up whenever the bike is parked.

Batteries are a tight fit and awkward to get at on some bikes. This alone is responsible for a great many failures. People are just too lazy to wrestle with a battery once a week like the book says you should. The best alternative to regular servicing of the battery is to have a gauge (volts or amps) mounted permanently on the motorcycle. It also helps to rig the battery to make service a little less difficult. "Soaping" or lubing the sides makes it easier to slide the battery in or out. You can also run a small strap of polypropylene (acid-proof) rope or webbing under the battery case to sling it out with if your fingers are too fat to get a grip on the little devil.

Perhaps the handiest electrical tool is the multitalented multimeter. You can use it on batteries to check basic voltage (with the engine off) and basic charging (with the engine on and revved up a little). The 14.4-volt reading you see here indicates that the charging system is fine on this bike. What some folks aren't ready for is that a fresh, hot battery will read 12.66 volts on its own (2.11 volts per cell times six cells). If you check regularly and one fine day find the battery has mysteriously dropped to 10 volts, you probably have a bad cell.

Some tips to help you keep your battery in tip-top condition:

- Install a voltmeter, ammeter, indicator kit (H-D No. 66009-87 for Harley-Davidsons), or some combination of these so you can monitor your charging system. It's amazing how few riders use a simple gauge to monitor the electrical system, yet throw oil pressure gauges on a lubrication system that virtually never fails.
- Use star washers to mount cable ends to battery terminals.
- Keep terminals clean and dry.
- Apply a little soapy water to the battery case if it will help you slip the thing in or out of the rubber battery tray.
- Don't drop a battery. Even a light bounce can crack the case and make for an acid leak.
- Baking soda neutralizes battery acid in the event of a spill.
- Always hook up the positive cable first—after you make sure the vent pipe is clear.
- Wet-cell batteries can only be (slowly) recharged from flat a small number of times, perhaps 8 to 10.

BATTERY FAULT-FINDING GUIDE			
	Good battery	Suspect battery	If suspect
Plates	+ Chocolate color − Grey	White sulfation on plates Plates buckled	Scrap
Sediment	Little or none	Deep sediment up to plate level	Scrap
Voltage	Above 12 volts	Below 12 volts	Test charge
Electrolyte	Normal level	Low, especially if one cell is low	Fill and Test charge
Specific Gravity	Above 1.200 in all cells. No more than 0.020 difference.	Below 1.100 or wide difference between cells	Test charge
Case	Sound and leek proof	Leaking case	Scrap Wash down affected bike parts in baking soda solution

SPECIFIC GRAVITY REQUIRED	PARTS OF DISTILLED WATER TO 1 OF CONC. SULPHURIC ACID
1.25	3.4
1.26	3.2
1.27	3.0
1.28	2.8
1.29	2.7
1.30	2.6

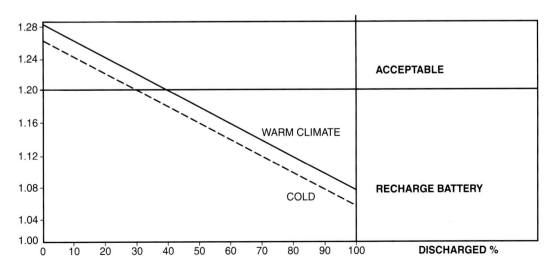

Project 22

Spark Plug Check and Replacement

TIME:	1 hour
TOOLS:	Sockets, screwdrivers, plug wrench, wire gap gauge, rags, anti-seize compound, compressed air, brass brush, magnet to retrieve plug
TALENT:	1
COST:	$
PARTS:	Spark plugs
TIP:	Blow off the top of the engine with compressed air to keep abrasives out of the cylinders
BENEFIT:	Smoother-running engine

If you look at your owner's manual, you'll find that spark plugs should be serviced about every 4,000 to 7,500 miles. Fortunately, the plugs don't often need replacing, just a quick brush off and back into the chamber of horrors they go.

Your bike's engine should be cold when you check the plugs. Place your bike on its side stand and remove the seat, tank, air box, or anything else, like bodywork, to gain access to the plugs. Some bikes (particularly those V-fours) may require a few tricks, so check your factory service manual first. While the air box is off, the carburetors are vulnerable to dirt, so cover them with clean rags or paper towels. Once you have access to the plugs, blow the top of the head off with compressed air to remove debris waiting to fall down the hole into your cylinder. Now, remove the plug wire from one plug at a time, labeling with masking tape which cylinder it goes to—you don't want to fire the engine with the wires in the wrong places.

Don't just jump in and remove the plug once it's exposed. Even though a cap has been covering the spark plug well, you should give it a quick blast with compressed air, too. You'd be surprised how frequently sand or pebbles pop out, and you sure don't want them in your engine. Once you've given it a shot of clean air, you can safely remove the plug. The tight quarters around the engine's head may require some patience to remove the plug. If you've unscrewed the plug completely and can't get a grip on it to pull it out, try using a magnet. Otherwise, a spark-plug socket with a foam liner will grip it so you can lift it out.

Look closely at the electrode and insulator. It should be a light tan or gray color. (Check the sidebar "Reading Your Plugs" for tips on what other colors mean.) Using a brass brush, clean the plug of any deposits. Next, measure the gap with a wire thickness gauge. The flat spade gauges don't give accurate readings unless held perfectly square to the gap. If the gap is too narrow or too wide, use the

Despite the manufacturer's best efforts, sand and pebbles work their way into remarkable places. Blow off the cylinder head before removing the plug caps, and blow out the plug wells, too.

If you must remove two or more plug wires at once, wrap them with tape and number them, unless the factory was kind enough to do it for you.

Use a brass brush to clean the electrode and insulator. Be sure to clean the plug again with compressed air before you reinstall it. Note: Some fine-tipped plugs cannot withstand this treatment.

The best way to check a plug's gap is with a wire gauge. This eliminates the requirement that the tool be held perpendicular to the electrode.

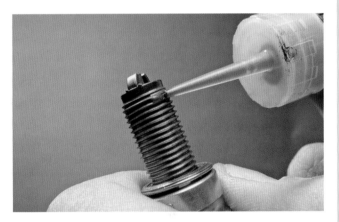

Spark plugs can sometime be ornery when you try to remove them because of cold welding between the aluminum of the head and the steel of the plug. Anti-seize helps to remedy the problem.

READING YOUR PLUGS

So, you've taken a plug out of its cubby hole, and you're wondering what to do with it. Impress your friends and neighbors by emulating famous race tuners: Closely examine the plug to see what it tells you about the state of your engine. Of course, you'll need some sort of comparison. The photos below will provide examples of what to look for. Remember, these are, for the most part, extreme examples meant to illustrate various plug conditions. Your plugs will probably have subtler symptoms.

 You want all your plugs to look as pretty as this one. Note the nice, even gray or tan on the insulator. The electrode exhibits only slight erosion.

 Carbon fouling shows up as dry, soft, black soot on the insulator and electrode. Although usually caused by a too-rich fuel mixture, other potential problems are shorting ignition leads and too-cold plug temperature. A badly carbon-fouled plug can lead to difficult starting, misfiring, and uneven acceleration.

 This plug has been subjected to severe overheating, as illustrated by the extremely white insulator and small black specks. If you look closely, you will see more electrode erosion than on a normal plug. When a plug overheats, the engine experiences a loss of power under heavy loads, such as at high-speed, high-rpm running. An overly advanced ignition, too-hot plug temperature, or poor engine cooling could be the culprits. Improperly torqued plugs can also overheat.

 Oil fouling is characterized by black, gooey deposits on the insulator and electrode. Have you noticed that your bike was difficult to start and that the engine missed frequently at speed? The oil came from somewhere, and the likely culprits are worn piston rings or valve guides.

***Sidebar photos courtesy of Denso Sales California Inc.

gapping tool usually attached to a set of wire gauges to carefully bend the side electrode outward—a little effort goes a long way.

When the gap is correct, spray the plug with contact cleaner; let dry, then apply a little anti-seize compound to them. Carefully, insert the plug into the plug hole. If you can get your fingers down into the plug well, rotate the plug counterclockwise until you feel the threads drop into synch. Then, using only your fingers, rotate it clockwise to engage the threads. Screw in the plug finger-tight, and then snug it down with a torque wrench. This step is vitally important, since some plug failures are associated with incorrectly torqued plugs.

Before reassembling your entire bike, start the engine to make sure all the cylinders are firing correctly. (Fuel-injected bikes may need the gas tank installed to maintain proper fuel pressure.) If anything sounds amiss, check all plug connections and also make sure all the wires are connected to the correct cylinders. When everything sounds right, button up your bike and go ride another 4,000 miles.

Chapter 5
Cooling System

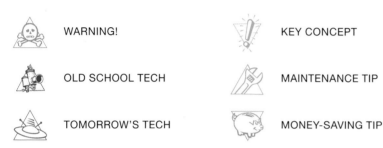

WARNING!

KEY CONCEPT

OLD SCHOOL TECH

MAINTENANCE TIP

TOMORROW'S TECH

MONEY-SAVING TIP

Modern four-stroke motorcycle engines are high-tech marvels. Liter-size motorcycles put out more than 165 horsepower at the rear wheel. With incredible output like this, it's shocking to realize how wretched they are at converting gasoline's chemical energy into mechanical power. Even with generations of development, they convert only about 20 percent of the energy generated by the burning fuel into horsepower. The other 80 percent is simply converted into heat. But there's nothing simple about that heat. Left unchecked, the heat of combustion would melt pistons like cheap candle wax. Consequently, there's a clear and present need for some type of cooling system to control operating temperatures and prevent your engine from going supernova.

Three types of cooling systems have been utilized over the decades: air, air/oil, and liquid. Liquid-cooled systems are erroneously abbreviated as water-cooled; virtually every such system utilizes a mixture of a coolant, such as the now-common ethylene glycol, and water. Ultimately, though, all of the excess heat an engine produces must be dissipated into the atmosphere.

Almost all earlier motorcycle engines were air-cooled, getting rid of their heat just via airflow over their finned surfaces. In 1985, Suzuki introduced its ground-breaking air/oil-cooled GSX-R750; the cylinders and head were finned like an air-cooled engine, but the bike also had a sizeable oil cooler as well. Some BMWs and Buells, among others, still use the system. But for all the simplicity (compared to liquid-cooled counterparts, anyway), light weight and reliability of air- or air/oil-cooled engines, they nonetheless tend to suffer from higher operating temperatures and the accompanying losses in performance and fuel economy.

These days, the vast majority of motorcycles use a closed liquid-cooling system. A pump circulates coolant through passages in the cylinder block and cylinder head(s), absorbing and carrying away excess combustion heat, and then to a radiator, which exchanges the heat into the atmospheric air moving past its cooling fins and cores.

To make the system more efficient, it is pressurized and thermostatically controlled. By operating the system at higher than atmospheric pressure—typically 7–15 psi—the boiling point of the water-based coolant rises to some 250 degrees Fahrenheit or higher. As a result, the coolant won't boil and loose efficiency at normal engine operating temperatures of 180 to 230 degrees Fahrenheit. The pressure is controlled by the pressure cap on the radiator or recovery tank.

Because internal combustion engines don't operate efficiently or cleanly (in terms of emissions) until they are up to full operating temperature, a thermostat in the system restricts flow of coolant until coolant temperature climbs into the normal range. From that point on, the thermostat will only restrict coolant flow if temperature begins to fall below the threshold of normal, typically around 190 degrees Fahrenheit.

COOLING SYSTEM MAINTENANCE

You cannot go wrong having your bike's cooling system flushed and refilled with fresh coolant every two years, as many manufacturers recommend—it's cheap insurance. With the cost of replacing failed cylinder head gaskets in the $600 to $1,200 range, routine maintenance of your bike's cooling system makes sense, and cents—lots of them.

Corrosion

If, however, you choose to take the cheapskate's way out and not put any effort into maintaining your motorcycle's cooling system, your main concern almost certainly will be corrosion.

Why does corrosion form in the cooling system? Simple: The cooling system is a chemical battery. The circulation of water across the surfaces of dissimilar metals creates an electrical potential, which is the definition of a battery. Modern engines feature components made from steel, aluminum, cast iron, copper, and other alloys, all washed by the flow of coolant. Over time, the acidity of the coolant increases, creating corrosion and debris that can clog and restrict flow, cause the engine to overheat, and destroy expensive parts.

A note on old coolant: Recycle! Most dealers and independent shops will recycle old antifreeze by cleaning and filtering it, adding a new anticorrosion and water pump lubricant package, and reusing the coolant in another vehicle. Keeps prices lower, prevents waste, and keeps the environment cleaner—all good things. Check with your local city hall for the nearest coolant recycler in your area.

Remember that coolant is extremely toxic to humans and animals. Unfortunately, its semisweet taste makes it somewhat attractive to critters, so make absolutely sure any spillage is cleaned up right away. Never allow antifreeze to spill into the street or storm sewer.

Radiator and Hose Care

Fresh coolant every couple of years is simple and inexpensive, but it doesn't completely take care of things. Hoses, the thermostat, and the radiator cap also need

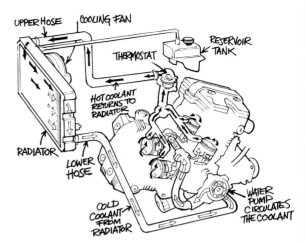

periodic attention. Replacing these components at every cooling system service is also good practice. Can these components last longer? Yes, but once again, look at the cost of replacing them as an insurance policy. What does getting stranded on the side of the highway with a failed cooling system, plus an overheated and possibly destroyed engine cost?

Check cooling system hoses with the engine cool or even slightly warm, but not fully cold if possible. You want to check them at temperatures above ambient so they're closer to their working temperature. Wear your gloves and feel each hose. It should be firm, not squishy, and should not bulge dramatically anywhere, particularly at each end where it fits over a coolant outlet. Any hardening or cracks warrant replacement—now.

Troubleshooting

Let's face it, the primary symptom of any cooling system problem is overheating. How do you know the engine is getting too hot? That big red warning light on the dash might be a hint, or the needle on the temperature gauge pegged into the red. Or engine roughness or loss of power. Or—heaven forbid—steam coming out from between your knees.

The first rule of thumb when dealing with overheating is deal with it now. If your engine begins to overheat, pull safely off the roadway, stop, and shut the engine off—immediately. Don't continue unless it's an absolute necessity for your immediate safety. Continuing to operate the engine will drive temperatures even higher and ultimately severely damage the engine. Remember, the engine is overheating because it is producing more waste heat than the cooling system can dissipate. So it's getting hotter . . . and producing even more waste heat . . . which can't be dissipated. It's a domino effect, so engine temperatures will continue to skyrocket until you stop and shut it off.

Do not open the radiator cap! Remember, the cooling system is under significant pressure. Releasing that pressure by opening the cap will cause the overheated coolant to boil instantly, potentially causing serious injury to you. Leave the cap and system alone and let it cool thoroughly.

Need something to do in the meantime? Call for assistance with your cell phone. Once the cooling system has cooled to ambient temperature, it's possible to inspect for the cause of the overheating. If it's a simple fix, make repairs, refill it with coolant, and be on your way.

Dealing with Leaks

If coolant is disappearing from the recovery tank—or ultimately the radiator—look for physical evidence of the leak. Wetness at the bottom of the radiator, dripping from the lower hose, or running down the sides or back of the engine indicate a significant leak . . . from something!

The most common leaks are:

• **Pump seal:** Coolant leaking down the outside of the engine

• **Radiator:** Bottom of radiator wet, but upper part of lower hose dry

• **Radiator hose:** Hose wet/damp with coolant near leak, puddle nearby?

• **Cylinder head gasket:** Loss of coolant into the recovery tank due to overpressure of system with combustion pressure; loss of coolant, overheating, coolant in oil, white smoke from exhaust—all potential symptoms of a blown cylinder head gasket

One final component in the cooling system is the coolant itself. Believe it or not, if pure cooling efficiency is the only criterion, water is the best choice. Its ability to absorb and transfer heat quickly and efficiently, along with its abundance and low cost, makes it the perfect coolant—with a few

exceptions. Water freezes at temperatures of 32 degrees Fahrenheit or lower, it tends to promote corrosion, and it doesn't lubricate the water pump and its seals as well as more specialized coolants.

To address such issues, most modern coolants are a mix of ethylene glycol, which is the antifreeze component in the coolant, and water. A 50/50 mix will protect cooling systems from freezing down to about 34 degrees Fahrenheit below 0. Is more better? Not really. Ethylene glycol works very well as antifreeze, but it's not quite as efficient as water in transferring heat. So there's no advantage or benefit from operating the cooling system with a mixture more than about 60 percent antifreeze and 40 percent water for the coldest climates.

To prevent corrosion in the cooling system, an additive package is blended into the coolant, including rust inhibitors and a water pump lubricant. Historically, the rust inhibitors have been phosphates, borates, and silicates.

There's also a whole other class of coolants, almost entirely used only for racing, and then specifically for roadracing. Why? Because ethylene glycol is as slippery as the legendary sinus drainage on a door-opening fixture. A coolant leak during practice or a race could have disastrous consequences. The same is true for lubricating oil, of course, but no one has been able to find a substitute for that—yet.

However, coolant substitutes are mostly propylene glycols, or similar solutions, and their use is required by virtually all road race sanctioning bodies. Propylene glycol coolants are claimed to be biodegradable, non-toxic and corrosion-resistant, and have antifreeze capabilities almost equal to that of their ethylene glycol counterparts. Such solutions include Maxima Cool-Aide, Cycle Logic Engine Ice, Martini SuperKool, Silkolene CCA, and Evans NPG Coolant.

COOLING SYSTEM TROUBLESHOOTING

PROBLEM	PROBABLE CAUSES	ACTION TO REPAIR	RELEVANT PROJECTS
COOLANT PUDDLES UNDERNEATH BIKE	Leak in coolant system	Determine what part of the coolant system is directly above the wet spot on the pavement. Inspect that immediate area for leaks If leak is from hose connection, tighten hose clamp Check for leakage/wetness directly below water pump If water pump is leaking, replace water pump Monitor rate of leak, as above	
COOLANT TEMPERATURE WARNING LIGHT ILLUMINATED	Pull safely off road and stop engine as soon as possible. WARNING: Continuing to ride with an overheated engine can lead to serious engine damage	Let engine cool 30 minutes or more; restart. If temperature light goes out, ride to dealership. If not, have bike transported	
ENGINE OVERHEATING, EMITTING STEAM TEMPERATURE GAUGE READS ABOVE NORMAL AND CLIMBING	Coolant leak, low coolant, blocked or failing radiator	Let engine cool 30 minutes or more. Check coolant level in overflow tank, add coolant/distilled water if necessary. Look for signs of leakage (puddles of bilious green fluid or wet hoses or connections). If you identify source of leak as hose or connection, replace hose or tighten connection. Test-ride bike to see if steam returns. If not, carefully monitor coolant level over next few weeks. If steam returns, let engine cool, refill with antifreeze or distilled water, and take to mechanic/dealership for repair	Project 23: Check your coolant
	Coolant leak, low coolant (NOTE: Once the gauge hits the maximum reading or red zone, you are heading for an overheat with steam coming from the engine. If that happens, see **Engine Overheating** section above	When your temperature gauge reads above normal, pull off the road to a safe location, shift into neutral, and run engine at a fast idle to increase coolant circulation	

COOLING SYSTEM

5

85

COOLING SYSTEM TROUBLESHOOTING

PROBLEM	PROBABLE CAUSES	ACTION TO REPAIR	RELEVANT PROJECTS
	Radiator fan not functioning	Check/listen for fan operation	
	Water pump failing	Replace water pump	
	Leaking coolant from hose connection	When engine is safely cooled down, identify leak area and tighten hose clamp(s)	
	Coolant hose ruptured	Remove, shorten, reinstall hose; replace hose	
	Punctured radiator	If radiator is punctured, add stop-leak product as short-term solution. Take bike to dealership to get radiator repaired or replaced	
		Pressure-test the system. NOTE: Do not loosen/remove radiator cap until engine is fully cool	
		Refill cooling system with 50-50 mix of antifreeze and distilled water, or distilled water	
		Replace radiator	

Project 23
Check Your Coolant

TIME:	15 minutes
TOOLS:	Antifreeze tester
TALENT:	1
COST:	$
PARTS:	None
TIP:	When adding water to the cooling system, only use distilled water
BENEFIT:	Keep your bike's engine alive and well

Your engine's aluminum internals are prone to oxidizing. Coolant and other products, such as Water Wetter, form a protective coating over the bare aluminum, inhibiting oxidation and thereby protecting against reduced efficiency from clogged passages. Coolant also lubricates the water pump and prevents foaming. Of course its most obvious function is to carry heat from your engine to the radiator, where airflow disperses it and allows cool liquid to return to the engine and keep it within operating temperatures. It is also blended to resist freezing and resultant expansion and engine damage.

Every fall, before outside temperatures begin to drop, you should test your antifreeze to make sure it will handle the cold. Although the overflow tank is the easiest to access for your annual coolant test, why not spend the extra time to expose the cooling system filler cap so you can test what's actually inside the engine? So, with your engine cold (never open a hot cooling system, which will spray scalding coolant at you), remove the filler cap. For the actual testing, you have a couple of choices.

Prestone makes clever throwaway test strips that you dip into the coolant, read the color, then toss into the trash. You can also use a testing tool that measures the specific gravity of the solution and displays the results with floating balls or a needle. While you're at it, check the color. If it's green like Mountain Dew, it's probably OK. Other colors may signal engine problems such as rust residue (red-brown) or oil residue (black).

If your bike has been regularly used and maintained, the coolant is probably good—clear and of proper concentration. If the concentration is off, or it's been two years since you changed it, proceed to Project 24 (Flush and Refill Your Cooling System).

Coolant usually pours out of the drain plug with a good deal of force, so be prepared. Make sure you have a container that will hold all your bike's old coolant, or you'll find out how hard it is to clean up antifreeze. Immediately transfer the poisonous liquid to a sealed container.

Check your antifreeze every fall, particularly if your bike is stored in an unheated garage. These test strips don't take up any room in your toolbox.

Project 24

Flush and Refill Your Cooling System

TIME:	15 minutes to 1 hour
TOOLS:	Sockets, ratchet, wrenches, screwdrivers, funnel, rags, antifreeze tester, drain pan
TALENT:	1
COST:	$
PARTS:	Coolant, new copper drain-plug washer, Water Wetter (optional)
TIP:	When adding water to the cooling system, only use distilled water
BENEFIT:	With Water Wetter, your engine should run cooler

C hanging the coolant every two years is also a good idea. Begin with your bike in gear on its side stand. Locate the drain plug (it's usually on the water pump cover). Place a container large enough to hold all the coolant under the plug. If you want to keep the antifreeze off your skin, wear latex gloves. Open the filler cap at the top of the system. Using a wrench, unscrew the plug. Before the plug is completely out, the coolant will start to leak past the threads, so be prepared. Pull the plug free and let the system drain. As soon as the system is completely empty, reinstall the plug and a fresh copper washer and torque to specs. Next, empty the expansion tank into the catch pan and get all the used antifreeze into a sealed container for transport to a recycling center or auto parts store. Don't leave it in the pan on the garage floor because it's fatal to humans and animals if it's ingested.

If you use a 50/50 mix of coolant and distilled water, mix the solution prior to pouring it into the filler. That way you're certain about the mixture, no matter how much liquid the system requires. Also, you'll have a container of the proper mixture if you need to top off the expansion tank in the future. If you want your cooling system to be more efficient, borrow a trick from the road race guys and buy a bottle of Red Line Water Wetter (or similar product). You should notice a slight drop in operating temperature.

Once you've filled the cooling system to the brim, you need to run the engine with the filler cap off. As the engine warms up, you'll see bubbles working their way out of the system. In fact, as the engine circulates the coolant, you may see the level drop quite a ways. Keep topping off the system as the level drops. When the engine starts to warm up, the coolant will start to expand out of the filler. Stop the engine and replace the radiator cap. Fill the expansion tank until the level is midway between the two lines. Now, take your bike for a short ride to get it completely up to temperature, then park the bike and allow it to cool off completely. Once the engine is cool again, top off the cooling system and button up your bodywork. You should now be good to go for at least another year.

24

FLUSH AND REFILL YOUR
COOLING SYSTEM

Chapter 6
Drivetrain

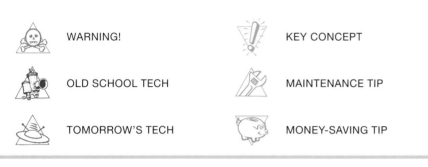

WARNING!   KEY CONCEPT

OLD SCHOOL TECH   MAINTENANCE TIP

TOMORROW'S TECH   MONEY-SAVING TIP

The simple fact is you can have an engine with enough horsepower to spin the Earth at 15,000 rpm, but without a drivetrain—a transmission and final drive—you and the rest of the motorcycle are as good as parked. All that power has to get to the rear wheel somehow.

That's the drivetrain's job: The drivetrain transfers power from the engine to the drive wheel. A number of components are involved in doing this job. The transmission (or gearbox, as it's also known) features several gear ratios—the difference between engine speed and the speed the vehicle is traveling—to keep the engine in its efficient power band over the bike's entire range of useable road speeds. From the transmission, power is transferred to the drive wheel by chain, belt, or a driveshaft (like a car).

In terms of maintenance, just keep it simple. With few exceptions (Harley-Davidson being just one), the majority of motorcycles share their engine oil with a unitized transmission. Apart from a motorcycle's high specific output, this is just one more reason to change your oil and filter perhaps a bit earlier than the manufacturer's recommendation; over time, transmission gear teeth literally shear the long-chain antiwear polymers in most oils' additive packages. For motorcycles that have a separate oil supply for the transmission (Harley and some European motorcycles), the manufacturer's recommendation should do nicely for replacement intervals.

Lubricate the chain religiously per the manufacturer's instructions in your owner's manual, and you'll rarely see a single problem. Belts require virtually zero maintenance, as do most car-style gear-case final drives. Given at least a modicum of decent care, your drivetrain should have a long, happy life. You'll have to R&R (remove and replace, to translate from mechanics' jargon) chain and sprockets when they wear out, but regular lubrication will keep that to the longest interval possible.

WHY A TRANSMISSION?

Why do we need a transmission in the first place? A transmission varies the ratio between engine speed and rear wheel speed. In first gear, your engine is more closely matched to the speed of the rear wheel. This means that when you are taking off from a dead stop, the engine will spin quickly through the rpm range and accelerate the bike more quickly.

Of course, once the engine spins up to redline—which can vary from 8,500 to 16,500 rpm on modern motorcycle engines—the motorcycle can't go any faster. So shift into second gear, and the same engine speed will give a much higher rear-wheel speed.

Note that the broader the engine's spread of power, meaning the range of rpm in which the motor makes

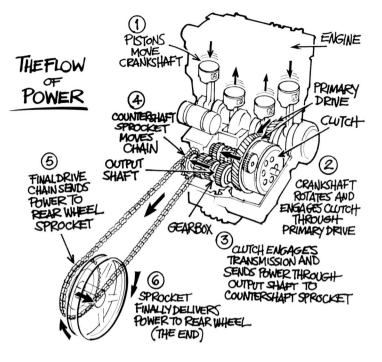

THE FLOW OF POWER

① PISTONS MOVE CRANKSHAFT

ENGINE

④ COUNTERSHAFT SPROCKET MOVES CHAIN

PRIMARY DRIVE

CLUTCH

OUTPUT SHAFT

⑤ FINAL DRIVE CHAIN SENDS POWER TO REAR WHEEL SPROCKET

GEARBOX

② CRANKSHAFT ROTATES AND ENGAGES CLUTCH THROUGH PRIMARY DRIVE

③ CLUTCH ENGAGES TRANSMISSION AND SENDS POWER THROUGH OUTPUT SHAFT TO COUNTERSHAFT SPROCKET

⑥ SPROCKET FINALLY DELIVERS POWER TO REAR WHEEL (THE END)

half is on the countershaft, or layshaft. The countershaft transmits engine power ultimately to the rear wheel.

Shifting

The transmission varies the ratio of engine speed to road speed through gear sets. Each gear set provides a specific ratio of engine to road speed, starting with the (numerically) highest ratio for first gear, and ending up with the (numerically) lowest ratio for high gear or overdrive. When you shift into any gear—first, second, third, or so on—the lever moves a shift mechanism that simply locks the chosen gears to their respective shafts, providing that ratio of drive. Unlike automobile transmissions, though, which can access neutral from any gear or speed, motorcycle transmissions are sequential. That is, whether upshifting or downshifting, you must select each ratio in order, with neutral available only between first and second gears.

Of course, there's also a clutch between the engine and transmission that the rider operates with his left hand. When the clutch lever is pulled back to the handlebar, the transmission is disengaged from the engine, which interrupts the flow of power briefly so shifts can be made smoothly. What's more, the clutch also allows the bike to remain stationary while the engine continues to run.

CHAIN FINAL-DRIVE

Once the engine's mechanical energy makes its way to the countershaft, via whichever ratio or gear set, it then has to jump the gap back to the rear wheel. Three different final-drive systems can accomplish

usable power, the fewer gears that are required to ride the bike. Most modern motorcycles have five- or six-speed gearboxes.

A few of the large-displacement cruisers have only four-speed transmissions, in part because large-displacement engines tend to have a broad spread of power. The four-speed transmissions on these bikes also make riding a bit more relaxed, as you have to shift less. In short, the transmission gives your bike's engine the flexibility to be used over your bike's entire range of road speeds. A self-driven lawn mower, by comparison, usually works best at a specific rpm, normally near its torque peak, and so it can couple directly to the drive wheels.

Motorcycle transmissions are almost universally manually operated, via the rider's left foot. There have been a couple of attempts to build (and sell) bikes with automatic transmissions, but they weren't true self-shifters like automobile automatics, and are no longer available. So, with manual transmissions completely dominant, that's what we'll focus on here.

All modern motorcycle transmissions are constant-mesh. That is, each pair of gears, or gear set, for each ratio or speed (as in a five-speed or six-speed gearbox), is always engaged. Half of each gear set is on the mainshaft, which receives power from the engine via the clutch; the other

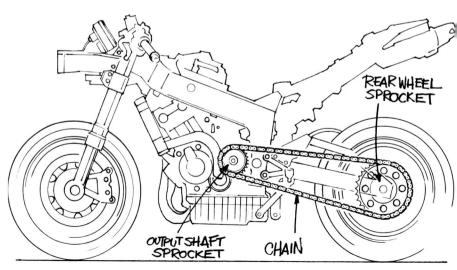

REAR WHEEL SPROCKET

OUTPUT SHAFT SPROCKET

CHAIN

that remarkable feat: chain, belt, or shaft. Each one has its pluses and minuses, as well as its own cadre of devotees and detractors.

Chain final-drive is perhaps motorcycling's most common system of the three currently used for transferring mechanical energy to the rear wheel. It is also the oldest of the trio for its use, coming as it did from the first successful safety bicycle, the 1885 Rover.

Power is transmitted from the engine via a roller chain and a pair of toothed wheels, or sprockets, one each on the countershaft and on the rear wheel. As the chain is drawn around the countershaft sprocket by that sprocket's rotation, the gear teeth mesh with each link; that action pulls the chain, which rotates the sprocket on the rear wheel in the same fashion. That is, the chain meshes with the rear wheel sprocket's teeth, turning it—and the entire rear wheel—around. *Et voila*, motion!

These days, there are two types of roller chains for motorcycles: O-ring and non O-ring. O-ring chain can be a bit of a misnomer. Rather than O-rings, manufacturers are using X- or Z-shape rings that help keep special, installed-at-the-factory lubricant inside the chain, and water, dirt, and other nasties out. Note that most high-quality chains used on motorcycles are O-ring (or X- or Z-ring) chains.

Chains by the Numbers

Even if you knew all of that, you might still be wondering if there's any significance to the numerical title given to each chain—420, 525, 630, and so on. Originally, the numbers referred to a specific dimension of the chain in eighths of an inch. The first number is the chain's pitch, or its center-to-center distance between the pins at each end. So a 5-series chain has that pitch at 5/8 inch, or, expressed today as 15.875 mm. The second and third numbers indicate the chain's width between the inner surfaces of the inner side plates. As with the first digit, higher numbers indicate greater strength.

Chain Gang: Virtues + Vices

There are several good reasons why you'd want your motorcycle to be a member of this particular chain gang. To begin with, chain final-drive systems are lighter than their other two counterparts—significantly so compared to shaft final-drives. They're more efficient, too, than big, heavy, power-sapping shaft final-drives, and narrower than belt final-drives. What's more, chain drives allow

owners to alter their overall gearing with relative ease. That's no small consideration, either, given that so many manufacturers overgear their motorcycles (so they run at lower rpm) in order to pass ever-tightening noise and emissions laws. In fact, chain final-drives are the most easily tunable of this trio in that respect.

Of course, nothing comes for free—chain drive has its disadvantages, too. It requires the most maintenance of the three by a long shot, what with periodic cleaning, lubrication and adjustment, as well as replacement. Indeed, when a chain and/or sprockets are worn out, you need to replace all three—chain, countershaft sprocket, and rear wheel sprocket. If you do not, the remaining part(s) will wear out the new one(s) astonishingly quickly.

Even today, people who should know better describe chain wear as "stretch," as if the chain were as elastic as the waistband in their shorts. Elongate would be a far better term. What happens is the pins wear; this creates the clearance inside the bushing that makes the chain physically longer. Inappropriately sized chain, excessive abuse with the throttle, lack of lubrication and/or adjustment, and not replacing the chain when it's obviously worn can all contribute to this apparent and seemingly excessive "stretch."

REAR CUSH-DRIVES

Shaft-drive vehicles—cars and motorcycles alike—usually have a spring- or rubber-type damper built into the driveline, oftentimes into the shaft itself. Such dampers take the brunt of the shock loads the driveline is subject to, rather than let them hammer away at the potentially fragile clutch, transmission, and final-drive gearcase.

Such devices' size and weight make them unsuitable for incorporating into a motorcycle's engine. So, what can be done for chain- and belt-drive bikes?

Plenty, actually. For such motorcycles, the damper—or rear cush-drive, as it is also known—has long been integrated into the rear hub, directly behind the sprocket. Most often, the hub has cavities cast into the drive side. Rubber blocks fit into those cavities, but not too tightly. The sprocket bolts to a carrier that has long, thin vanes that fit into the hub, against each of the rubber blocks. Consequently, the rear sprocket and carrier can move slightly, in the same direction the wheel rotates. One other solution is for the sprocket carrier to have fingers that slip into rubber bushings in the hub. Blocks or bushings, either one provides some damping for the to-be-expected driveline shock loads.

⚠️ Over time, the drivetrain's relentless rain of shock loads simply wears out these rubber dampers so that they must be replaced. You'll be able to tell when you detect a far-larger-than-usual windup in the driveline when you open the throttle; the driveline will feel noticeably sloppy. If you can rotate the rear sprocket more than about 5 to 10 degrees, the rubber dampers have likely turned to dust. At least they're easy to replace, usually . . .

BELT FINAL-DRIVE

🔧 Belt final-drives were also popular in motorcycling's infancy. They were leather belts, though, and when it rained they slipped horribly, which did little to endear them to motorcyclists. In the 1980s, however, technology made belt final-drive a viable solution once again, with the advent of toothed rubber-and-Kevlar belts, so that they functioned similarly to chains and sprockets.

You Want a Belt?: Virtues + Vices
In totaling up their pluses and minuses, belt final-drives seem to split the difference neatly between chain and shaft drives. In particular, belts require practically zero maintenance, much like shaft-drive systems; adjustments are virtually unheard of, no lube is necessary (which also helps make belts far less messy than chains as well), and belts don't rust. Belts are also comparable in weight to chains, and in efficiency. They're quieter, too, and when a belt finally does need to be replaced, it's not necessary to replace both cogwheels.

🔧 When you do have to replace a belt, it's an epic job, requiring removal of the swingarm (you can't split a belt like you can a chain). What's more, it's virtually impossible to change overall gearing with a belt, and—admittedly a minor point by comparison—belt drives are invariably wider than chain drives.

SHAFT FINAL-DRIVE

Automotive-style shaft final-drives are the third in our

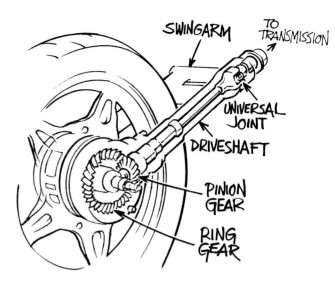

triumvirate of ways to transfer the engine's mechanical energy. They are instantly identifiable, with a hollow output shaft (basically a piece of tubing) extending back from the engine to the rear wheel, terminating in—again—a very automotive piece of hardware: a differential, or gearcase. The pieces inside the gearcase are virtually identical to their four-wheel counterparts; at the end of the shaft itself is a pinion gear, which meshes with a ring gear that completes the power transfer to the wheel. Yes, it's bulky and heavy, but it's also pretty much bulletproof, something crucial to the touring riders to whom shaft final-drives are almost invariably marketed.

⚠️ Just looking at a shaft final-drive should provide you with some clues as to its advantages. The massive size hints at a long-term, high-mileage reliability that makes chains and belts seem almost frivolous by comparison. Plus, where chains and belts put their working parts on display, a shaft drive hides almost every working part. That characteristic suggests a rider might not have much in the way of regularly scheduled maintenance to perform—and that's precisely the case. Indeed, shaft final-drives require the least amount of upkeep, compared to belts and chains.

And, of course, just as with its compatriots, trade-offs are inevitable. There's a (literally) heavy price to be paid for such stoutness, as shaft drives possess far more avoirdupois than the other two final-drive styles. Nor can a rider change gearing with a shaft drive in any way that might be characterized as easy or convenient. And, lastly, shaft drives can have an unwanted effect on a motorcycle's handling. It's called chassis-jacking, and it

PROBLEM	PROBABLE CAUSES	ACTION TO REPAIR	RELEVANT PROJECTS
CLUTCH SLIPPAGE/ SHUDDER	Dry clutch: overheating	Allow to cool off; normal service should then resume. If not, take the bike to the dealership for diagnosis	
	Wet clutch: fiber/friction plates could be dried out due to lack of use, prolonged storage	Remove clutch plates; soak fiber/friction plates in clean motor oil; reassemble	
NO/INCOMPLETE CLUTCH DISENGAGEMENT	Wet or dry clutch: worn-out clutch plates	Inspect clutch plates (and check wear on clutch basket) and replace as necessary	
	Air trapped in hydraulic clutch slave/master cylinder	Check fluid level in clutch master cylinder reservoir	
		Bleed clutch/replace clutch slave and master cylinder	
NOISY, GRINDING, OR STIFF GEARSHIFTS	Poorly adjusted clutch (cable-actuated system)	Adjust clutch properly	
	Incomplete clutch disengagement	Take to dealership for diagnosis	
FINAL-DRIVE CHAIN NOISY	Poorly lubricated and/or misadjusted chain	Adjust and lubricate drive chain	Project 6: Adjust your chain
	Chain and sprockets worn out	Replace chain and sprockets	Project 25: Chain and sprocket replacement
FINAL-DRIVE CHAIN SKIPS OVER SPROCKET TEETH	Excess slack in final-drive chain and/or excessive wear to countershaft and rear wheel sprockets	Adjust final-drive chain, and/or replace final-drive chain and sprockets	Project 25: Chain and sprocket replacement

occurs when the rider opens the throttle, which makes the ring gear in the final drive try to "climb" the pinion gear, and causes the rear of the bike to rise.

Still some riders will gleefully put up with such short-comings just to have the convenience and utter reliability of a shaft drive.

DRIVETRAIN

6

Project 25
Chain and Sprocket Replacement

TIME:	2 hours
TOOLS:	Sockets, big half-inch socket to fit countershaft nut, big socket for axle nut, ratchet, air-powered impact driver or breaker bar, torque wrench (lb-ft), wrenches, locking pliers, flathead screwdrivers, punch, chain cleaner or WD-40, contact cleaner, blue Loctite, rags, rotary tool and cutting wheel, chain breaker (or hacksaw), chain rivet tool, section of pipe or 2x4 lumber, assistant to work the brake pedal
TALENT:	2
COST:	$-$$
PARTS:	Countershaft and rear sprockets, O-ring chain with rivet master link, countershaft nut lockwasher
TIP:	Loosen the countershaft sprocket before removing old chain
BENEFIT:	The ability to tune your power delivery based on your preferences or a particular track

The easiest way to determine that you need a new chain is from wear on the sprockets. If your sprocket's teeth are worn to sharp points, hooked, or unevenly shaped, it's time to replace the chain and sprockets.

Another symptom is a clicking sound as you accelerate from a stop. This is the sound of the drive system taking up the slack. Sometimes this problem can be fixed by adjusting the chain tension (see Project 6). If the chain can be adjusted back to factory slack, the sound disappears, and any tooth wear is minimal, you can get more miles out of the chain. Otherwise swap out the chain and sprockets—together, because they wear together.

The first step in this process is not removing the chain. You need to free up the countershaft sprocket while you still have a way to lock it down.

Once the countershaft sprocket is loose, you can remove the chain. Clip-style master links are easy—too easy—to remove. Slip the clip free with a flathead screwdriver. Next, walk the removable plate off the pins by prying the ends alternately with your screwdriver. Eventually, the plate will pop free. With endless chains or

riveted master links, if you don't have a chain breaker, a hacksaw will do the trick. If you have a chain breaker, you may or may not (depending on the strength of the breaker and the size of the chain) need to grind off the head of the roller pin.

Before you install the new chain, you'll need to replace the sprockets. To remove the rear wheel, first loosen the chain adjusters three full turns and snug up the locknuts to hold them in place. Remove the axle nut and axle. Lay the wheel down sprocket up. Using a socket, remove the nuts from the studs securing the sprocket in a crisscross pattern. Slide the old sprocket free. If the stud threads are greasy, clean them with contact cleaner. (Now is also a good time to clean your wheel.) Swap in the new sprocket and torque the nuts to spec.

Since you've already loosened the countershaft sprocket, you should be able to spin the nut free. While you have the sprocket off the countershaft, take a quick look at the seal with the engine case. You shouldn't see any leakage. Clean all the encrusted chain goop from the surrounding area. Clean the countershaft with contact cleaner, paying particular attention to the threads for the

Countershaft sprockets are usually secured one of three ways: a pair of bolts securing a plate to the sprocket, a big clip that slips into a groove in the countershaft itself, or a really big nut. For the pair of bolts, simply put the engine in gear, press on the brake pedal, and unbolt them. Follow the first two steps for the clip, but slip it off with a flathead screwdriver instead. The really big nut provides the biggest challenge. Using a punch or big flathead screwdriver, bend the tabs on the lockwasher that have been folded against the flats of the nut.

Since the nut was torqued to at least 65 lb-ft and may have thread lock on it, you'll need to secure the rear wheel before you attempt to break the nut free. Slip a piece of pipe or 2x4 through the rear wheel just above the swingarm. Now, when you muscle the nut free, the wood will keep the wheel, chain, and sprocket from moving. Be prepared to sweat a little. Of course, you could resort to the lazy man's method of pulling the trigger on a (pneumatic) impact driver—no sweating involved.

nut. Once the contact cleaner is dry, slide the sprocket onto the shaft. Don't worry about the nut(s) yet. You'll torque it down once the chain is installed. Clip-type sprockets can have the clip pushed into place with a big screwdriver.

Wrap the new chain around both sprockets. If the chain has not been cut to length, turn the chain adjusters in equal amounts until the middle of the adjustment range is indicated on the swingarm. Snug up the axle nut to keep the axle from moving. Pull the chain taut and fold the chain over where it meets the other end. Your goal is to mark the rivet that needs to be removed so you can slip the master link into position. Remove the rivet as described earlier.

If your chain came with a clip-type link, replace it with a rivet master link, which will not come free.

If your chain includes a tube of grease, apply a hefty amount to the pins, O-rings, and plates. Install the O-rings included with the master link on the pins. Push the pins of the master link through the chain from the back. When you're happy with its position, check and install the O-rings on the front of the chain and press the outer plate on with your fingers. Use your chain tool to finish installing the link. Then use it to flare the ends of the roller pins so your new link stays put.

To secure the countershaft sprocket nut, add a few drops of blue Loctite to the threads and torque to spec.

Be sure to double-check the chain slack after 100 miles or so. As the chain breaks in, it will lengthen. And breaking in the chain is the most fun part.

To make it easier to press out the roller pin, grind off the top of the rivet with a rotary tool and cutting wheel. If you are removing a riveted master link so that you can reuse the chain in the future (common when gearing change at a track requires a longer chain), you'll want to grind off both pins. Usually, the midpoint between the two sprockets will be the most unobstructed place to break the chain.

Motion Pro's Chain Cutter & Riveting Tool is about the best one around. Install the correct-size breaking tip in the tool, making sure that the tip is withdrawn at least 2 mm inside the alignment bolt. Center the pin in the tool and tighten down the alignment bolt with a 14-mm wrench to hold the tool in position. Using the 14-mm wrench, crank the extraction bolt so that it pushes the breaker tip and the roller pin out of the bottom of the tool. When the pin falls free, back out the extraction bolt until the tip is back inside the alignment bolt. Loosen the alignment bolt until the chain falls free. Repeat if necessary for a master link.

If you're using the same-size sprockets, lay the old chain down beside the new one to mark the length. Now, pop the pin out of the new chain to cut it to the correct number of links. For different sprocket sizes, you'll measure the chain to length once the sprockets are mounted. If you're changing to different sprocket sizes from your previous setup, measure the proper chain length by wrapping it around both sprockets. Mark the pin where you have to bend the chain as it meets the other end—that's the pin you will remove to set the chain length.

CHAIN AND SPROCKET REPLACEMENT

Place the new sprocket on the studs. If you're unsure of the orientation, the number of teeth on the sprocket is usually stamped on the side facing out. Screw the nuts down finger tight. Set your torque wrench to half of the value specified in your factory service manual and tighten the nuts in a crisscrossing pattern. Once all nuts are torqued halfway, set the full torque value on your wrench and tighten the nuts again. If you tighten the nuts down to their full-torque setting in one step, you run the risk of stripping the threads. Remount the wheel and loosely fasten the axle nut.

Tighten the rivet tool until it distorts the roller pin. The goal is to make it impossible for the outer plate to be able to back away from the inner plate.

Even though you used Loctite compound on the threads, a new locking washer is required to assure that the countershaft nut doesn't spin free. Make sure the washer is bent so that it is firmly against the entire side (not just one point) of the nut. Note the rivet on the master link, too.

CHAIN AND SPROCKET REPLACEMENT

Project 26

Replace the Drive Belt

TIME:	A full day
TOOLS:	Common hand tools, plus tools required to remove and install the primary drive
TALENT:	3
COST:	$$$$
PARTS:	
TIP:	Now is the time to consider any driveline repairs or upgrades
BENEFIT:	This is generally a maintenance issue. Obviously, a worn or damaged belt is both unsafe and unreliable

Replacing a worn or damaged drive belt is another one of those dirty dishes chores. There is no way to sugarcoat it. On Harley-Davidsons you'll need to remove the primary drive, as well as several of the frame parts on the left side of the motorcycle before you can remove the old belt. The manual goes into great detail as far as replacing the belt; therefore, I'll only discuss in general the belt replacement process.

Obviously, the number-one reason you'll be replacing the belt is because it's either worn out or damaged. If so, take a very good look at the sprockets. It's even money that if the belt is worn out so are the sprockets. By the same token, a stone or other foreign object that may damage the belt can tear up the pulleys just as easily. Given the magnitude of the job, you may want to bite the bullet and replace the pulleys and belt as a unit, rather than do the job twice.

Belt Inspection

Start by checking the edge of the belt for cuts, tears, or odd wear patterns. Pay attention to the outer edge of the belt; typically you'll find some beveling there. In and of itself, this isn't a serious problem, although it does indicate some sprocket misalignment. Inspect the outside of the belt for stone punctures. These can be difficult to spot, so look carefully. Take a good look at the inside of the belt. When the belt is new, a layer of nylon facing and polyethylene covers the tensile or structural cords. Once the facing wears away, the only thing holding the belt together is the tensile cords. If the tensile cords are visible, the belt is worn out, and chances are excellent that the pulleys also are kaput. At this point, the belt is in

serious danger of wearing through. When the belts are new, the thin polyethylene coating is very obvious; however, it can quickly wear off as it is burnished into the belt. This is a normal situation and alone does not indicate belt wear.

Lastly check the belt teeth for damage, particularly for cracks at the base of teeth. The H-D service manual incorporates a very good chart that details belt problems and their solutions, as well as common sprocket problems. Use it as a guide before rushing out to buy a new belt.

A picture is worth a thousand words, and in a word this belt is shot.

Chapter 7
Suspension

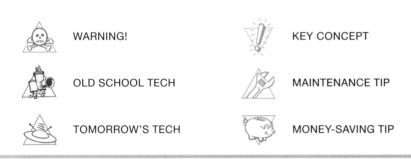

WARNING!

OLD SCHOOL TECH

TOMORROW'S TECH

KEY CONCEPT

MAINTENANCE TIP

MONEY-SAVING TIP

Some riders want to learn about their bike's suspension in the worst way possible. Unfortunately, that often turns out to be precisely the case, as they try to wrestle their frontal lobes around another rider's suggestion to add 40 clicks more prebound to the rear shock, or a road test's grave pronouncement that their mount's front fork is in dire need of reduced high-speed spring repression, as any fool could plainly see.

But, wait! As we'll soon discover, your bike's suspension really isn't that difficult to crack. Yes, suspension tuning invariably rewards the slow, methodical, thinking approach rather than the impatient one that wants to make six to eight changes at once to speed things up a little. No, it doesn't take a particularly deep understanding of physics—or even math—to figure this stuff out. And, yes, if you find yourself hopelessly in the weeds (metaphorically speaking, of course), you can always return to home; that is, the recommended settings in your owner's manual.

SPRINGS & DAMPERS

Springs (almost always coil-type for motorcycle suspensions) are analogous to batteries: They both store energy. Fork and shock springs absorb the impact energy as a wheel/tire hits a bump or pothole. In doing so, the spring compresses as the wheel is driven upward by the impact, and then releases that energy, pushing the wheel downward so it maintains contact with the pavement. Without the spring, the wheel/tire would literally bounce off the road, up and down, until it finally expended all the energy from the initial bump or pothole.

To control the bouncing (compressing and rebounding) of the wheel/tire on the springs, there needs to be something to damp (not dampen; that would mean making it damp, or wet) the uncontrolled bouncing. That device would be called a damper, otherwise known as a shock absorber; the front fork functions essentially the same way. The damper gets rid of the spring's excess energy through hydraulic friction. The damper is a fluid-damped piston inside the shock that works inline with the spring. This piston moves in the same direction and at the same speed as the spring. The piston has an opening, or orifice, facing a reservoir of hydraulic fluid, in this case oil. As the piston moves back and forth, the oil gets rudely shoved back and forth through the piston's orifice. Fluids, being incapable of being compressed, resist flowing easily through the orifice, causing hydraulic friction. That, in turn, is what causes the damping effect.

Apart from making wheel movement possible over paving imperfections, the springs' other job is to support the weight of the motorcycle and rider, plus (if applicable) a passenger and luggage. Given the wide range of types of motorcycles and their weights (also true of their riders and passengers), it shouldn't come as a surprise that springs come in different rates, or weights. Springs are rated according to the amount of weight it takes to compress one a specific distance, such as pounds-inch or kilograms-meter. So, a 100 lb-in spring requires 100 pounds to compress it 1 inch, 200 pounds to compress it 2 inches, and so on. A shorthand way of referring to springs is simply by the weight, so that our 100 lb-in spring comes to be called simply a 100-pound spring.

Compressing the spring slightly while at rest (or installed in a fork, or mounted to a shock) is known as pre-load. Preload ensures the bike doesn't sag over much under the rider's weight. Similarly, additional preload accomplishes the same end should you add a passenger and/or luggage. In short, spring preload maintains the proper chassis attitude and prevents bottoming-out of the suspension. Adding preload, however, does *not* make the spring stiffer. Nothing can do that. Additional preload simply means it will require more weight just to get the spring to move.

> Preload is used to set the sag, meaning how far the suspension compresses when loaded with just the bike (unladen sag) and with the rider aboard (laden sag). Setting the sag is the single most important adjustment you can do with your suspension.

Front Fork

The simplest kind of commonly used front suspension these days is the conventional telescopic fork, with the same kind of single-orifice damping system described earlier; it's called a damper-rod fork. In truth, this fork actually has one hole each for compression and rebound damping, but because they're different circuits (compression to assist the spring over bumps, rebound to damp the spring's energy as it extends after a bump) it's still, technically, a single-orifice damping system. Damper-rod forks have been used for generations, and they're still in use today, usually on cruisers and cheaper and/or smaller-displacement bikes—generally, motorcycles that don't put a premium on ride quality or handling.

Why? Because such systems are far too progressive. That is, the change in their damping qualities is too extreme. They provide overly soft damping over small, gentle road imperfections, but turn way harsh over larger, more square-edged ones. It's not quite the worst of both worlds, but it is close.

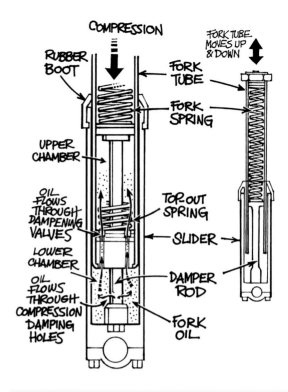

> That's the main reason the conventional damper-rod fork's place has been taken by the cartridge fork, which has become standard issue for any motorcycle whose audience values a measure of sophistication in the way their front suspension works. It's because of the way a cartridge fork can (generally) be calibrated to provide just the right combination of compression and rebound damping for the bike it's bolted to, whether that's a hardcore sport bike or a mile-munching touring rig.

Such tuning is possible because a cartridge fork's internals are basically the same as that of a rear shock. The cartridge itself consists of a tube, largely filled with oil, that has a piston that travels up and down the tube's length. A damping valve, normally for rebound, is added or incorporated into the piston. At the base of the cartridge is the compression valve.

For the most part, both fork legs contain one of these cartridges. However, on some bikes, only one leg has a cartridge. On others, each of the two legs contains a cartridge unit, but with only a single valve, so that one side handles solely compression-damping duties, and the other solely rebound.

> One other physical change accompanied the switch to cartridge forks for most motorcycles, that being the larger diameter of the fork tubes moving from the bottom of the fork to

the top, where they're bolted into the triple clamps rather than holding the front wheel as before. These came to be known as male-slider forks, or upside-down forks, for what should be obvious reasons. It was a logical change, as the bending forces imposed on the upper fork leg are enormous. It just makes sense to put the larger-diameter tube in the triple clamps, because as a tube's diameter increases, its stiffness jumps dramatically; simple physics.

Still, it's the cartridge fork's valving that makes it such a huge leap forward over the previous damper-rod fork. In place of a crude, single fixed-orifice each for compression and rebound, the cartridge fork's compression and rebound valves are made up of a stack of flexible washers called shims. As the fork moves up and down, oil gets forced through holes in the valves. On the opposite side of the valves are the shim stacks. The oil then forces the shims to deflect, or bend slightly, to provide the damping effect.

All well and good, you might say, but so what? Well, in the first place, the shim stack, by bending, provides an infinitely variable orifice, which in turn guarantees much less-progressive damping than is the case with a damper-rod fork. In the second place, changing the number, thickness, and/or diameter of the shims provides the cartridge fork's all-crucial tuneability, so that it can respond properly to paving imperfections both small and gradual, or large and sharp—and to just about anything in between.

One other advantage that tagged along with the cartridge fork—one seen first on rear shocks because their construction is similar to that of cartridge forks—is adjustable damping. Yes, shim stacks can allow damping adjustments as well, but it's not necessarily possible with all OEM forks. Besides, tuning suspension via the shims requires far more knowledge and experience than most owners are willing to take on.

Instead, the adjustments come from so-called "clickers"—essentially needle valves, with detents, that thread into the top of the fork (for adjusting rebound, usually) or the bottom (for adjusting compression, likewise). Each detent provides a tactile and sometimes audible click, largely to make it easier to adjust the suspension more precisely than would be possible by just counting turns of the needle valve. The needle valves restrict or open the flow of oil for each damping circuit. Spring preload is also a common fork adjustment, accomplished via a threaded collar in the fork caps. Turning the collar clockwise increases preload; counterclockwise decreases it. Some forks offer all three

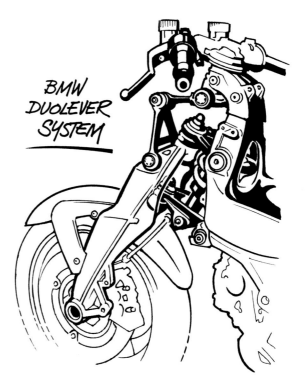

BMW DUOLEVER SYSTEM

adjustments (spring preload, compression, and rebound damping), while others adjust only for preload, and some have no adjustment capability whatsoever. Cost is normally the limiting factor; more expensive motorcycles tend to offer more adjustability, especially if they're sport bikes.

Alternative Front Suspensions
Whatever its form—damper-rod or cartridge-type, right side up or upside down—the telescopic fork has long reigned as motorcycling's first choice for front suspension. There are a number of reasons for this. For instance, the telescopic fork is relatively simple, it's been developed for generations, and it's familiar to riders, both in its appearance and in how it makes motorcycles handle.

However, if you look at it logically, the tele fork verges on being disastrous. Suspension and braking loads affect the steering, for example, and its vast, relatively unsupported length can make it very flexible.

And those are the very reasons that many bright thinkers have come up with alternative solutions to the tele fork, notably hub-center-steering versions such as Bimota's Tesi and Yamaha's short-lived GTS1000, and variations of a double-wishbone front end such as those created by Norman Hossack and a host of others. The only alt front ends that have had any real success (defined here as being used on mass-produced motorcycles for more than just a few model-years) have been BMWs Telelever and Duolever. The two are variations on Hossack's design, and are generally well regarded (especially the Duolever) for their ability to separate the effects of braking and suspension from actually steering the motorcycle. However, most riders who have grown up riding bikes with telescopic forks find the steering on these BMWs lacks a certain feel—one that's difficult to define but is particularly confidence-inspiring during spirited cornering. In short, they're not for everyone—yet—and the telescopic fork's reign is relatively safe—for now.

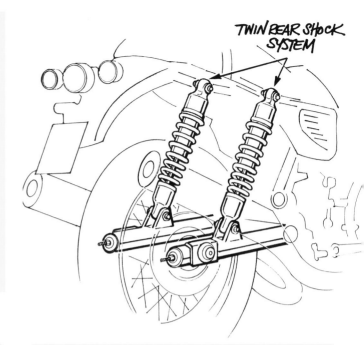

SHOCK ABSORBERS & REAR SUSPENSIONS

Well, if you've been able to grasp how cartridge forks work—and, hopefully, you have—then you should also have a pretty good idea of how shock absorbers work, as the principles are the same, even if the physical sizes of the two are not.

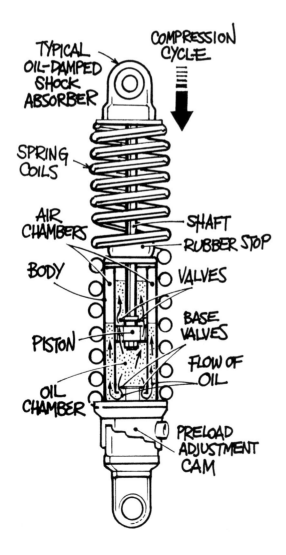

Of course, there are some differences between the two. For example, high-quality rear dampers are almost universally pressurized De Carbon–types, where cartridge forks almost always work at atmospheric pressure. A De Carbon shock/damper is a single-tube unit (regular/conventional hydraulic shocks such as Konis have double-tube construction) with a sliding piston that separates the damping oil from a high-pressure (360 to 430 psi) inert gas, usually nitrogen. Why use such a design? Because, characteristically, De Carbon dampers consistently respond immediately to paving imperfections, unlike conventional hydraulic shocks whose construction can provoke aeration or cavitation of the damping fluid, which reveals itself as inconsistent or nonexistent damping. They also stay cooler, thanks to their single-tube (also known as mono-tube) design.

Those are relatively minor differences, though, compared to the massive changes motorcycling's rear suspension has gone through in the last several decades. Here are some of the variations that have made it into mass production:

Twin Shocks

Back in the day, all motorcycles' rear suspensions were configured like this, with a conventional, unbraced swingarm shaped like a U, with one damper on each side of the rear wheel, positioned relatively upright and with the bottom mount on the swingarm roughly in line with the rear wheel's axle. In that position,

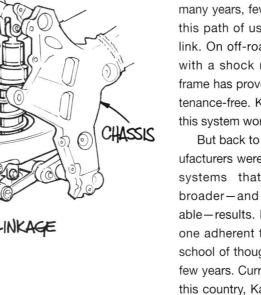

SHOCK ABSORBER

SWINGARM (SINGLE-SIDE STYLE)

SPRING

CHASSIS

LINKAGE

many years, few manufacturers went down this path of using a single shock with no link. On off-road bikes, a linkless system with a shock mounted lower in the rear frame has proved to be effective and maintenance-free. KTM, in particular, has made this system work very well.

But back to the early 1980s. Other manufacturers were busily working on link-type systems that could be tailored for broader—and supposedly more desirable—results. Honda's Hawk GT 650 was one adherent to the single-shock/no-link school of thought, but only produced for a few years. Currently, of motorcycles sold in this country, Kawasaki's Ninja 650R is one of the few road-going motorcycles to use such a system.

the ratio of shock travel to rear wheel travel was about 1:1. That is, if the damper moves 10 mm over a bump, the rear wheel does likewise.

This setup works perfectly adequately for the majority of riders. But when they start pushing harder on bumpy back roads, the swingarm starts to flex and the previous generation (or older) dampers start to show their limitations. It is possible to get much better results with a modern aftermarket pair of shock absorbers.

Single Shock/No Link

Readers might recall Yamaha's mid-1970s YZ Monoshock motocrossers as being the first mass-produced motorcycles with a single rear shock. They didn't have a link; it was mounted directly to the frame and the swingarm at a roughly 2:1 ratio. That is, if the rear wheel moves 1 inch, the damper/shock stroke moves 0.5 inch.

In truth, Vincent's Series A motorcycles from the early 1930s had an almost identical setup, so it wasn't exactly a new idea.

> Regardless of who came up with it first, the advantages remain steadfastly the same: it eliminates any potential differences between two shocks in a conventional twin-shock rear suspension; it helps make the swingarm stiffer; and it moves the damper and spring forward for better mass centralization. It also reduces the damper's travel in relation to wheel travel. That's significant because it inherently reduces the aeration (foaming) of the hydraulic fluid.

Still, with no link, the motorcycle is stuck with whatever damper/ wheel ratio that was designed into it. For

Single Shock with Link

This is what modern rear suspension looks like. They're so widespread that riders have come to expect them on current motorcycles.

Single-shock link-type rear suspensions have all of the advantages listed above—plus one important extra: the ability to tailor, with the link, a suspension that's either progressive (becomes stiffer or softer) or linear in its action.

The general thinking behind links—for street bikes, anyway—is that it's best to have one that provides a progressively stiffer rear suspension. That is, as a shock nears the end of its travel, the link's leverage decreases, so that its response becomes stiffer. Consequently, a rider can take on a passenger and/or luggage, and not have to worry about the rear suspension bottoming. For racing or high-performance riding, a linear-rate link is most often the best solution.

SUSPENSION TUNING

> Before we even get started, you need to know and understand one bedrock truth: There is no one universally perfect suspension setting for all riders of one particular motorcycle. There's no lost chord, there's no Atlantis, no Santa Claus, no Easter Bunny, and no one perfect setup. Sorry to be the one to break this to you.

Unfortunately, if you want the best suspension setup for your motorcycle that suits your weight and riding style, you're going to have to root it out through trial and error. That means writing down the settings and your resulting riding impressions in a notebook. This information will be invaluable when you invariably make too many adjustments at once, and you're completely lost. If that happens, though, you can return the settings to something you liked previously, or at least to the stock settings.

You should also know it's not that scary or difficult. Honest. It just takes time and requires you to pay careful attention to how your motorcycle is working.

First things first: You need to get your sag measurements correct, front and rear. All this does is determine how much preload your front and rear springs require to keep the fork and shock(s) in their most useful range of travel. If you have too much or too little sag/preload, adjusting the damping won't have anywhere near the desired effect. In fact, you're more liable to sink into a morass of conflicting damper settings, and your bike will handle like a spavined cow.

In general, most experts suggest setting your bike's sag at about one-fourth to one-third of your bike's total travel, front and rear. That usually works out to roughly 25–30 mm for both ends. Consult your owner's manual for the recommended sag. Also, you'll find setting sag much easier if you recruit two buddies to help you with this.

For the front, get the front wheel completely off the ground so the suspension is fully extended. Use a metric scale tape measure to get the distance from the dust seal/wiper to the bottom of the triple clamps (conventional fork) or to the top of the casting that holds the axle and brake caliper(s) (upside-down fork); call this F1. At the back, measure from the rear axle to a point directly above the rear axle, with the suspension completely extended; call this R1.

Then get the same measurements, first with the motorcycle resting on the ground (unladen sag) and then with yourself in the saddle, fully dressed in your riding gear (laden sag). You'll need at least one person to steady the bike, and another would be helpful to get the measurement, using the same procedure. If F1-F2 or R1-R2 is less than 25 mm, you'll want to reduce preload; if F1-F2 or R1-R2 is more than 30 mm, you'll want to increase preload (see Projects 27 and 28 for a slightly more precise method of measurement).

Adjusting Damping
Now, on to damping. First, a couple of caveats.

Make only small changes; no more than two clicks at a time. Plus, these are suggested guidelines, and should be considered as such. If any of this is beyond your understanding, or even after following these suggestions your bike still doesn't feel right, then you should either seriously consider unlimbering your credit card and simply buying upgraded suspension components, or—at a minimum—return your bike's suspension settings to those recommended in your owner's manual. And, if after that you still feel there's a problem, definitely take your motorcycle to a dealer so they can find out what the problem is.

The first damping adjustment to make is rebound, as it has the greatest effect on your bike's handling. Try to dial in only as much as is necessary to keep the bike feeling planted and stable. At either end, if ride quality is excellent at lower speeds, but as you go faster, the front and/or rear start to feel loose or unstable and wobble or weave sets in, you need more rebound damping. However, if the ride is harsh, and at higher speeds the front starts to wobble and/or the bike tends to run wide exiting corners, you should reduce rebound.

For compression damping, try to use as little as possible. Symptoms of too little compression damping include excessive front-end dive under hard braking, a mushy feel to the front or rear, and any bottoming over big paving imperfections at speed. Too much compression damping is characterized by a harsh ride (although not quite as bad as having too much rebound), and when paving imperfections are felt immediately and directly through the chassis.

Some race-replica-quality sport bikes these days are coming with adjusters for both high- and low-speed compression damping adjusters. What's important to remember here is that the speed referred to is how fast the suspension has to react—not your road speed. In general, low-speed compression damping affects ride quality, especially in fast corners, and overall stability; high-speed compression damping affects the bike's ride height, and ride quality over small ripples. Adjust accordingly after a series of test rides.

It's worth repeating here that there is no one universal setting that will make your motorcycle a veritable handling demon. The procedures outlined in this chapter are merely general suggestions to get you started on the right path.

SUSPENSION TROUBLESHOOTING

PROBLEM	PROBABLE CAUSES	ACTION TO REPAIR	RELEVANT PROJECTS
POOR RIDE QUALITY	Improperly inflated tires	Check tire pressure and inflate to motorcycle manufacturer's recommended psi	Project 37: Check tire pressure
	Improper sag	Set sag	Project 27 & 28: Measure sag and adjust preload front/rear
DETERIORATING RIDE QUALITY/ HANDLING	Worn-out oil in shock(s) or fork	Drain and replace fork oil. Have shock(s) rebuilt at dealership, if possible	Project 31: Change your fork oil
EXCESSIVE PLAY IN REAR SWINGARM	Linkage bearings in rear suspension worn out	Rebuild and/or replace bearings	

You'll need to decide for yourself if the resulting settings are correct for your weight and riding style, or if you need to go further one way or the other.

Also bear in mind your settings will work well on a particular stretch of pavement. In an ideal world, you'd change the settings for different types of surfaces and riding conditions. Racers do this—you probably won't!

Stick with it, use the same stretch of pavement or racetrack to make your evaluations, and don't forget to keep copious amounts of notes. Best of luck.

Measure Sag and Adjust Preload: Front

TIME:	30 minutes–1 hour
TOOLS:	Two assistants, riding gear, metric tape measure, open-ended wrench or socket, shock preload adjusting tool or long screwdriver and hammer, hacksaw or pipe/tubing cutter (for PVC spacers), jack
TALENT:	1
COST:	$
PARTS:	PVC pipe to cut spacers
TIP:	Adjust the preload to suit the load the bike will carry—rider, passenger, gear, etc.
BENEFIT:	With preload adjusted for proper sag, your suspension will be able to do its job better

The load on your suspension when you ride solo is different from the load with two riders and luggage. If your bike is to have adequate suspension travel to absorb pavement irregularities, you will need different suspension settings for the two scenarios. This is the world of sag and preload. Sag is the amount your bike settles under its own weight (free sag), and loaded for the riding you plan to do (static sag). Preload is the amount of tension dialed into the spring; preload regulates sag.

Too little sag and your bike will be prone to topping out the suspension as it extends to its limit; too much sag and the suspension can bottom out, giving you and your passenger a harsh jolt. Once your sag is set, you can determine whether your suspenders' spring rate is correct for your weight and size.

While measuring sag is a comparable procedure front and rear, setting preload is as different as the two suspension systems. In this project, we will address the front of the bike. Then, in Project 28, we'll bring the back up to speed.

Measuring Sag

In order to measure static sag, you'll need two assistants. A metric tape measure will also make the calculations easier than an SAE one. Before you mount the bike, you need to measure the suspension when it's completely topped out. Lift on the grips until the front wheel begins to come off the ground. On traditional forks, measure from the stanchion wiper to the bottom of the triple clamp. (If your bike has fork covers, you'll need to measure from the top of the fender to the bottom of the triple clamp. Also, make sure you measure from the same location every time.) Measure from the wiper to the top of the axle clamp on inverted forks (like those found on the Yamaha Warrior and Kawasaki Mean Streak). Name this number L1 and write it down.

Now have one of your assistants hold the bike from the rear while you get into your riding position. (If you're setting sag for riding two-up or with a full load of luggage, be sure to have these on the bike for this measurement.) The other assistant should push down on the fork and let it slowly rise up until it stops. The distance it moves will be called L2. The front end should now be lifted and allowed to settle slowly down until it stops, a range of movement forming measurement L3. Exactly in the middle of measurements L2 and L3 is the point where the fork would want to live in a frictionless system. So, the average between the measurements would be (L2+L3)/2.

To determine static sag for the front of the bike, subtract the average measurement calculated above from L1. In mathematical terms, static sag = L1-(L2+L3)/2. Suspension gurus generally agree that between 25 to 30 mm (1 to 1.2 inches) is optimum static sag—even if

This inverted fork makes measuring sag easy. If your bike has fork covers that prevent access to the stanchion, measure the sag from the fender to the bottom of the triple clamp.

instructions on how to do this, if you're lucky enough to have preload adjusters.

Changing Preload

Some of the bigger, touring-oriented cruisers have air pressure adjusters to set front preload. Even forks that don't have external adjusters can have their preload altered. It just takes a little more time.

If you want to adjust the preload on a fork that doesn't have factory adjusters (and most cruisers don't), you can create custom spacers by cutting them out of the largest PVC pipe that will fit inside the fork. Although you don't have to take the front end off the ground, removing the pressure from the front suspension will make reassembly easier. When changing spacers without jacking the front end up, only remove the cap from one side of the fork at a time, or the bike will crash down to the bottom of the fork travel.

Begin with your bike on a jack or a lift. If you don't support the front end, the bike will drop on the fork as you remove the cap of each tube, leaving you no recourse but to lift the front end when you want to put the cap back on.

Next, remove any parts that may interfere with your access to the top of the fork legs, such as windshields and handlebars (lay them on a pad on the tank without removing the cables or hoses). Loosen the bolt on one side of the top triple clamp to relieve pressure on the cap's threads. Remove the fork cap either by unscrewing it with a wrench or by pressing down on the cap and removing the circlip. The cap is under pressure from the spring, so be prepared for it to pop out. Remove the stock spacer and measure its length. Since the amount of sag you need to gain/lose is almost a

you're bigger or smaller than the average rider. If you have too much sag, you'll need to increase the fork's preload. Conversely, if you have too little, back off on the preload a bit. See your factory service manual for

With the rider in position, extend the suspension and let it settle slowly back into its sag. Next, press down to let it rise up into place. The average of those two measurements will give the true reading.

If your bike has air adjustable preload (front or rear), all you need to change the preload is this nifty pump from Progressive Suspension. *Photo courtesy Progressive Suspension*

Once you remove the fork cap, you'll see the top of the spacer. Any length you add to your new spacer will make it that much harder to reseat the fork cap.

one-to-one ratio to the amount you need to remove/add to the spacer, you can easily approximate the right length with simple arithmetic. While you've got the saw out, cut a couple sets of PVC spacers in quarter-inch increments on either side of your calculated length. File down any rough edges on the PVC and clean the spacers of any grit. Label the spacers with a Sharpie. Slip the new spacer into place with any washers you may have also removed with the stock spacer. If you've increased the preload, expect to work a bit to get the

fork cap in place. Don't forget to torque the screw-on caps and the triple clamp's pinch bolts back to spec.

A final note about preload: If you take the time to measure the preload required for solo riding and two-up, write down the settings. When you need to change the preload for different riding situations, all you'll have to do is take out the wrenches and make the changes to the shock. (Since most cruisers don't have fork preload adjusters, set the preload for the kind of riding you do most and leave it.)

Make sure your cuts on the PVC spacers are square. A miter box or pipe cutter will help with this. Also, cut, clean up, and label three or four spacers to ease the swapping process as you dial in the front end.

MEASURE SAG AND ADJUST PRELOAD: FRONT

Project 28
Measure Sag and Adjust Preload: Rear

TIME:	30 minutes
TOOLS:	Two assistants, riding gear, metric tape measure
TALENT:	1
COST:	None
PARTS:	None
TIP:	Set the sag wearing the gear you usually wear, while in your normal riding position
BENEFIT:	With preload adjusted for proper sag, your suspension will be able to its its job better.

This project continues the work we started in Project 27. Moving to the rear of the bike, it's time to measure sag and adjust preload if necessary.

Measuring preload at the back of the bike uses the same procedures, and the same math, you applied up front. The key to good numbers is to pick a good measuring point, such as the rear axle. You can measure straight up from this to, say, the bottom of your rear fender. Just use the same two points, and go straight up and down, with each measurement. We're looking for static sag of 25–30 mm. As with the front, if you have too much rear sag, you need to increase preload; too little and you'll need to reduce preload a bit.

Changing rear shock preload is fairly easy on all bikes. Most stock shocks will have either a stepped adjuster or threaded, locking-ring adjusters. The stepped adjusters usually ramp the preload over five or six settings. Using the tool supplied in the factory toolkit, simply lever the collar onto the proper step. The process should take less time than it took to get the tool out from under the seat. Then measure the sag again to see if you reached your goal. Locking-ring adjusters can also be altered with a tool. Motion Pro makes a clawed adjuster that mounts to a 3/8-inch ratchet. Many aftermarket shocks also ship with an adjuster. If you don't have a tool, a long screwdriver and hammer will work in a pinch.

Begin by loosening the locking ring (the one farthest away from the spring). Using a Sharpie or a scribe, mark the adjusting ring so that you can count the number of

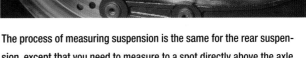

The process of measuring suspension is the same for the rear suspension, except that you need to measure to a spot directly above the axle.

Notice how the locking ring has been loosened from the adjusting ring. The black mark will make it easy to keep track of how far the ring has been turned.

turns you increased/decreased the preload. The fine-pitched threads move the adjusting ring approximately 1 mm per revolution. When you're roughing in the preload, make adjustments in full-turn increments. Fine-tuning the preload will be done with much smaller increments. Once the preload is set, tighten the lock ring down to keep the adjusting ring from backing out. Don't jam the lock ring down more than a quarter-turn, or you may have trouble loosening it next time you adjust the preload.

Now that the static sag is set, you can measure the free sag to make sure your bike has the correct rate springs. Measure the amount the bike sags under its own weight. The free sag should be between 0 and 5 mm. Simply lifting the weight of your bike to see if it moves up slightly before topping out the suspension will give you an idea of how much free sag it has. While this may not seem to make sense, if your suspension has no free sag, your spring rate is too soft. The soft rate forced you to use too much preload to get the desired sag. If you have a bunch of free sag, your spring is too stiff. Changing the rear spring will require a trip to your local suspension guru or aftermarket company.

While changing the preload doesn't get any easier than using a stepped adjuster, you can't fine-tune the preload the same way you can with a threaded collar.

Project 29
Adjust Damping Settings

TIME:	Minutes to hours to days to weeks to years of twiddling
TOOLS:	Screwdriver, brain, pen, paper
TALENT:	3
COST:	None
PARTS:	None
TIP:	Write down the setting and symptoms religiously
BENEFIT:	A bike that makes you feel like a hero

When you initially set up your bike's damping, start with the sag properly set. If you don't, you won't get a good baseline. Also, consider the condition of your suspension components. If it's been a couple of years since the fork oil was freshened or you've got a couple of hard seasons on your shock, do that maintenance first. Similarly, if you've squared off your tires with the daily commute or your last three-day sport tour, spoon some new rubber onto the rims.

Begin by setting your bike's damping adjusters to the factory-specified positions. Damping adjusters measure their settings one of two ways: clicks or turns. If your bike uses clicks, turn the adjuster all the way in (clockwise) and unscrew the adjuster the correct number of clicks. For turns, do the same thing but count the turns instead of clicks. From here, you'll set your suspension's rebound before you ride and then modify the compression and rebound based on your riding impressions.

To test your fork's rebound damping, stand your bike straight up. Press firmly down on the center of the triple clamp—not the handlebar. Be sure not to hold the brake. The suspension should rebound back to its starting point and not beyond. If it bounces back beyond the original position, you need to increase damping by screwing in the rebound adjuster on top of the fork. Generally, make adjustments in single clicks or half turns. If the fork rises back directly to its original position, press on the triple clamp and time how long it takes to rise back. You want the rebound to take about a second. Adjust the rebound damping until you feel the timing is right. Follow the same procedure in the rear, pressing on the center of the seat. The shock's rebound adjuster is usually on the bottom of the shock body.

You'll find the compression-damping adjuster on the bottom of the fork, generally.

The best way to test your suspension settings is to repeatedly ride the same section of road. Dial in the front and rear suspension separately. First, ride your test road with the compression set to the factory specs to form a baseline. Next, go a couple of clicks firmer. Did the handling improve or get worse? Now try a couple clicks softer than stock. Which of the three settings do you prefer? Keep experimenting. Take notes. When you're satisfied with the front suspension, continue the process with the rear.

If you're having trouble figuring out what signals your bike is giving you, consult the "Suspension Troubleshooting Symptoms" sidebar.

As your riding-and suspension-tuning skills improve with time, don't be surprised to find that your settings need to change, too. You may find yourself developing bumpy and smooth road settings or canyon and commuting settings. Have fun, and give yourself a pat on the back for knowing your bike and your riding so well.

Riders are more familiar with the fork rebound adjusters than any others. Perhaps it's because they're in plain sight every time you ride.

Contrary to the fork adjusters, the shock rebound adjuster is on the bottom of the shock.

You'll find the shock compression adjuster either on the top of the shock or on the reservoir.

SUSPENSION TROUBLESHOOTING SYSTEMS

Here are some basic symptoms of suspension damping problems. Remember, these are extreme examples; your symptoms may be more subtle. You may also have to find an acceptable compromise on either end of the adjustment spectrum. It all depends on how the bike's handling "feels" to you.

Lack of Rebound Damping (Fork)

- The fork offers a supremely plush ride, especially when riding straight up. When the pace picks up, however, the feeling of control is lost. The fork feels mushy, and traction "feel" is poor.
- After hitting bumps at speed, the front tire tends to chatter or bounce.
- When flicking the bike into a corner at speed, the front tire begins to chatter and lose traction. This translates into an unstable feel at the clip-ons.
- As speed increases and steering inputs become more aggressive, a lack of control begins to appear. Chassis attitude and pitch become a real problem, with the front end refusing to stabilize after the bike is countersteered hard into a turn.

Too Much Rebound Damping (Fork)

- The ride is quite harsh—just the opposite of the plush feel of too little rebound. Rough pavement makes the fork feel as if it's locking up with stiction and harshness.
- Under hard acceleration exiting bumpy corners, the front end feels as if it wants to "wiggle" or "tankslap." The tire feels as if it isn't staying in contact with the pavement when you're on the gas.
- The harsh, unforgiving ride makes the bike hard to control when riding through dips and rolling bumps at speed. The suspension's reluctance to maintain tire traction through these sections erodes rider confidence.

Lack of Compression Damping (Fork)

- Front-end dive while on the brakes becomes excessive.
- The rear end of the motorcycle wants to "come around" when using the front brakes aggressively.
- The front suspension bottoms out with a solid hit under heavy braking and after hitting bumps.
- The front end has a mushy and semi-vague feeling—similar to lack of rebound damping.

Too Much Compression Damping (Fork)

- The ride is overly harsh, especially at the point when bumps and ripples are contacted by the front wheel.
- Bumps and ripples are felt directly; the initial hit is routed through the chassis instantly, with big bumps bouncing the tire off the pavement.
- The bike's ride height is affected negatively—the front end winds up riding too high in the corners.
- Brake dive is reduced drastically, though the chassis is upset significantly by bumps encountered during braking.

Lack of Rebound Damping (Rear Shock)

- The ride is plush at cruising speeds, but as the pace increases, the chassis begins to wallow and weave through bumpy corners.
- This causes poor traction over bumps under hard acceleration; the rear tire starts to chatter due to a lack of wheel control.
- There is excessive chassis pitch through large bumps and dips at speed, and the rear end rebounds too quickly, upsetting the chassis with a pogo stick action.

Too Much Rebound Damping (Rear Shock)

- This creates an uneven ride. The rear suspension compliance is poor and the feel is vague.

- Traction is poor over bumps during hard acceleration (due to lack of suspension compliance).
- The bike wants to run wide in corners since the rear end is "packing down"; this forces a nose-high chassis attitude, which slows down steering.
- The rear end wants to hop and skip when the throttle is chopped during aggressive corner entries.

Lack of Compression Damping (Rear Shock)

- There is too much rear-end "squat" under acceleration; the bike wants to steer wide exiting corners (since the chassis is riding rear low/nose high).
- Hitting bumps at speed causes the rear to bottom out, which upsets the chassis.
- The chassis attitude is affected too much by large dips and G-outs.
- Steering and control become difficult due to excessive suspension movement.

Too Much Compression Damping (Rear Shock)

- The ride is harsh, though not quite as bad as too much rebound; the faster you go, the worse it gets, however.
- Harshness hurts rear tire traction over bumps, especially during deceleration. There's little rear-end "squat" under acceleration.
- Medium to large bumps are felt directly through the chassis; when hit at speed, the rear end kicks up.

Reprinted courtesy of *Sport Rider Magazine*—www.sportrider.com.

ADJUST DAMPING SETTINGS

Project 30
Adjust Ride Height

TIME:	1 hour
TOOLS:	Tape measure, ruler or caliper, wrenches, sockets, torque wrench, screwdrivers, Allen keys, jack or lift, assistant
TALENT:	3
COST:	None
PARTS:	None
TIP:	Lowering a bike can dramatically affect ground clearance, so be careful what you wish for
BENEFIT:	A bike that steers the way you want it to

Adjusting the ride height can be an important step toward getting your bike to behave the way you want it to. Changing the ride height can help with speeding up or slowing down steering, altering rear wheel traction, keeping the chassis attitude the same after changing to a different tire profile, or simply lowering the bike for a shorter rider.

As with any suspension change, little alterations can have big effects on your bike. Take careful notes, beginning with the baseline measurements. After that, make sure you record every change you make.

To find your baseline rear ride height, measure from the center of the rear axle to a spot on the frame or bodywork directly above the axle with your bike's rear suspension topped out. Write down both the measurement and the point measured to, so you can ensure repeatability. For the fork, measuring a change in ride height is easy. Since the fork tubes extend through the triple clamp on most sportbikes, you simply measure how far they protrude above the triple clamp.

Be clear on what you are seeking with changes to ride height. The factory settings are designed as a compromise to handle most situations a rider is likely to encounter. For example, if you drop the front end to steepen the rake angle and speed up the steering, you may get a bike that turns in quickly but is unstable in a straight line and wants to shake its head over every little road imperfection. You can also experience the same behavior if you raise the rear of the bike to increase

ground clearance. The general rules of thumb concerning ride height can be summarized as:

Bike is nose high (front too high or rear too low):
• Chatter or poor grip on front tire exiting corners
• Difficult to steer or change direction
• Motorcycle runs wide exiting corners

Bike is nose low (front too low or rear too high):
• Motorcycle unstable at high speeds
• Unstable, tries to swap ends under hard braking
• Lack of grip from rear tire

See "Suspension Troubleshooting Symptoms" in Project 29 to determine whether your problem involves ride height or damping. Because symptoms can be similar, you may want to talk to a bike suspension expert for a second opinion.

Typically, you change the front's ride height by sliding the triple clamp up or down on the fork legs. Use a rear stand to stabilize the bike. Place a jack or lift under the front of the bike and crank it up until the fork is fully extended. This takes the pressure off the fork and makes it easier to slide the legs up and down inside the triple clamp.

Altering a bike's rear ride height can be a bit more complicated than the front. If you've already installed a spiffy aftermarket shock with an integral ride-height adjuster, simply loosen the locknut and crank the adjuster up or down until the desired height is reached.

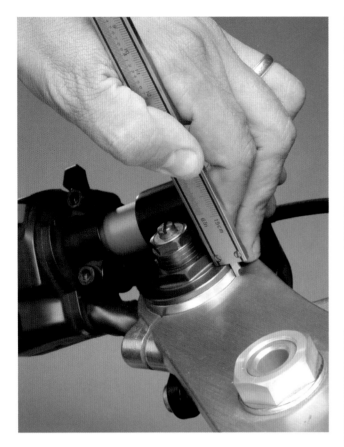

This ZX-6R has a factory spacer already installed. The two washers (right) will allow the shock to be lengthened or shortened in 2-mm increments, which should be more than adequate.

Although you can measure the height of a fork leg above the triple clamp with a ruler, a caliper will lock into position and allow you to accurately compare the height of both fork legs. Working on one leg at a time, loosen all of the triple clamp pinch bolts except one. Prepare for the front to drop when you loosen the final bolt. You can assist a fork tube in slipping through the triple clamp by twisting it slightly. If the triple clamp will not slide down on the fork leg, a retaining clip may be hidden under the top triple clamp. You'll need to raise the clamp and remove the clip before you can lower the triple clamp. When the front has been lowered or raised the proper amount, tighten one bolt and carefully measure the fork height. If you are raising the triple clamp on the fork, lifting the bike slightly on the jack may help. Don't raise the triple clamp on the fork so high that the fork cap is below the clamp's top surface. If you get to this point, move to the back of the bike and lower the rear. Some bikes with inverted forks have registration marks on the top of the tube to assist in setting the height, but you should still double-check the height with a ruler or caliper. When you're certain of the height, retorque all of the pinch bolts and move on to the second fork leg.

This Penske shock has an integral ride-height adjuster. Just loosen the lower locknut (as shown) and turn the adjuster to lengthen or shorten the shock length. Don't forget to tighten the locknut.

However, make sure that you don't alter the height beyond the shock manufacturer's recommended range. You don't want the shock's piston rod to fail, do you?

Those of you with nonadjustable shocks have two choices for altering the rear ride height. You can change the length of the shock, or change the suspension tie rods (or dog bones). Both of these options offer compromises. First, changing the length of the dog bones will change the progression rate of the entire rear suspension.

If you lengthen the dog bones to drop the bike, the progression rate will increase, giving a stiffer ride. While you can alter the rear ride height by changing the shock's sag, you will compromise its ability do its job.

To keep the progression rate the same on a lowered or raised bike, altering the length of the shock or the shock mount is the preferred way to go. Some bikes, such as the ZX-6R shown in the photos, have the top shock mount bolted to the frame with a spacer. You'll

A bike lift eases the process of adjusting the front ride height by taking the bike's weight off the front suspension. You can also use the lift to assist in raising or lowering the triple clamp on the fork tubes.

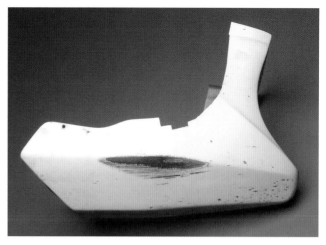

Although dragging bodywork is relatively benign, beware: Hard parts usually aren't far away. To increase the ride height without altering the chassis attitude, the front and rear of this bike needed to be raised an equal amount to eke out some more clearance on a tight and bumpy track.

need to remove the shock to gain access to the mounting bracket. Next, take the bracket (or the spacer) to your local hardware store to find washers that fit the

mount. By combining washers of varying thicknesses with the stock spacer, you will be able to raise or lower the rear ride height. Keep the changes small. Current rear suspension linkages have a leverage ratio of about 2:1. So, a 2-mm spacer will raise the rear about 4 mm.

After each change—either front or rear— reassemble your bike and ride it to make sure you haven't created handling problems. If you have, reset your suspension to its previous settings. If you have lowered the bike, remember that you have decreased your cornering clearance.

LOWERING CAUTIONS

Anyone with a shorter inseam looking to get better footing while straddling his or her bike needs to be aware of the compromises involved in lowering a bike. First and most importantly, you will decrease your cornering clearance. To put it in plain English, you can no longer lean your bike over as far as its designers intended. If you even occasionally scraped your footpegs or any other part of your bike while riding, you should avoid lowering your bike. Try reshaping your seat or buying a lower aftermarket seat. Also, consider simply getting more comfortable with only one foot on the ground at a stop. Look at the grid of any AMA National, and you'll see lots of jockey-sized riders in perfect control of their machines with only one foot down.

The maximum you should ever consider raising the fork tubes in the triple clamp is 15 mm. The increasingly compact sporting packages built today won't allow much more than that. Even then, you should test to make sure that full fork travel doesn't allow the fender or tire to contact the triple clamp or other components, such as the radiator. Since you'll be lowering the front and rear the same amount to maintain chassis attitude, you'll most likely be pretty safe lowering the rear 15 mm, but you should check to make sure that your rear wheel doesn't hit the rear fender when fully compressed.

Lowering your bike any more than the 15 mm will require installation of lowering blocks in the fork. You'll also need to shorten the fork springs to deliver the appropriate rate over their new, shorter

travel. Lengthening the tie rods also makes the rear linkage significantly more progressive (i.e., stiffer) and limits your shock's effectiveness. If your shock doesn't have ride-height adjusters, you should consider buying a shorter shock or having a suspension company shorten your shock's shaft. Otherwise you risk significantly compromising the suspension's function.

Other lowering considerations include shortening the side stand. You need to make sure the stand allows the bike to lean over far enough to remain stable and not fall over. Finally, if you do lower your bike, carefully build up to your new maximum lean. Flicking your bike into a corner before you know where the hard parts will drag could have you touching down hard enough to lever a wheel off the ground— and then you'll really touch down.

Project 31
Change Your Fork Oil

TIME:	1–2 hours
TOOLS:	Wrenches, sockets, torque wrench, screwdrivers, Allen keys, metric tape measure, jack, circlip pliers or jeweler's screwdrivers (for non-screw-on caps), press (for non-screw-on caps), caliper or ruler, Ratio Rite or another graduated container, spring compression tool (for inverted forks)
TALENT:	1 to 3
COST:	$
PARTS:	Fork oil
TIP:	Overfill the fork slightly if you are using a suction-type tool to set oil height
BENEFIT:	Consistent damping from year to year

Fork oil, like motor oil, loses viscosity over time. If ignored, the fork will cease to perform properly and internal components such as the slider bushings will begin to wear. If you're not planning to upgrade your front suspension, replace your fork's slippery stuff every two years or 15,000 miles, or at the interval your factory service manual recommends.

To replace the fork oil on newer bikes, remove the fork from the chassis. First remove the front wheel. Then remove the front fender by unbolting it from the fork legs.

Bikes with fork covers require that the fork covers be removed, too. Remove the top triple clamp (with the bar still attached) by unscrewing the bolt or nut securing the top clamp to the steering stem. Wiggle the bar front to back as you walk the triple clamp free. Once it slips off, lay the bar on a thick piece of padding on the tank. Now unscrew anything securing the fork cover to the lower triple clamp and follow the above directions to extricate the fork legs from the lower triple clamp.

Screw caps should be removed with a socket or wrench. Holding a rag securely over the fork cap is good advice—even for those with screw-type caps. As you reach the last thread, the cap will tend to fly off. If you're not holding on to it, you or the cap could suffer.

Damping rod forks are slightly easier to prepare for an oil change. With the cap off, pull out the spacer and any washers and lift out the spring. Turning the spring counterclockwise as you lift it out helps to free it of excess oil, but you'll still want to wipe it off and place it on a clean rag.

Cartridge forks (including inverted forks) require a different approach: disconnect the fork cap from the cartridge piston rod by loosening the locknut securing it to the cap with a wrench on the nut and socket on the cap. Next, remove the nut from the piston rod to free up the spacer, spring, and washers. (Note their order for reassembly.)

If you can't see the nut at the base of the fork cap, your bike requires a cartridge fork compression tool (available as a factory service part from your bike's manufacturer, or from an aftermarket company such as Race Tech) to compress the fork spring to reveal the locknut securing the cartridge to the cap. Once the preload spacer is compressed enough to reveal the nut, use a pair of wrenches, loosen the locknut, and spin the cap off the cartridge piston rod.

Empty the oil into a suitable container for transport to a recycling center. In order to make sure that all the old, dirty oil is expelled from the fork, you'll need to pump the slider up and down a minimum of 10 times. Cartridge forks (both standard and inverted) require that the piston rod be pumped to expel the oil. If you can't grip the locknut on the end of the rod while pumping it, you can

31

CHANGE YOUR FORK OIL

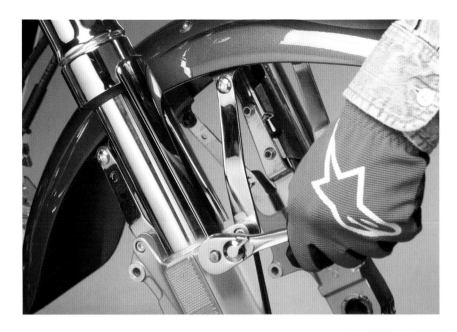

After you remove the front wheel, unbolt the fender. You may need to squeeze the sides slightly to remove it. Beware, the paint scratches very easily.

buy the screw-on factory part intended for this job, or call Race Tech.

Measure out the amount of oil recommended by your factory service manual before adding it to the fork. If you plan on using a fork oil level tool, add between half an ounce and an ounce of extra oil. If you're using the dipstick method, follow the manufacturer's recommended amount. Pour the oil into the fork and fill the system by pumping the fork and piston rod a minimum of 10 times. Keep pumping until you no longer hear air escaping.

Measure fork oil height with the fork fully compressed and no spring installed. You can use a coat hanger or a more sophisticated fork oil level tool sold in the aftermarket.

Don't worry about torquing fork caps into the fork tubes until the unit is reinstalled in the triple clamp with the lower clamp bolts torqued to spec. Before you tighten the triple clamp pinch, make sure that the top of the fork tube (not the cap that sits on top of it) is flush with the top of the triple clamp (that is, unless your factory service manual specifies otherwise). Folks with fork covers can save this step until after the second leg is mounted. Just don't forget to do this final tweaking once the top triple clamp is in place and torqued to the steering stem. Now move on to the other leg. Before you ride, return the air preload (if you have it) to your preferred settings.

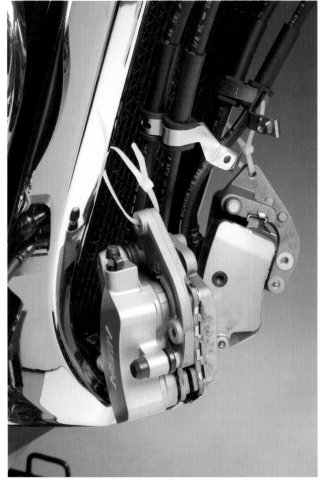

Whenever you do any work that requires removing the calipers, don't leave them hanging by the brake lines.

On bikes with air-adjustable preload, release all the pressure by pressing the pin in the center of the valve. If the handlebars will prevent you lifting the spring straight out of the fork leg, remove the bar from its clamps and lay it on some padding placed on the tank. Loosen the bolt(s) securing the top triple clamp to the fork leg. Bikes with screw-on caps only need to have the caps unscrewed with a wrench or deep socket. Caps secured with a circlip or retaining ring must be pressed in to take the pressure off the circlip. Two tools can make this much easier. Some automotive part pullers will hook over the triple clamp and press in the cap via a thumbscrew. A woodworker's corner clamp can achieve the same result for much less money (usually around $5). Press down on the cap just enough to take the strain off the circlip. Using a jeweler's screwdriver or pick, remove the circlip, and slowly ease the cap out with the press. You will want to hold a rag over the cap, as it may jump out from the force of the spring. Cruisers without fork covers only require that you loosen the bolts on the upper and lower triple clamp and slide the fork free.

For damping-rod forks, once you remove the cap, pull out the spacer and any washers and lift out the spring. Turning the spring counterclockwise as you lift it out helps to free it of excess oil, but you'll still want to wipe it off and place it on a clean rag. Folks with cartridge forks need to go through one or more additional steps to free the spring and spacers: You will need to disconnect the fork cap from the piston rod by loosening the locknut securing it to the cap with a wrench on the nut and socket on the preload adjuster. Then simply unscrew the cap from the rod and remove the spacer, spring, and washers. (Note their order for reassembly.)

CHANGE YOUR FORK OIL

Project 32
Change Fork Springs

TIME:	1 hour
TOOLS:	Wrenches/sockets, torque wrench, circlip pliers or jeweler's screwdrivers (for non-screw-on caps), press (for non-screw-on caps), claw-type pick-up tool to grab cartridge piston rod (optional), saw with miter box or lpipe cutter, rags, jack or front stand
TALENT:	2 to 3
COST:	$$$
PARTS:	Fork springs, PVC tubing
TIP:	If your fork is more than four years old, this is a great way to freshen up your ride
BENEFIT:	Improved ride and handling

So, you set your sag only to find that your spring rate was wrong. Or perhaps your stock springs are tired from a couple years of riding. Either way, you're looking at installing a new set of fork springs. Swapping springs in traditional forks, be they damping-rod or cartridge units, is easy. Inverted forks may require special tools and techniques, but the process is still pretty easy.

Refer to the previous project, which details the process for removing the fork from your bike. When you disassemble a cartridge fork on a cruiser, you may notice something funny about the fork's internals. Yep, often only one of the legs will have a cartridge. The other one will only have oil and a spring. When you consult your factory service manual, you may also discover that the factory has different requirements for oil volume and height for each leg.

Although you may be tempted to drop your new springs into place, don't—unless you want to wipe up the fork oil that splashes out. If you are using progressive-rate springs that are wound more tightly at one end than the other, some manuals will recommend placing the spring with the tightly wound end down. Why? According to the folks at Progressive Suspension, the direction of the spring wind makes no mechanical difference, though sometimes orienting the spring this way will lessen the spring noise. Racers, on the other hand, recommend keeping the tightly wound section up to

To keep your bike clean, slowly pull the spring out of the fork leg. Turning it counterclockwise can also help leave the oil in the fork.

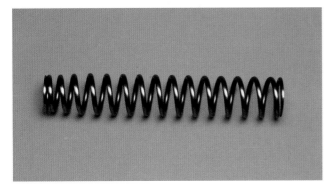

Progressively wound springs can be identified by how the wind is tighter at one end. This helps the spring to function at one rate fully extended and a stiffer one as it compresses.

make it part of the bike's sprung weight (the part of the bike supported by the suspension) instead of the unsprung weight on the wheel that must track over pavement irregularities. Either way, the spring will work the same—you decide.

If you need to make your own preload spacer to fit this spring, use the largest PVC that will fit inside the fork leg. You will need to cut the spacer perpendicular to the tubing. A miter box or pipe cutter will help, but isn't necessary. Those with nonadjustable forks will want to make a variety of spacers in quarter-inch increments on either side of the spring manufacturer's recommendation to aid in setting sag. Use a knife and a bit of sandpaper to deburr the spacers. Wipe both the interior and the exterior of the spacers clean before installing them. Don't forget to write their length on them with a Sharpie, so you don't have to measure them each time you change them. Make sure that the preload spacer is the length specified by the spring manufacturer before placing it, and any necessary washers, into the fork leg. Reassemble the freshened fork in the reverse of the way you disassembled it.

The rare cruiser fork with rebound adjusters requires special assembly techniques, so consult your factory service manual for the recommended method. To finish up your fork, make sure you torque the fork caps, and don't forget the pinch bolts on the triple clamp. Once you've reset your sag, you should feel a noticeable improvement in your suspension.

Although you can remove a circlip fork cap by pressing down on the cap with a screwdriver while simultaneously removing the circlip, this cheap woodworking clamp makes the job much easier.

These precut and labeled spacers will speed the setting of your bike's preload if you don't have adjustable forks.

Project 33
Install Aftermarket Shocks

TIME:	1 hour
TOOLS:	Wrenches, sockets, torque wrench, socket extenders and/or universal joint, bike jack or lift, zip tie, an optional assistant
TALENT:	1 to 3 (depending on shock location)
COST:	$$$ to $$$$
PARTS:	Aftermarket shocks
TIP:	Mounting a single shock inside the chassis requires more finesse than dual shocks
BENEFIT:	Better control of your bike's rear suspension, better grip, better handling

Stock cruiser shocks haven't kept up with the march of suspension technology. For the way that many cruisers are ridden, this hasn't really made a difference. Still, many riders prefer the styling of aftermarket units. Other riders, thanks to their riding ability, can sense the limitations of the OE units. Whatever your reason for swapping shocks, you'll generally get a sexier-looking, better-performing bike with an aftermarket suspender or two. Even if you're not adding an aftermarket piece, this project will be helpful to those who need to remove their shock to send it off for revalving, a simple rebuild, or installation of a different rate spring.

Begin by putting your bike on a jack or bike lift. Next, you'll want to secure the front end so that it doesn't roll away while you're elbow deep in the bowels of your bike. While some people perform this modification with the front wheel snugged up against a wall, I've found that a zip tie around the front brake lever works just fine for a simple shock swap.

If your bike will be sitting without a shock while it's out for freshening, you should consider finding a way to secure your bike. Regardless of how long you expect the project to take, don't lie under your bike until you're certain that it is safely supported. Remove any parts (like the seat, saddlebags, side covers, or the exhaust system) that block unfettered access to the area around the linkage. During this project, you'll be adjusting the height of the bike on the jack or lift to allow the eyelets on the shock to line up with their mates on the bike.

Cruisers with the shock attached to some sort of linkage require that you partially disassemble the linkage to get to the shock. Begin with the base of the shock. Look closely at the bolts securing the tie rods (or dog bones). On many bikes, you will have difficulty removing the bolts for either the top or bottom end of the rods. Determine which bolt is easiest to remove and lower the linkage out of the way. Remove the bolt securing the top of the shock to its mount and carefully lower the old shock out past the swingarm.

Carefully place the new shock in position. Some shocks are easier to slip into place from above the swingarm rather than from below. Place the top

Lift your bike so that the shock fully extends, but the rear tire doesn't leave the floor.

Space is really tight, but with the rear wheel supported, the shock should slip right into position. You may have to adjust the bike lift up or down slightly to get the eyelets on the shock to line up with the chassis.

mounting bolt through the shock's eyelet and let it hang in place. If your new shock has a remote reservoir, you need to find a place to mount it. If the shock's instructions don't have a recommended position, find a place where you can securely mount the reservoir so that it does not interfere with the rear wheel travel or with the rider's leg or foot. Using the supplied rubber spacers and hose clamps, loosely mount the reservoir and check that the shock's braided stainless-steel line doesn't abrade the frame or any other part of the bike. You can buy covers that wrap around the line like a spring at your local bike shop. Once you are certain about the reservoir position, tighten the hose clamps.

Reassemble the suspension linkage in the reverse order of your disassembly. A light coat of grease on the bolts' shafts (while keeping the threads clean) will help them slip into place and prevent corrosion. You may find that you have to rotate the shock shaft slightly to help the clevis slide over the linkage. If you have trouble lining up the bolt holes, adjust the length of the bottle jack supporting the rear of the bike. Proper torquing of the bolts is essential for keeping everything where it belongs.

Before you can get back on the road, you need to set the sag and damping to the shock manufacturer's recommendations.

Many aftermarket shocks will have rebound damping adjusters that allow you to modify the shock's behavior as it extends after absorbing a bump.

Dual shocks are almost too easy to replace. Simply unbolt one and install the other. You still need to support your bike with a jack, though.

Chapter 8
Frame

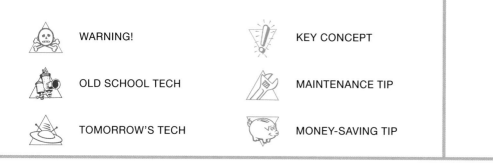

WARNING!

KEY CONCEPT

OLD SCHOOL TECH

MAINTENANCE TIP

TOMORROW'S TECH

MONEY-SAVING TIP

Just as the human spine serves as the main support structure for your body, your motorcycle's frame serves as the main support for the rest of the bike. Unlike your spine, however, your bike's frame can take many forms—steel or aluminum, pressed or trellis, cast and/or welded, and so on.

STEEL VS. ALUMINUM

Paper or plastic? Regular or decaf? Chocolate or peanut butter?

Life presents us with a variety of choices daily, but few of them are as well defined as the choice between steel or aluminum as a frame material. Each one presents its own unique blend of advantages.

For instance, steel is quite stiff and strong compared to aluminum, but much heavier. Given identical lengths, overall diameters, and wall thickness, a piece of steel tubing is roughly three times as stiff, three times as strong, but three times as heavy as a piece of aluminum tubing. Steel is easy to weld (at least until you get into more exotic molybdenum-alloy steels), and fairly easy to fabricate—that is, make tubes from it, castings, sheets, extrusions (think of toothpaste being squeezed from a tube), and a host of other forming methods. And while aluminum requires more skill to weld, its soft, plastic (ductile) nature makes it a natural for fabrication.

What's crucial, though, is that strength and stiffness are also primarily functions of diameter and wall thickness. Consequently, by using more material (thicker tubes

or larger spars), a designer can create an aluminum frame that's as strong and stiff as its steel equivalent. What firmly tips the balance in the favor of the material used for soda pop cans, however, is that the steel equivalent would almost certainly have paper-thin tubes or spars, which could be easily damaged and extremely difficult to weld if a repair is needed. A rider might not have much confidence in a frame that he could poke his finger through as if it were a piece of rice paper. All of that is why aluminum has become the material of choice for frames designed and made for most high-performance motorcycles. Recent advances in technology, such as extremely accurate and thin-wall vacuum die-casting techniques, have made aluminum frames so prevalent.

STEEL TUBE FRAMES

In the beginning (when dinosaurs roamed the earth, etc.), proper motorcycle frames were welded up from collections of steel tubing. The earliest versions were little more than glorified bicycle frames, with a single backbone tube and a single-cradle tube that extended down from the steering head, then underneath the engine. The next variation simply doubled the downtube into what's called a double-cradle frame, with the front of the engine bolted solidly between the two down-tubes for added rigidity.

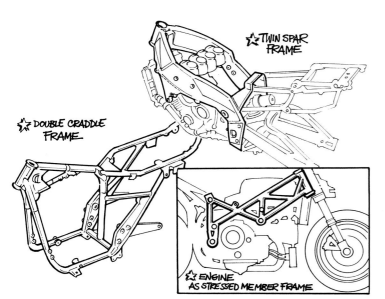

TWIN SPAR FRAME

DOUBLE CRADLE FRAME

ENGINE AS STRESSED MEMBER FRAME

One other steel tube iteration is the spine or backbone frame, which utilizes a large-diameter tube or fabrication running from the steering head, over the top of the engine, with no downtubes whatsoever. Such a design can be one of the simplest and least expensive to manufacture. Yet despite their seeming lack of sophistication, backbone frames can be extremely effective. Perhaps the most recent example is Honda's 599, introduced in the United States as a 2004 model, and a few years earlier in Europe as the Hornet 600. Whatever you call it, the bike's backbone frame works well, and the bike immediately gained a reputation for its excellent, confidence-inspiring handling.

For the most part, the double-cradle design went on to become a near industry standard. And the most famous of all such steel tube frames is the Norton Featherbed. According to legend, the McCandless brothers from Northern Ireland were wizards with tubes and torches, especially brother Rex. Supposedly, in 1949, Rex simply gave Norton his latest double-cradle frame design, complete with swingarm and dual-shock rear suspension—quite a breakthrough then. Norton racer Harold Daniell is credited with giving the frame its illustrious name. After sampling a McCandless-frame Norton Manx, Daniell likened the experience to "riding on a featherbed." At the time the Norton's handling was indeed head and shoulders above the rest, and the Featherbed went on to inspire dozens of copies, most coming from the nascent Japanese motorcycle industry.

After the Featherbed, however, steel tube frame design on production bikes virtually stagnated for most of a generation. It wasn't until 1983 with the advent of Honda's V45 Interceptor that manufacturers seemed interested in trying something new or different. Even then, the most interesting thing about the Interceptor's frame was its use of silver-painted square and rectangular steel tubing in an attempt to make a visual connection with Honda's NS500 two-stroke V-3 Grand Prix road racer. Yet while the two frames looked somewhat similar at a distance, the NS500's was constructed of aluminum tubing.

Why the near-total absence of changes to steel tube frame design in such a long period of time? Simply because it's a mature technology; the flaws have long ago been identified and subsequently rectified. It's a new version of the old saying, "If it ain't broke . . . " Steel tube

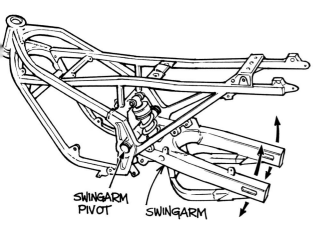

SWINGARM PIVOT

SWINGARM

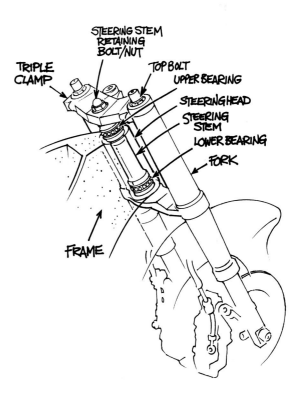

STEERING STEM RETAINING BOLT/NUT

TRIPLE CLAMP

TOP BOLT

UPPER BEARING

STEERING HEAD

STEERING STEM

LOWER BEARING

FORK

FRAME

frames continue to be used extensively on the majority of motorcycles below premium price-points, and for good reason. Well-designed ones can provide excellent handling for all but the most demanding of riders, and they can be reasonably cheap to make. In short, there will always be a place for such frames in motorcycling.

Having just disparaged steel tube frames from use at the very top of, say, the sport bike food chain, it's worth mentioning one boutique brand in particular that employs the seemingly dated design throughout its entire lineup, even for its most expensive and highest-performance sporting tackle—namely, Ducati. The Italian brand long ago realized the importance and romance of its own history, and that much of those qualities are wrapped up in its signature trellis frame. Continued development year after year has evolved Ducati's steel tube structure into something that's easily the equal of more-sophisticated aluminum frames. In fact, Ducati uses steel frames on its MotoGP race bikes.

PRESSED-STEEL FRAMES

Apart from the sizable initial costs of making the stamping dies, manufacturing pressed-steel frames is perhaps the most economical way to mass produce such items.

Simply put, sheets of relatively thin-gauge steel are stamped (pressed) into shape, and cut or punched from the dies. Then they're usually secured into position in a jig of some sort and spot welded. Pressed-steel construction is quick, too, because the procedure easily lends itself to robot welding.

However, without the benefit of a continuous weld (at a minimum), such frames can tend to suffer from flexing and broken welds when used harshly.

For all of these reasons, pressed-steel frames are most often employed on small-displacement motorcycles or scooters, vehicles that won't stress the frames overmuch.

As a point of history, Honda began using the pressed-steel manufacturing process for its 1949 Dream D, partially for the process' speed and convenience of manufacturing, but also because it was difficult to get steel tubing of sufficient quality. Moreover, pressed-steel construction has been in use since the 1920s.

ALUMINUM FRAMES

Aluminum's current near-total dominance as the most popular material for sport bike frames can be traced directly to its meteoric ascendance in the same role in Grand Prix road racing. In the early 1980s, aluminum frames took up permanent residence in GP paddocks nearly overnight. Why the change *en masse*? Precisely because of the phenomenon described in the "Steel Vs. Aluminum" section at the start of this chapter: that strength and stiffness are more profoundly affected by material diameter and wall thickness than they are by the material itself (steel or aluminum, given otherwise identical pieces).

Moreover, by the early 1980s, frame stiffness had become a Holy Grail to GP bike designers. Aluminum allowed them to create stiffer frames—and, so they thought, better-handling ones—but without a huge weight penalty. Interestingly, it is possible to create a frame that is too stiff, and frame design has shifted a bit to incorporate a bit of flex.

In motorcycling, racing success tends to drive development of mass-produced products. So it was only a matter of time before such frames made their way onto street bikes. The first mass-produced aluminum-frame production bike was Suzuki's 1983 RG 250 Gamma, and others soon followed. If this first wave had any identifiable shortcoming, it was only that the bike's engineers—just like the ones for the 500 GP bikes—basically duplicated the previous generation's steel tube frames with aluminum tubes, and hadn't yet gone far enough to realize the material's advantages.

In short order, though, race bikes began sprouting massive, deep-section twin-spar frames, with the spars fabricated from sheet aluminum and extending from the steering head back to the swingarm pivot in as direct a line as possible. Such a design created the straightest possible load path with a structure best suited to withstand those loads. And, of course, that thinking quickly made its way to mass-produced street bikes.

The next big jump in frame theory and design was controlled flex. Several manufacturers had already built what were considered to be totally rigid frame structures. As it turned out, such frames made a motorcycle almost unrideable; it chattered and skipped over midcorner bumps like a flat stone thrown across a still pond.

What engineers discovered is that, when a motorcycle is leaned over, such as through a turn, bump forces come at angles the suspension simply can't cope with; result—chatter. So, they deduced, the chassis (frame, fork, wheels, and tires) *has* to flex a little, and in a controlled way in such situations.

PROBLEM	PROBABLE CAUSES	ACTION TO REPAIR	RELEVANT PROJECTS
BIKE DOESN'T WANT TO RESPOND SMOOTHLY, EVENLY TO SMALL STEERING INPUTS AT SLOW SPEEDS	Steering head bearings too tight	Check and adjust steering head bearings	Project 34: Check steering head bearings, Project 35: How to repack or replace steering head bearings
FRONT END/ STEERING FEELS LOOSE AND IMPRECISE; KLUNK CAN BE HEARD AND FELT THROUGH HANDLEBAR OVER BUMPS AND WHEN COMING TO AN ABRUPT STOP	Steering head bearings too loose	Check and adjust steering head bearings	
CAN FEEL A DEFINITE DETENT THROUGH THE HANDLEBAR(S) WITH THE FRONT WHEEL POINTED STRAIGHT AHEAD	Flat spots in bearings/rollers and/or races of steering head bearings	Replace steering head bearings	
DISTURBINGLY IMPRECISE STEERING; AT HIGHER SPEEDS BIKE WALLOWS AT A POINT THAT SEEMS DIRECTLY BELOW THE RIDER	Loose swingarm pivot bolt	Torque according to shop manual figure(s). If unsuccessful, have a dealership diagnose the problem	

Assisting them in their design process was increasingly sophisticated technology associated especially with high-pressure/high-vacuum die-casting and spark erosion techniques, for example. Both processes permit creation of remarkably accurate, precise, and thin-wall aluminum parts, which, when welded together, permit fine-tuning of the desirable portion of frame flex, without also getting the disastrous kinds of flex that destroy handling. Honda was the first to trumpet the arrival of such thinking and technology on its street bikes, and the other manufacturers have quickly followed suit.

And for the cynics who believe the only people who benefit from such advances are sport bike pilots, they might feel heartened to know those selfsame influences spread through each manufacturer's lineup more completely each year. The connection between racing and road bikes has never been shorter, or more direct.

Project 34
Check Steering Head Bearings

TIME:	2-plus hours, depending on what maintenance is required
TOOLS:	Wrenches and sockets, rear stand, bike jack
TALENT:	3
COST:	$
PARTS:	Replacement bearings
TIP:	All parts that could exert any force on the front end (brake lines and cables) should be removed before checking the steering head bearings
BENEFIT:	Seamless response to steering input; longer service

Every time you turn, the steering stem moves inside the steering head. As time passes, portions of the bearing races can become dented from the bearings' balls or rollers transferring loads from the fork to the frame. The result is steering that wants to self-center the bearings to those familiar dents. Can you ride a bike with this condition? Sure. As with any neglected system, your bike can push on for a while delivering substandard feel and performance. But why settle for that?

Bikes have come a long way in terms of performance and responsiveness. Riding one that is in top tune when you've let yours get ragged is a lot like hopping on a new bike when you've only ridden classics. The payoff is crispness, smoothness, responsiveness—a more exciting and rewarding ride. If you love to ride, why not make that experience the best it can be? Talk to high-caliber race teams and you'll find that they place such a high priority on how the bike steers that they will check and adjust the steering head bearings before every race weekend.

While street riders may scoff at that type of maintenance schedule, they should be forewarned that if they don't make a point of checking their steering head bearings every 10,000 miles, or at least once a season, they may suffer from a couple of handling maladies. First, they may notice that their bike will shake its head under normal deceleration under hard braking, or if their hands are removed from the grips. Also, as the steering head binds and requires increasing effort to overcome the internal friction, riders may find themselves weaving at low speeds as they oversteer. (This symptom is similar to having a steering damper set too tight.) According to Chuck Graves, race team owner, gifted tuner, and long-time fast guy at Willow Springs, overtight head bearings will also affect turn-in on the brakes at corner entrances—and give the bike the tendency to run wide. One last sign of bad bearings is that riders may actually feel a clunk in the grips as the steering stem shifts in the steering head.

1. For an accurate check of the steering head bearings, the bike needs to be on a rear stand with the front wheel off the ground. To check for loose or damaged bearings, grasp the base of the fork legs and move it front to back. If you feel any movement or the telltale clunk and your steering stem is properly torqued, your bike needs new bearings. For the subtler but equally important tests, remove all components that could impart a force on the fork—the brake lines, throttle cables, and clutch cables.

2. With the fork stripped of all but the clip-ons and wheel, begin testing the bearings by turning the bar full-lock to one side. When the bar is turned approximately 15 degrees toward center and released, the fork should fall back to the stop, barely bounce, and settle down. If the bearing is

too tight, it won't reach the stop. A loose bearing results in a couple of bounces on the stop. This is called the fallback test.

3. The next test is to lightly hold the front wheel between your fingers and move it back and forth across the center of the travel. You should feel no notchiness or restriction of movement, which would signal worn spots on the bearing races. Finally, turn the fork just a couple of degrees off center and release it. The fork should not move. If it tries to self-center, the bearings are worn.

4. Now that you're armed with information about the bearings' condition, you know what you need to do. If the bearings are fine, and you are on a regular maintenance interval (as in checking the bearings before a race weekend), bolt the front end back together, and you're good to go. If you're doing your 10,000-mile or annual maintenance, and if the bearings passed every test, disassemble the triple clamp, lube the bearings, and retorque your front end. If your bike failed any of the tests, it's time to replace the bearings. (See Project 35.)

Project 35

Repack or Replace Steering Head Bearings

TIME:	2-plus hours, depending on what maintenance is required
TOOLS:	Wrenches and sockets, large socket, steering nut wrench, torque wrench, rear stand, bike jack, torch, rubber mallet or dead-blow hammer, drift, blow torch, bearing grease, bearing race puller, safety glasses
TALENT:	3
COST:	$
PARTS:	Replacement bearings
TIP:	Heating the steering stem makes removing and installing the races much easier
BENEFIT:	Renewed steering performance

Like any bearings, those in the steering head need to be lubricated periodically to maintain smooth performance. If the checks you performed in Project 34 showed excess play or binding, you will need to adjust the bearings for proper bearing tension. Either condition may likewise herald the need to replace the bearings and races. Even if everything checked out fine and you've traveled 10,000 miles since you last serviced them, it's time to repack the steering head bearings to keep them in top condition.

Repacking the bearings will involve disassembling the head, removing the bearings, and cleaning all the old grease from them and the bearing races—the cups pressed into the head tube on which the bearings move. With all the grease removed, you can inspect both the bearings and the races for wear. If reusing your old bearings, repack them with grease and reassemble. Set the tension according to the fallback test.

If replacing the bearings and races, you can knock out the races yourself with a hammer and drift, or take them to a machine shop if you don't trust yourself not to dent your bike or yourself. Pack full of grease, reassemble until you get a passing fallback test, then get out and enjoy your perfectly steering bike.

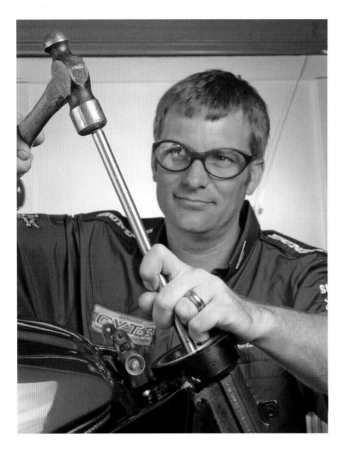

Removing the races from the steering head will appeal to your destructive side. Reach through the steering head with a metal drift and locate the back of the lower bearing race. With a ball-peen hammer, walk the race out of the frame by hammering on alternating sides of the race. (Some mechanics like to heat the steering head with a blow torch, but it only seems to make a noticeable difference on race installation, not removal.) To remove the top bearing race, repeat the process with the drift reaching from the bottom of the neck. Be cautious, though. You're hammering up and don't want to dislodge the bike from its supports. Here the mechanic demonstrates how to knock the lower race out of the steering head. If you're not comfortable with your hammer technique, have a machine shop remove the races for you. When installing new bearings, you can use a bearing-driver set or a socket that has the same outer diameter as the outer edge of the race. If you're unable to find a suitable socket, you can always flip the old race upside down and use it as the driver. To ease locating the races in the steering head, utilize temperature to expand and contract solid objects. Place the new races in the freezer for a couple of hours. Before you remove each from its bed amongst the frozen peas, heat the steering stem until it is hot, but not so hot that it discolors. Quickly place the race in the neck and drive it into position. With the difference in temperature, you should only need a couple of whacks to bottom the race.

To pack the bearings—whether ball or tapered rollers—you want to push grease into them until it oozes out the other side of the cage. When the bearings lift out of the races, as with steering head ball bearings, the job is easy. Just put a healthy dollop of grease in the palm of your hand and press the bearing into it, forcing the grease into the gaps between the cage and the balls. You'll do the same for the removable tapered roller bearing often used at the top of the steering stem. For tapered roller bearings affixed to the stem, press the grease into the rollers until you see it start to ooze out of the top of the roller cage. Here note how he presses the grease from the inside of the bearing so that he can see when it begins to ooze out of the spaces between the balls and the cage.

Before torquing the steering stem, you must have the fork legs and wheel properly reinstalled and torqued. Also, the front wheel should be raised off the ground. Remount the steering stem to the frame and finger-tighten the stem nut. Mount the fork legs and make sure they are aligned so that the axle will slide easily from one leg into the other. Torque the triple clamp pinch bolts. Mount the front wheel and torque the axle down. You're now ready to perform the stem bearing adjustment. If your steering head uses ball bearings, the job is pretty simple. Using a steering nut wrench or one of the cool steering nut sockets sold by Komoto Draggin Racing, torque the steering nut down to the factory-specified initial tightening specification to set the bearings in the races. This number will be quite a bit higher than the final torque setting. (For example, the R6 factory service manual specifies 38 lb-ft) Once you set the seating torque, turn the fork back and forth a few times to distribute the grease.

Install the top triple clamp, torque it down, and recheck with the fallback test to make sure that you haven't affected the steering. Tapered roller bearings are much more finicky, and you'll have to adjust them by hand. Tighten the stem nut down to set the bearings, then loosen them back up. Now begin tightening the nut. After each adjustment, give the fork the fallback test you used at the beginning of this project. Once the fork passes the test, carefully lock down the stem nut with the locknut. Different bikes use different locking methods, so consult your factory manual. (For example, some bikes use a locknut clamping down directly on the stem nut, while others, such as Yamaha, have a rubber spacer between the nut and the locknut.) This steering nut tool sold by Komoto Draggin Racing (above) takes some of the guesswork out of torquing the stem nut. You simply place it over the nut and torque it down like any other fastener. It's worth every penny to those who practice regular steering maintenance.

Project 36
Swingarm Pivot Bearing Replacement

TIME:	2 hours
TOOLS:	Wrenches, sockets, torque wrench, screwdrivers, pliers, circlip pliers, bike lift or jack, hammer, drift, bearing driver, propane torch, red Loctite, vise
TALENT:	3
COST:	$$
PARTS:	Replacement bearings
TIP:	Heating the bearing sleeve makes driving the bearings out much easier
BENEFIT:	Less stiction in swingarm movement, better suspension performance

Perhaps the most overlooked item on motorcycles is the lowly swingarm pivot. Well, if you've spent money and time upgrading and dialing in your suspension, don't you think it's a good idea to take as much of the fluid-movement-sapping stiction out of the swingarm travel? Bikes that have been ridden in wet weather or near the ocean are particularly susceptible to having corrosion damage in any bearing—not just the swingarm bearings.

How do you know when the swingarm bearings need replacing? Well, if you lubricate your bearings on a regular basis, check them before you regrease them. What to look for at those times are wear marks or rust on the pivot shaft. If you see any divots on the shaft, you can bet the bearings aren't happy about it either.

You'll need to strip off your bike's lowers if you're planning on using a jack under the engine. Also, be careful where you place the jack—don't crush your exhaust pipe. Follow the directions in your factory manual for removing the swingarm.

Once you have the swingarm free, place it in a soft-face vise to hold it steady while you work on it. Remove the collars, pivot, and dust seals with a screwdriver and replace any ripped or torn seals. If a circlip is present, remove it. Heat the swingarm outside of the bearing, but not so hot as to cause it to discolor. Using a drift, reach through from the opposite side of the swingarm and place the edge on the seam between the crush tube and the bearing. If you can't catch the lip of the inner race because of the internal spacer, you may find

Heating the outside of the swingarm around the bearing will ease its removal.

that a flathead screwdriver will help get the bearing started. With the drift on the inner race, give the bearing a whack or two until it moves slightly. Now switch to the other side of the bearing and repeat. Essentially, you are walking the bearing out of the hub. When the bearing pops out, set the crush tube aside for later. Flip the swingarm in the vise and tap out the remaining bearing. Remember, after you've rapped a bearing with a drift just once, the bearing is junk.

Opinions vary on how best to drive a bearing into place. Some people freeze the bearing for several hours and then heat the part on which it will be installed. Others lubricate the outside edge of the bearing with

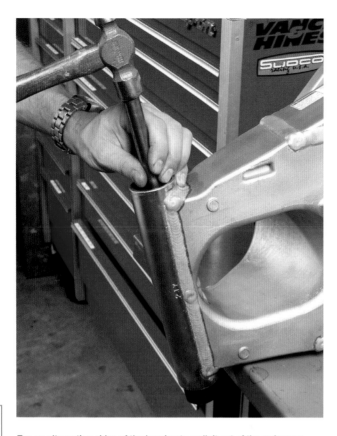

Tap on alternating sides of the bearing to walk it out of the swingarm.

This mechanic prefers to use red Loctite as the lubricant between the bearing and the swingarm.

assembly lube. The mechanic from Trac Dynamics featured in the photos here uses red Loctite. He feels that the Loctite helps lubricate the two metal surfaces when wet and makes the bearing stay in position better when it dries. You choose your preferred method.

If you have a bearing driver set, use it to install the bearings. Otherwise, find a socket that has the exact same outer diameter as the outside edge of the bearing. If you're unable to find a suitable socket, you can always use the old bearing. The key is never to hammer directly on the new bearing itself. Tap the bearing until it is seated in the pivot flush with the outer edge (or the edge below the circlip housing). Slip the crush tube into the pivot and install the other bearing. Don't forget to reinstall any circlips you removed.

When replacing bearings, consult your factory service manual for proper bearing orientation. Some bearings need to be placed in certain ways. For example, on a ZX-6R the ball bearings need to be oriented with the manufacturer's markings pointing out, but needle bearings require that the markings face in. Getting oriented before you tap the bearings in will save you time and money.

Once the bearings are installed, you'll need to pack them with grease. This serves two purposes. It helps the metal parts move against each other, and it keeps out corrosive moisture. Using healthy dollops on your finger, mash the grease into the spaces of the rollers. Keep

Packing needle bearings completely full of grease takes patience, but it will keep corrosion away.

doing this as you work your way around the bearing, until it is completely filled. Wipe a thin layer of grease on the pivot sleeve and slide it into the pivot. Apply a bit of grease to the grease seals and press them onto the swingarm. Finally, place the collars into the seals. The swingarm is now ready to be mounted back in the frame.

Chapter 9
Tires and Wheels

WARNING!

KEY CONCEPT

OLD SCHOOL TECH

MAINTENANCE TIP

TOMORROW'S TECH

MONEY-SAVING TIP

To some riders, tires are merely round and black, and nothing more. If they give their tires a thought, it's only because they're dangerously close to being flat or bald, and can no longer be ignored. Truth is, *nothing* on your motorcycle is as crucial to your safety and your bike's overall handling as your two round, black friends. Because, through two contact patches roughly the area of a credit card each, they transmit information about acceleration, braking, and turning. That's precisely why you need to provide them with—at the least—slightly more attention than you would a pet goldfish.

As with most things, in the universe of tires some items change and others stay the same. Just like the earliest pneumatic tires, modern ones are still made from rubber (synthetic rubber, anyway), stout textile (or steel) cords, and they pump up with good old-fashioned air. However, today's tires also feature extremely sophisticated technology and space-age materials, which allow them to develop much higher levels of performance. In fact, current supersticky D.O.T.-approved race tires are better than dedicated race rubber of a little more than 10 years ago. Even today's far-less-specialized tires are vastly superior to the best street-legal rubber of just a few years ago.

TIRE CONSTRUCTION
Don't make any bar bets on this assertion, but for our purposes there are essentially just two kinds of construction for motorcycle tires: bias-ply and radial. Yes, each of those has a variant that borrows heavily from the other type of construction, but for clarity's sake, we'll limit the discussion of construction to two.

BIAS-PLY CONSTRUCTION

Bias-ply tires amount to old school thinking, really. They've been around almost as long as the pneumatic tire itself, which is credited to being invented by J. B. Dunlop. J. B., a Scottish veterinarian living in Belfast, Ireland, came up with his invention, it is said, to give his grandson's tricycle a smoother ride. (Actually, another Scot, Robert Thomson, invented the first vulcanized pneumatic tire in 1845, but apparently no one cared, as it was Dunlop's that ended up creating the tire industry.)

All pneumatic tires have an underlying structure called a carcass. A bias-ply tire's carcass is made up of layers (plies) of strong textile cords, each ply's cords embedded in a matrix of rubber. All the cords in a ply are parallel; the plies are placed at angles between 30 and 45 degrees from the tire's center, and each successive ply alternates direction. That is, if the first ply angles to the right, the next will angle to the left, then right, left, and so on.

135

As a result of its construction, a bias-ply tire is made up of quite a number of elements, all of which flex as the tire rolls down the road. Such flex inevitably generates heat—and heat is a tire's enemy number one. What's more, being made up of so many plies and pieces also means a bias-ply will be heavy, which can also contribute to heat buildup.

With so many seemingly inherent shortcomings, one might wonder why bias-ply tires continue to exist. Well, radial motorcycle tires are a relatively recent technology. Consequently, there are a lot of motorcycles still out in the world (and some still being built) that came with bias-plies as original equipment. And because motorcycle and tire manufacturers alike rarely recommend retro-fitting a radial to such bikes, there's a huge market for bias-ply tires. Simple economics, in other words.

RADIAL CONSTRUCTION

Italian tire maker Pirelli was the first company to bring out a radial motorcycle tire, in 1983. It was called the MP7, and Honda used it to equip its big, heavy, and powerful VF1000R. Since then, virtually every motorcycle tire company has come out with its own lineup of radials for two-wheelers of almost every engine displacement extant.

Several things distinguish a radial tire's construction. To start with, a radial's carcass usually consists of just a single ply (again, parallel textile cords in a rubber matrix) with the cords running from bead to bead, 90 degrees to the direction of travel. Radials also typically employ a textile or steel belt (or belts) running circumferentially underneath the tread. For a tire to have true radial construction, the belt(s) must be placed at 0 degrees—parallel to the tires' direction of rotation, and 90 degrees to the carcass' ply.

Not all radials, though—for cars or motorcycles—utilize such so-called true radial construction. Depending on a tire's application, it might have a pair of belts arranged bias-ply-style. These belts, along with extensive choices of materials, make the sidewalls more or less stiff, and allow fine-tuning a tire's grip, feel, stability, agility, service life, and so on.

Whether true radial construction or belted hybrid, one of the biggest claims to fame a radial has over a bias-ply is that it runs cooler, a happy consequence of both requiring fewer pieces and (as a result) being lighter. By its very nature, a radial tire is also extremely flexible. Engineers exploit this trait with some clever fine-tuning to yield satisfying jumps in grip and tread wear. In short, where the bias-ply tire offers shortcomings, the radial tire offers solutions.

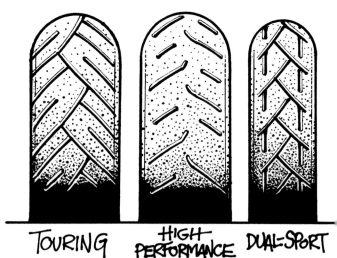

TOURING — HIGH PERFORMANCE — DUAL-SPORT

TIRE CHOICES, AND HOW TO MAKE SMART ONES

Today's motorcyclists are all but spoiled for choice, and that phenomenon is especially evident in the current selection of street tires. What would you like, cousin? Radial or bias-belted? D.O.T. race tires or sport tires? Or sport-touring? Single-compound? Or double or triple? Which is most important to you: Ride quality? Long tire life? Or pure, leech-like grip? Regular or decaf? With so many choices, accompanied by the relentless, yelping din of marketing hype, the uninitiated might be bewildered at best.

Basically, there are only four types of tires a street rider needs to consider: racing/track day, sporty road, sport-touring, and dual-sport.

Racing/track day tires lie at the radical high-performance end of the street-bike tire continuum. Although they still have tread, with water-shedding grooves, they have precious little, and almost none on the farthest part of the shoulders, for exceptional grip at extreme lean angles. Such tires often have rather pointy profiles for quick steering-response, and to put a bigger footprint on the road at those same lean angles. They tend to have stiffer carcasses as well, to better deal with higher cornering loads. And their primary calling card is sheer, unalloyed grip, especially on smooth, dry roads, particularly after they've been brought up to their proper operating temperatures

Many street riders (and you know who you are) are utterly convinced they need racing tires, either because they just know they ride fast enough to warrant them, or because they're equally certain a racing/track day tire will allow them to ride that quickly. They could hardly be more wrong.

Why? Because with so little tread, racing/track day tires have a real shortage of grip on wet pavement; the pointed profile can make a bike feel nervous and twitchy on the street, where a rider rarely finds the opportunity to just flick the bike over on its side; the stiffer carcass shortchanges ride quality; and the street environment makes it extremely unlikely such tires would be able to sustain the temperatures necessary to make them work properly, let alone get them up to that temperature in the first place. And, even if a rider could get past all that, racing/track day tires are designed to work for a relatively small number of heat cycles (one heat cycle is getting the tire up into its operating range, and then cooling off).

Make no mistake: racing/track day tires are superb in their chosen environment—the racetrack. If you can afford a track day and a pair of such specialized tires, you won't believe the level of grip they provide. It's not far removed from that of pure racing slicks from barely a decade ago.

Sporty road tires, on the other hand, are far more suitable for everyday street use, although some of them also force similar compromises on the rider as do racing/track day rubber. That's fairly easily discerned, as several manufacturers specify if a particular tire is for 70 percent track/30 percent street use, down to 30 percent/70 percent track/street.

Generally, for the more street-oriented tires, imagine clipping 30 to 35 percent off the track performance characteristics, and 40 to 45 percent of the worst attributes of such tires' street performance characteristics of racing/track day tires, and you'll get a rough idea of what you might be able to expect from sporty road tires. For the most part, they're far more forgiving on the street than such tires' harder-core brethren, and they don't lose that much in pure performance; they're still suitable for the odd track day if you so desire.

As for sport-touring tires . . . well, unfortunately, too many motorcyclists, when they hear the word "touring," invariably think of someone the age of their grandfather (or older) who rides a Honda Gold Wing, very slowly. Thing is, today's sport-touring rubber isn't *that* far removed from sporty road tires. One crucial difference is that you're almost guaranteed sport-touring tires will have a nice, uniformly rounded profile that makes cornering more predictable and, thus, more confidence-inspiring than the sudden drop-in of a bike wearing the more triangular profile of most race/track day tires and some sporty road tires. Plus, sport-touring tires will wear much longer than the other two—much longer.

Sadly, though, fashion and peer pressure are both powerful incentives, and powerfully difficult to resist. So,

if you find yourself in such a position, where your riding buddies are giving you stick for being so uncool as to ride a bike with *sport-touring* tires, just ask them how cool it is to save money—especially as they'll be replacing their pricey race/track day tires in 1,000 to 2,000 miles.

Lastly among our tire choices are those for dual-sport motorcycles. And it's more than likely that if you have such a bike, you probably know exactly what you want from your tires. Which is fortunate, as a dual-sport's typical wheel sizes—19- or 21-inch-diameter front with a 17-inch rear—doesn't leave you with quite the tire choice of riders on pure street bikes or pure dirt bikes. What you do get is the choice between a fairly aggressive-looking off-road-type tire with rather tall, widely spaced knobs, and something that far more resembles a street tire, with larger, but much shallower tread blocks. Ultimately, they all must be street-legal, and it's up to you to pick the tire that best suits the type of riding you do.

SIDEWALL HIEROGLYPHICS AND HOW TO DECIPHER THEM

For those who understand them, the symbols, letters, and numbers on a tire's sidewall are as clear and easily decipherable as their own native language. To the rest of us, though, they look like something you'd have to drink a case of Ovaltine for, so you could get the right magic decoder ring.

In truth, a tire sidewall's markings aren't really that hard to figure out. Let's take a look at one:

180—nominal section width, or cross-section, in millimeters; the actual width of the tire from inner sidewall bulge to outer sidewall bulge

60—aspect ratio; the ratio of the tire's sidewall height to its nominal section width; 60 defines a tire with a sidewall height 60 percent of its section width

R—radial construction; the tire is built with its structural cords or belts laid across the shortest distance from bead to bead, perpendicular to the rolling axis of the tire; radial tires perform far better and are in the process of replacing bias-ply tires

- indicates bias construction; B indicates bias belted construction

17—nominal rim diameter in inches

77—tire's load index; defines the maximum load, in pounds, the tire can vertically support safely when inflated to a specific pressure

TL—tubeless; no inner tube should be used

TT—tube type; use an inner tube

Z—speed rating of tire; defines the maximum speed for which the tire is rated; a Z rating indicates a maximum speed of 149 miles per hour and higher (other speed ratings: S, 112 miles per hour; H, 130 miles per hour; V, 149 miles per hour

Rear (or front)—indicates fitment to rear (or front) wheel

directional arrow—indicates direction of rotation when tire is mounted correctly

TIRES: BUY 'EM LOCAL OR FROM THE WEB?

It doesn't take a rocket scientist—or a butcher, a baker, or even a candlestick maker—to figure out that tire prices at your local dealer are almost always going to be higher than those at mail-order or Web sites. For the most part, it's straight-up business economics: The mail order or Web sites sell greater volumes than your dealer. Consequently, they don't need to make as big a profit per unit; what's more, because they sell so many tires, they have to buy vast numbers of them from the manufacturers, which usually warrants a discount of some kind, and ethical companies often pass those savings on to the customer.

It's a very different situation for dealerships. They simply can't buy into that economy of scale. And they do have to make a reasonable profit, because a lot of people at the dealership—the parts department, the service department, and so on—are depending on it, so *they* can earn a living.

In addition, the dealership's service department will almost certainly have an area set aside devoted just to tire mounting and balancing, with the proper tools to ensure your rims don't get end up looking as if they'd been gnawed by angry beavers, and a dynamic balancer to ensure your wheel/tire is precision-balanced. On top of that, if you purchase a set of tires from your dealership, often they will discount the mounting and balancing costs, another way for a customer to save money rather than through buying tires from a mail-order house or Internet site. Sheer bandwidth and ease of ordering your tires is generally a poor substitute for genuine service.

Ultimately, of course, it's up to you. If you have the three Ts—time, tools, and talent—to mount and balance your own tires, then maybe it does make sense to get your rubber rolling stock at the cheapest possible price.

But, if you depend on your dealer for that sort of work, you might want to think real hard before you pick up the phone or click on that mouse to get your next set of tires from someplace else.

THE GREAT MOUNT & BALANCE ACT: WHAT TO EXPECT

So you took the plunge: bought a pair of the finest examples of the tire manufacturer's state of the black art, just right for your bike and riding style, then had them professionally mounted and balanced by your local dealership. Congratulations.

Now you've returned home to assemble all the pieces in, as they used to say in old service manuals without a hint of mirth, reverse order. Presumably you've got your bike well supported on a pair of paddock stands, or one of the Abba Superbike Stands, as mentioned in the first chapter.

Supposedly, a few words to the wise are sufficient, so: It will be advantageous to you later if you put a thin coat of light grease on each of the axles, front and rear. Then, when you get your next set of tires, you won't need to hammer the axles out because they seized to the axle spacer inside the hub. Similarly, all the fasteners, axle nut(s), and pinch bolts will live together in far greater harmony if you torque them to the specs in your service manual.

Before setting out on your first test ride, there's one more tip to follow: Don't even leave the driveway without giving the front brake lever a couple of squeezes, and depress the rear brake pedal as well. To install your wheels it's quite likely you needed to (gently) pry the brake pads apart so the brake rotors would slip between them. Discovering you have no brakes at your first stop—and then possibly far more than you wanted after frantically pawing at the lever and stomping on the pedal—can take the gloss right off your day.

Speaking of gloss, you might have noticed a slight sheen on the tread surface of your new tires. This should tell you the tires aren't going to have anywhere near the grip they should until they've been run-in. That means no applications of full power or maximum braking for (depending on the manufacturer) some 50 to 200 miles. You also should *gradually* increase your lean angle on both sides until that smooth surface has been abraded away. Then? Let 'er rip.

TIRE PRESSURE

Inflation pressure is another key factor in tire performance. Check the swingarm, under the saddle, or in the owner's manual for the manufacturer's recommendations for the correct tire inflation pressures for your motorcycle.

Note that each tire will also carry a maximum pressure for maximum load rating (usually on the tire's sidewall), but the correct tire pressures for your bike are those recommended by its maker.

Most tires' specs call for between about 32 to 42 psi. For those who require such advice, the simplest approach is to never let tire pressures drop below approximately 32 psi while cold. At 32 psi or above, the tire sidewall will be sufficiently stable and responsive to quick steering inputs, the tread surface ought to maintain near-optimal contact with the pavement, operating temperatures should remain stable and safe, and the tire will deliver near-maximum traction and mileage. This is an acceptable rule-of-thumb you can follow; but again, check the exact pressure recommendations from the bike's maker.

HIGH ANXIETY

LOW PRESSURE

Maintain correct tire pressures by checking them at least once per month. Tires have a funny habit of losing pressure slowly. Air can escape through the microscopic porosity of the tire itself—or a not-so-microscopic nail hole. Air can also leak from the rim/bead area—where the tire meets and seats to the rim—and through the porosity of the rim itself, particularly with aluminum and alloy wheels. Lastly, tire pressure will drop simply due to changes in air temperature. In fall and winter, tire pressures will drop roughly 1 pound per 10-degree reduction in air temperature. That means a tire with slightly low air pressure, perhaps 25 psi in August, might have less than 20 psi in January—a prime candidate for a flat tire at a most inconvenient time and place, after work in a dark, freezing parking lot.

AFTERMARKET WHEELS: CARBON FIBER, MAGNESIUM AND ALUMINUM! OH, MY!

It might not seem intuitive at first, but lighter aftermarket wheels can be one of the most complete bolt-on modifications you can make to your motorcycle. By complete, we mean a modification that has the most (beneficial, of course) far-reaching effects on the motorcycle, influencing performance in as many ways as possible.

Lighter aftermarket wheels definitely qualify in that respect. Almost to a man, riders comment on how such hoops improve their bikes' acceleration; provide quicker steering and lighter handling; and help suspensions track better over rough pavement. Such benefits aren't all that surprising, given the weight savings—up to some 4 pounds for the front wheel and up to around 7 pounds for the rear wheel, depending on the application—and their location as unsprung weight.

Yes, such baubles can be expensive. For now, carbon-fiber wheels define the market's upper end, at up to $4,500 for a pair. Still, have you priced engine work lately?

Carbon fiber also establishes (currently) the upper end for weight savings, too. In descending order, the processes/materials run: carbon fiber, forged magnesium, cast magnesium, forged aluminum, and cast aluminum.

And, if you can afford it, the best suggestion appears to be forged magnesium, with weight reductions within a pound or two (nominally) of carbon fiber, and pricing that's potentially double that of stock wheels, but approximately $1,000 less than carbon fiber.

You'd be hard-pressed to get a similar performance boost—especially such a comprehensive, well-rounded one—from any other relatively priced single aftermarket component.

CARING FOR BEARINGS

If either the front or rear of your bike develops a weave, or feels like a tire is low on air pressure, and none of the corrective measures you take cures the symptoms, or even relieves them, then it's pretty likely the culprit is a failed—or failing—wheel bearing.

And it just so happens that removing your bike's wheels in preparation for some fresh tires provides an excellent opportunity to check up on those bearings. If you've yet to pull off the wheels, grab the fork or swingarm with one of your hands and the wheel with your other. Forcefully try to move the wheel from side to side. If you notice any play that shouldn't be there—say 2 to 3 mm or more—then it's a reasonable bet those wheel bearings are history.

If you had any doubt as to the bearings' condition, you can find out for certain once you get the wheel off. Just stick a finger into the axle hole of the bearing (there are generally bearings on both sides of the front hub; the same at the rear, but often there's a third bearing in the sprocket carrier). If any of the bearings makes a distinct crunching sound and feel as you rotate it—and it's a much worse sound than stepping on a June bug, or breaking a tooth—then that bearing is definitely toast.

A final note: Even if only one bearing has failed, or is on its way there, most mechanics feel it best to replace all the bearings in a hub. Also, check a local bearing supply house before paying full-pop price at your dealer. Often as not, the bearing supply house will have the proper replacement for a fraction of the OE part.

Project 37
Check Tire Pressure

TIME:	Minutes
TOOLS:	Tire gauge, notepad
TALENT:	1
COST:	None
PARTS:	None
TIP:	Trust the tire (and bike) manufacturers to know what pressure works best
BENEFIT:	Better grip and longer tread life

Tire pressure plays an important role on your motorcycle. First, the tire is an important part of the suspension. Air pressure can stiffen or soften the ride qualities in undesirable ways. Perhaps the most important effect tire pressure has for sport riders is controlling the size of the contact patch and, by extension, the life of the tire.

As a tire rolls down the road, it goes from being almost perfectly round to flat where it engages the tarmac. This flat oval of rubber constitutes the contact patch. To form this flat spot that moves around the tire with each revolution, the carcass actually bends in two directions. It begins by bowing out slightly before it bends back on itself under the force of the road. This bowing and bending back and forth creates heat inside the tire. Tire manufacturers use this heat buildup to their advantage by designing rubber compounds that reach their peak effectiveness at a particular temperature. Air pressure helps the tire develop and maintain that temperature.

A side benefit of using the proper pressure is that the front tire will feel more precise and turn in quicker. If you run your tire pressures too low, you can easily overheat your tires simply riding in a straight line. Remember, lower pressures yield a larger contact patch, which is

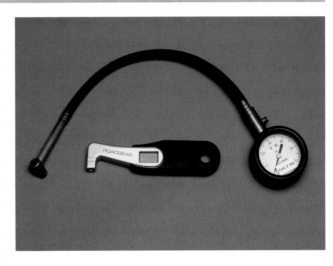

Just because one tire gauge is more expensive than the other doesn't mean that it is more accurate. The budget Roadgear digital gauge on the left has been spot-on since its package was opened. The dial gauge on the right has been consistently reading 2 pounds low since it was new. Compare your gauge to one of the tire vendors' at your local track to see how yours stacks up.

created by the carcass flex. The same process happens when you're not cornering, too. Take your bike out on an extended interstate ride with too little air, and all that flexing of the tire can cook the life right out of it.

TIME:	1 hour
TOOLS:	Tire pressure gauge, tire repair kit
TALENT:	1
COST:	$
PARTS:	Progressive Suspension tire repair kit, extra CO_2 cartridges
TIP:	Check your kit every couple of months—vulcanizing glue has a habit of hardening all by itself
BENEFIT:	Finish the ride you started

Project 38
Flat Fix

Unfortunately, flat tires seem to occur at the most inconvenient place and time, like on a remote section of road, 150 miles from home, with no cell service to call a friend. Since bikes don't carry spare tires, we're usually at the mercy of luck—or our planning. Carrying a tire repair kit with CO_2 cartridges can help turn getting back to civilization into a mere inconvenience rather than a day-long event.

When you suspect you have a leaking tire, before you attempt to assess the damage, make sure you're well away from the side of the road. Now begin by checking your tire for visible damage. If you find a nail, don't pull it out right away. Instead, rub some spit on it where it enters the tread to see if it bubbles. If it doesn't, leave it for now. You may have a leak somewhere else. (If you find a leak somewhere else, go back and pull the nail and check that you don't have two leaks.) Keep looking for your leak. A generous application of saliva to any holes you suspect in the rubber will reveal the culprit.

Once you've found the hole, free it of any debris. Open your flat-fix kit and assemble the pieces, but don't puncture the CO_2 yet. Coat the metal portion of the plug

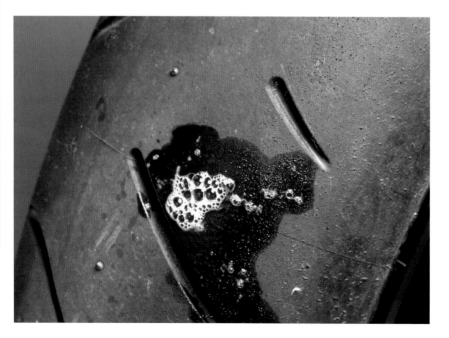

The most effective means of finding a leak out on the road is to look for impressions or debris in the tire and administer a liberal application of saliva.

Rotating the plug tool inside the tire performs two services: It reams the puncture to a uniform shape and coats the surface with cement.

Don't skimp when applying vulcanizing cement to the plug. You want to be sure that the entire surface is covered.

tool with vulcanizing cement. Insert the tool into the hole. (You may have to push fairly hard.) Now rotate the tool back and forth in order to clean out the hole, coat it with cement, and give it a uniform shape.

Remove the plug from its protective casing and place it snugly on the tip of the tool. When you unwrap the film protecting the sealing portion of the plug, be sure not to handle the sticky section, as doing so may weaken the plug's seal. Coat the plug with the vulcanizing cement. Push the plug firmly into the puncture. You want the sticky ring around the plug to be solidly pressed into the tire's carcass, with the plug's adhesive strip in the center. Remove the tool. Some of the plug should remain on the outside of the tread. Just prior to

inflating the tire, cut the excess rubber from the plug, leaving about 1/8 inch protruding from the tire.

Although the vulcanizing cement will dry fairly quickly, you should wait at least 15 minutes (longer in temperatures below 60 degrees) before you pressurize the tire with the CO_2. Stop at the first gas station you find to check for further leaking and set your tire to the correct pressure.

A plug is a temporary fix until you can get to a shop and have your tire replaced. Progressive Suspension recommends not exceeding 45 miles per hour with a plug in your tire. If you decide to ignore that advice, don't ride any faster than you're willing to tumble down the pavement.

143

Trim the excess plug, leaving 1/8 inch above the tread.

While keeping the CO_2 cartridge upright, inflate the tire to a workable pressure. You will probably need more than one cartridge.

Project 39
Removing Wheels

TIME:	15 minutes–1 hour
TOOLS:	Various sockets, various Allen sockets, open-end wrenches, torque wrench, breaker bar, front and rear stands, tape measure, grease, rags
TALENT:	1
COST:	None
PARTS:	Cotter pin
TIP:	Plan ahead for when you need to remove the front wheel by buying or building the correct-size hex key
BENEFIT:	Save $$$ when you change tires by removing the wheels at home rather than having your shop do it

Many repairs or maintenance procedures require you to remove one or both wheels. While the process seems complicated the first time you do it, with a little practice you'll be able to cut down the time it takes dramatically, and you'll think nothing of pulling the rear wheel to swap out the sprocket with less than a half-hour before the next track session.

Front Wheel

Begin with the bike on the rear stand only. Loosen the axle nut with a breaker bar while the front tire still rests on the ground. To prepare to loosen the axle, loosen the axle clamp bolts at the bottom of the fork leg. The trick is to loosen only the bolts that pinch the nut and not the axle. While the correct pinch bolts are usually on the right side, glance at your service manual to confirm.

If you're lucky, your bike will have an axle with a separate nut. However, in recent years, manufacturers have been installing axles with increasingly large hex heads.

Installing the front wheel is the reverse of removal—with a couple of additional steps. Wipe the axle clean and apply a thin coat of high-temperature grease to it. Before

Loosen the axle pinch bolts before you attempt to remove the axle.

After you've slid the axle free of the swingarm, move the wheel forward and remove the chain from the sprocket.

With the hub hanging on the axle, lift the opposite side of the wheel until the holes line up. Then push the axle home.

you torque the axle nut, snug it up and take the bike off the front stand. Pump the brakes up, squeeze the brake lever, and bounce the front end a few times to make sure that the wheel is centered in the fork. Torque the axle nut and the pinch bolts to factory specifications.

Rear Wheel

For single-sided swingarms (VFR750/800, for example), remove the big, honkin' nut or nuts securing the wheel, then pull the wheel free. You may need to move the exhaust can, though. Standard swingarms require just a little more work. Some swingers don't mind if the chain adjusters are left the way they are. Others won't let you pull the axle free without some work—and you can just

forget about getting the axle back in. So, first try removing the wheel without changing the chain adjusters. If you find that you do have to loosen them, give the adjusters three full turns of slack and retighten the locknuts. Once you get the wheel back on the bike, tighten the adjusters those three turns.

So, you've removed the cotter pin and spun the axle nut off the axle. While holding the wheel in position (to take the strain off the axle as you slide it free), remove the axle. Now, push the wheel forward to create some slack in the chain. Remove the chain from the sprocket and hang it on the swingarm. The wheel can now be lowered out of the swinarm. You may have to support the rear caliper to pull the wheel free.

Big axle heads require special tools. Some aftermarket companies have started selling adapters that fit these axles, and you can sometimes get a spark plug socket to do the trick. If you can't find an Allen key big enough, you may be able to use a spark plug socket to free up the axle. If you weren't able to find a tool to fit the axle, another trick is to keep the pinch bolts on the axle locked, loosen the pinch bolts on the nut, and, using a smaller hex key, loosen the nut. On virtually all bikes, you'll have to remove the calipers first. Even on those that don't require it, remounting the wheel will be much easier if you do. Remove the calipers and support them with something other than the brake lines. Now, use the front stand to support the bike.

When you're ready to put the wheel back in the swingarm, begin by spreading the brake pads with a flat-head screwdriver. Next, clean and grease the axle. Carefully slide the wheel into the swingarm and lift it up in the forward position it was in when you removed the chain. You may need to try a couple of different angles to get the disc in the caliper. Once the disc is in the caliper and the chain is on the sprocket, pull the wheel backward until the hole in the hub lines up with the hole in the swingarm. (Having the axle hanging in the swingarm eases the next step.) Slide the axle into the hub far enough to support the wheel. Move to the opposite side of the bike, where you can see through the swingarm to the hub. Lift the wheel until the hole lines up with the swingarm. Tap the axle through using your hand or a dead-blow hammer.

Snug down the axle nut. If you had to loosen the chain adjusters, reset them. If you haven't adjusted your chain in a while, now is a good time. Verify that the marks on the chain adjusters match up on both sides before torquing down the axle nut. Verify that everything is in place and the wheel turns freely. Pump up the rear brake lever to make sure the pads aren't dragging. Finally, add a fresh cotter pin to the axle nut if your bike requires one.

Tightening the axle nuts to the proper torque specification is vital for your safety. Cranking them down too tight can compress bearing spacers and lead to bearing failure. Leaving them too loose can let them spin free, with disastrous results.

Project 40
Tire Change

TIME:	2 hours
TOOLS:	Front and rear stands, bead breaker, rim protectors, tire irons, valve stem tool, milk crate or oil drum, spray container with soapy water, tire pressure gauge, compressed air, gloves (or Band-Aids)
TALENT:	3
COST:	$–$$$
PARTS:	Front and rear tires
TIP:	Use a dedicated bead breaker
BENEFIT:	Superior traction, particularly in wet or dusty conditions

Changing tires is relatively easy—once you have the right tools. Rider Wearhouse (www.aerostich.com) offers a complete tire changing set containing everything you need, or you can piece your own kit together, filling the gaps in your current tool selection. Still, the first time you attempt it, you may swear up and down that you'll never do it again.

Begin with your bike on front and rear stands. Once you've removed a wheel, unscrew the valve core with a valve stem tool. After the tire has finished its lengthy sigh, place your wheel on your milk crate or oil drum. (Although milk crates are easier to come by, oil drums put your wheel at a more comfortable working height.) Whatever support you use, you want to make sure the wheel is not resting on a brake disc while you're working on the bead. Discs bend all too easily and are quite expensive.

Slip the bead breaker through the center of the wheel. If you're worried about scratching the wheel, wrap the support beam of the bead breaker with a rag. Working carefully will also help avoid scratches. Expect to exert some effort to break the "interference fit" between the bead and the rim. You'll know the bead has let go when it stops resisting.

Remove the valve core from the valve stem and let the tire deflate.

The rim center has a depression to allow the rest of the bead to loosen. Using the section of tire bead already in the wheel center, work the bead loose by pressing your way around the tire with your hands. Once the entire bead is in the depression, flip the wheel and break the bead on the other side.

Your next chore will be lifting the bead over the lip of the rim. Lubrication makes this job infinitely easier, but don't use anything that you can't wipe away or air-dry. So, leave the WD-40 and silicone lubricants on the shelf. A spray bottle of diluted dish detergent works just fine. Spray the outer edge of the bead and the rim with enough fluid to cover the surface. Next, wedge a tire iron between your shiny rim and the rubber.

If you're worried about marring your rim's finish, using rim protectors or wrapping duct tape around the tire iron can help—but nothing can prevent rim damage if you pull an Incredible Hulk routine while operating the irons. Slip the edge of the tire iron under the bead, and using the rim as the fulcrum, carefully lever the bead over the lip. With your second—and possibly third—hand, make sure the rest of the bead (on both sides of the wheel) is still in the center rim depression.

Taking your second tire iron, lift the bead over the rim a couple of inches from the first iron. Moving an inch or two at a time, work your way around the rim until the bead pops off the wheel. Don't get impatient while levering the bead, though; you can easily scratch the paint off the rim. Turn the wheel over, and you should be able to push the second bead off the rim by hand. If you have trouble, give the bead an assist with one of the tire irons.

Wipe off the excess lube from the wheel before mounting the new tire. Spray the first bead you'll slip onto the rim and line up the painted spot (the lightest point on the tire) with the valve stem, obeying the arrow on the tire showing direction of rotation.

Although you should be able to get the first bead over the rim most of the way by hand, the tire iron will work in a

Be sure to set your bead breaker so that it will not scrape the rim as you press the bead toward the center of the wheel.

pinch. Now, lube the other bead, and, while keeping the first bead in the rim's center depression, work the second bead over the lip. Finish off with the tire irons, keeping the beads opposite the iron in the wheel's center depression.

Screw the valve stem valve core back into place. You should hear each bead pop into place as you inflate the tire. Check to ensure it seated evenly. If not, deflate and reseat. Don't forget to balance your wheels before riding. And remember, new tires—though they feel sticky to the touch—are extremely slippery for the first few miles, so no funny business, OK?

Working your way around the tire, press the bead into the center depression in the wheel. Flip the wheel and repeat.

Work deliberately with the tire irons. Your discs, knuckles, and rim paint will be much happier.

Before you attempt to lift the bead over the rim, spray down the bead with a diluted dish detergent solution.

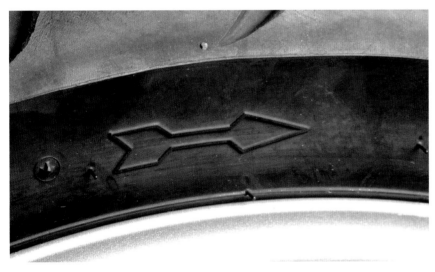

Make sure the rotational direction of the tire is correct. Otherwise, bad things could happen.

When mounting the new tire, you should be able to press most of the bead over the lip by hand. On the second bead, keeping the first one in the rim's center depression will help.

TIRE CHANGE

Project 41

Valve Stem Replacement

TIME:	30 minutes
TOOLS:	Valve stem tool, open-end wrenches, pliers, contact cleaner or organic cleaner, nonhardening silicone sealer
TALENT:	1
COST:	$
PARTS:	Metal valve stems
TIP:	Angled valve stems can ease tire inflation with some bikes
BENEFIT:	Tires that don't lose pressure at high speeds

With the tires off your wheels, begin by simply pulling the rubber valve stem out of the wheel. Clean the mounting surface with contact cleaner or your favorite nontoxic cleaner. After drying the wheel's orifice, check for proper fit of the new valve stem, particularly angled ones.

An angled valve stem can make the job of checking air pressure easier.

Consider how the valve actually works inside the stem. The air chuck presses the valve down toward the tire to allow air to flow. Let your mind wander a bit further to what happens to your wheel as you travel at the hypersonic velocities of which your sportbike is capable. The centrifugal forces want to fling the wheel components toward the outside of the wheel. The forces of high-speed riding could, conceivably, force the valve into releasing pressure. Metal valve stem assemblies usually sport a metal cap with a rubber O-ring to help

Once you're satisfied with the location, remove the stem and apply non-hardening silicone to the inner surface of the stem where it will contact the inside of the wheel. Similarly, apply a small amount to the gasket that will be held in place by the exterior washer and nut. Insert the stem and rotate it into position. Snug the nut down finger tight. Use an open-end wrench to finish the tightening, but not so tight as to distort the delicate threads on the stem. Wipe off the excess sealant, and you're ready to mount your tires. Once the tires are inflated, spread a soapy water solution around the base of the valve stem to make sure that the seal is airtight. Now, you can break the sound barrier without worrying about your valve stems letting you down.

seal the valve closed, thus preventing high-speed air loss. Even though this scenario is unlikely—and applicable only to track-speed riding—swapping out your rubber stems for metal ones also ensures that dry rot never strikes them, and allows you to fit bent stems if that would make access, and regular inflation mainte-nance, easier.

Chapter 10
Brakes

⚠ WARNING!

🪖 OLD SCHOOL TECH

🛸 TOMORROW'S TECH

❗ KEY CONCEPT

🔨 MAINTENANCE TIP

🐷 MONEY-SAVING TIP

When it comes to brakes, it seems too many motorcyclists tend to reflect the view of famous carmaker Ettore Bugatti, who responded to criticism of his cars' lack of braking ability with the line, "I build my cars to go, not stop."

Considered rationally, though, the brake system on your motorcycle *has* to work properly and stop you quickly and safely every single time you need it to, or you will be in a world of hurt. How do they work? Think of the brake assembly on each wheel as a small engine, but in reverse.

Your bike's powerplant converts fuel's energy into heat by combustion, and then converts that heat into mechanical work to propel the bike, right? Well, each brake assembly is an engine that just happens to work backward—so to speak—through friction. The brakes convert the energy of motion into heat, and dissipate that heat into the atmosphere.

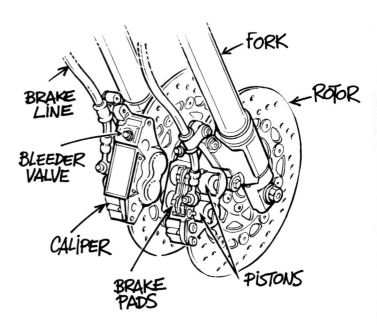

FORK

ROTOR

BRAKE LINE

BLEEDER VALVE

CALIPER

BRAKE PADS

PISTONS

HYDRAULIC BRAKES

🪖 Honda's revolutionary CB750 was the first mass-produced motorcycle to have a hydraulic disc brake, a single-rotor unit on the front wheel. Such a system remains the foundation of brake technology on today's motorcycles. Even with the application of anti-lock brakes (ABS), and/or linked brakes, the fundamental basics of hydraulic brake systems have not changed over the decades.

WHY HYDRAULICS?

Physics says a fundamental property of liquids—in this case hydraulic fluid or oil—is that they are not compressible. When you apply pressure to the brake lever or pedal, a mechanical linkage moves a pushrod in the master cylinder (which is filled with hydraulic fluid) that forces a piston down the bore of that cylinder. The piston's movement generates hydraulic pressure, which is transmitted through an interconnected series of brake lines to the individual brake assembly at each wheel. The

153

pressure reaching each wheel's brake assembly—a caliper in a disc brake system—pushes the pistons toward the rotor, or disc. The pistons act on brake pads, squeezing them against the rotor, which creates friction that generates heat, dissipates energy, and slows the motorcycle.

The harder you pull the lever or push the pedal, the more hydraulic pressure is generated, the more force pushing the pads' friction material against the rotors, the faster the energy of motion is converted into heat . . . and the quicker your bike stops.

The beauty of a hydraulic brake system is its basic simplicity. It has very few moving parts, is relatively self-contained and sealed, is remarkably consistent in operation, and is amazingly reliable.

MECHANICAL DRUM BRAKES

As simple as hydraulic brakes are, mechanical brakes are even simpler. And several smaller-displacement motorcycles (as well as many older bikes) still have a mechanical drum brake on the rear wheel. The drum is cast as part of the rear hub. A mechanical linkage or cable system transfers motion of the rear brake pedal to a cam, which forces the brake shoes (faced with friction material) against the inside of the drum. As the rider presses on the pedal, the energy of motion is again converted to heat, and your bike decelerates. Nothing to it, right?

Why do some motorcycles retain old-school drum brakes? Because in virtually every situation the vast majority of braking work is done by the front wheel; it's not as crucial for the rear wheel to have the greater sophistication and stopping power of a hydraulic disc. Besides which, mechanical drum brakes work perfectly well in that role. Lastly, on some bikes that have been in production for some time, the tooling is already paid for, which helps keep down the bike's retail price.

HOW TO DETECT WORN PADS

Unlike those in automobiles, motorcycle brakes don't provide an audible warning that your pads are worn. Instead, they have what can only charitably be called a visual warning system; the rider expected to visually verify the pads' condition periodically. It's certainly easy enough to do.

Virtually all brake pads will have a groove or line marked into the pads' perimeter; generally the groove or line is red or yellow in color, or at least something that contrasts vividly with the color of the pad material. The groove or line indicates the amount of remaining pad material, generally 2 mm or so. By looking at the leading edge of the caliper, or through inspection/access ports located on top of the caliper, you'll be able to see the groove or line in the pad. Once you see the groove or line butting up against the rotor, you should plan on changing your brake pads soon, if not immediately.

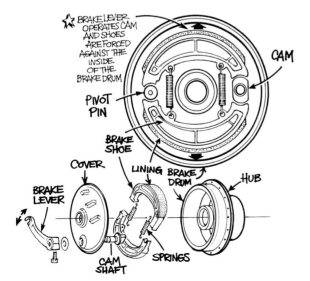

If you do not periodically check your pads, and you wear away all the friction material, then the pad's backing plate will begin to cut into the rotors. When this happens, you'll hear a loud screeching every time you apply the brakes. If you hear that noise, you'll need to replace both the pads and the rotor. Go any farther and you increase the damage, the repair bill, and the possibility one of the pistons will get pushed too far out of its bore, then cock slightly so that it wedges against the rotor, instantly locking the wheel.

BRAKE PADS: HOW TO PICK MR. RIGHT

Flip through the pages for brake pads in most any big parts distributor's catalog, and you're liable to mutter something to the effect of, "No free society needs this many choices of brake pads." The choices can be overwhelming: Are organic pads really, like, you know, *organic*? Like green beans? What's the difference between semi-metallic and sintered? Here's some that racers use! Can't go wrong with that, can you?

Well, yes, you can.

This is a good time to consider sticking with stock, original-equipment parts. Manufacturers generally do a superb job with every piece of the motorcycle, and especially so with brake pads, selecting the right friction material that will provide the best characteristics of stopping power, feel, and wear. There's a reason several racing teams use OE brake pads in classes where calipers and rotors must remain stock.

To some, however, such an approach might seem terminally uncool, So we'll offer some information on the various types of pads, but with a caveat: The following contains a host of generalities, because there can be a massive difference in materials and performance between one manufacturer's sintered pad, for instance, and another's. Firm, easy-to-follow recommendations are all but impossible to give, and it would be foolish to do so. With that said, let's proceed. Pads can be broken down by material:

• **Organic**—A material matrix held together by heat-resistant resin (glue, essentially). Early on, organic pads used asbestos as a binding material, and to make them more heat-resistant. We all know asbestos has gone the way of the carrier pigeon, dodo, etc., and now Kevlar has largely taken its place. In general, organic pads are said to work well right from cold (first applications), and some riders

like the lever feel they provide. They're also fairly friendly to discs, as they don't cause the scoring that can occur with more aggressive all-metal compounds. But organics tend to fade at lower temperatures than other pads.

• **Semi-metallic**—Basically an organic-type pad with metal particles, either in powder form or finely chopped wire; tin, brass, bronze, iron, and other metals are commonly used. The addition of metal makes these pads somewhat more heat-resistant than organic pads, and they wear less quickly. They're also harder on brake rotors than organic pads.

• **Sintered**—These pads consist of an all-metal powder formed under extremely high heat and pressure, with very little binding material. Generally they consist of brass, bronze, copper, and some iron, again for better performance at higher operating temperatures, said to offer good, consistent stopping power. However, those same higher operating temperatures get transferred from the pad to the rotor, which can cause warping with some aftermarket pads. Sintered pads also cause the most wear on rotors, and most brands should never be used on cast-iron rotors. They also tend to leave a potentially corrosive black dust on wheels, requiring more frequent cleaning. The majority of OE pads are sintered.

• **Carbon**—Essentially a semi-metallic-type pad, but with the addition of carbon rather than metal. Such pads are reasonably kind to rotors, but they're primarily remarkable for having perhaps the broadest range of operating temperatures; carbon pads tend to approach organics for their performance from cold, and work exceptionally well at higher temps, too. By its very nature, carbon is extremely heat-resistant. They do tend to be more expensive than other pads mentioned here, though. (Readers should know these are *not* the amorphous carbon pads used in MotoGP racing and on the space shuttle.)

If you still have to have a recommendation, here are some: First, use the same type of pad (organic, sintered, etc.) your bike came with, if not the OE pad itself. Second, resist the temptation to go with racing-only pads; such pads tend to work properly only at the elevated temperatures found in competition on a racetrack. Third, ask other owners what they've discovered through their experimentation. There are dozens of forums on the Web where you can find out what other owners have used successfully. But, unless you have a lot of time and money, let someone else experiment with brake pads on their motorcycle first.

WARNING SIGNS OF THE NEED TO BLEED

To stay in tip-top condition, a motorcycle's brake system really does need more frequent servicing than many riders might imagine. For instance, most manufacturers recommend replacing the brake fluid every two years or approximately 24,000 miles. There are a lot of mechanics, however, who will tell you one year is more appropriate.

In some instances, though, your bike's brakes will let you know they'd like your attention right now, if not sooner. One such instance is when you notice a sponginess or mushiness at the front brake lever or rear brake pedal when you apply the brakes. Mind you, there will always be a small amount of give in a bike's stock brake system simply because there's some flex in the lever and the OE rubber hoses tend to swell slightly at extreme lever-pressures. But the sponginess we're talking about here can be felt as more than an inch or so of lever play without significant pressure being applied at the pads, and resultant loss of stopping power.

What's going on? Air has managed to get into the hydraulic system, and with it water vapor, because all air has some measure of water in it. How did it enter the system? Pretty easily, actually. Air gets in through seals and rubber brake hoses, which are surprisingly porous in that respect.

Conventional glycol-based DOT 3, DOT 4, and DOT 5.1 brake fluids are hygroscopic, which means they absorb water. If sufficient water enters the system (as vapor that accompanies air) and the brakes get used hard enough, the water will actually boil near the calipers (source of greatest heat), releasing gas bubbles into the fluid. And while liquids can't be compressed, gases most certainly can. That's what you're feeling as excess motion at the lever or pedal.

CHOOSING THE RIGHT BRAKE FLUID

There are two basic types of brake fluid you can buy: traditional glycol-based as mentioned in the last section, and silicone-based. All brake fluids for sale in this country come with a Department of Transportation (DOT) that rating corresponds to that fluid's required minimum boiling temperatures. The temperatures are indicated as dry, which is fresh fluid, straight out of the container, and wet, which is after the fluid has absorbed a percentage of water. Higher numbers show a higher capacity for heat before they begin to boil. So, we have DOT 3, DOT 4, DOT 5 (silicone-based), and DOT 5.1.

Now, not only do glycol-based fluids absorb moisture from the air, but they also have the ability to keep that moisture in suspension so that they retain reasonably effective braking performance. Plus, by preventing water from separating to collect at the lowest point in the system, they reduce its fiendishly corrosive effects. In addition, such brake fluids have a degree of lubricity, which helps prolong seal life and makes them suitable for anti-lock brake systems (ABS). They also tend to change color gradually according to the amount of moisture they've absorbed, providing an indication of how contaminated they've become. However, glycol-based fluids are extremely destructive to paints and plastics.

The sole silicone-based brake fluid available is DOT 5, which has the same required minimum boiling temperatures as the more recently introduced DOT 5.1. Unlike the other fluids, DOT 5 is not hygroscopic; that is, it doesn't absorb moisture. Sounds good, right? Well, hold on—instead, the moisture that inevitably enters any braking system tends to form globules that drop to the bottom of the system with predictably corrosive effects. That's one of the reasons DOT 5 fluids require the most maintenance of any brake fluid. What's more, DOT 5 is more easily aerated and doesn't have their natural lubricity; both are reasons why DOT 5 isn't recommended for use with ABS. To its credit, DOT 5 at least isn't harmful to paint or plastics.

Just as with brake pads, it's all but impossible to offer a trustworthy, reliable recommendation for brake fluid. The best suggestion is to stick with what your owner's manual specifies. If it says to use DOT 4—and most do these days—then find a brand you like and stay with it. Don't experiment with brake fluids once you've chosen one.

In fact, don't mix brake fluids at all if you can help it. If you absolutely must do so, mix only glycol-base fluids. Never, ever mix glycol and silicone fluids. They will clot up, rendering your brakes unusable and require extensive stripping and cleaning, along with replacing every rubber seal in the system.

BRAIDED BRAKE LINES

If you're serious about upgrading your motorcycle's brake system, and don't have a particularly large budget, the best place to start is to replace the standard rubber hoses with braided steel lines.

> With a fairly small outlay of cash, you can replace both front and rear rubber hoses with braided steel lines that will immediately provide you with a firmer response at the lever, reduced effort for the same amount of stopping power, and better overall lever-feel as well.

First off, though, let's take care of the misnomer: Although they might be called braided steel lines, stainless-steel lines, etc., the steel description does not refer to the actual hoses that transfer fluid. Those are Teflon PTFE (polytetrafluoroethylene) hoses. They're surrounded and reinforced, however, by braided stainless-steel hose. The end result is virtually zero expansion even if you're squeezing the brake lever with both hands. Such minimal expansion guarantees all your effort is going into stopping the bike, and not swelling the hose.

There are several aftermarket companies that will sell you brake line kits with premade hoses, every piece of hardware you'll need, plus your choice of a rainbow of colors for the vinyl covering that goes over the steel braid (to keep it from scratching your bike). Some even give you a choice of colors for the fittings at the end of the hoses. And, lastly, virtually every brand of braided brake lines will last the life of your motorcycle.

AFTERMARKET BRAKES' ADVANTAGES

If you're rich as Croesus, then the sky's the limit if you really want to upgrade your bike's brake system to the highest degree possible. As with most things, excellence merely requires the application of a stack of Grovers.

And what would one get for a pile of greenbacks with the picture of our 22nd and 24th president on them? To start, you could have your choice of rotors: the latest petal-style discs from innovators Galfer or Braking, for better initial bite, better cooling, and lighter weight than OE rotors. Or perhaps some particularly fine ductile cast-iron rotors from Brake Tech, which promise not only a 40 percent weight savings over OE discs, but unparalleled feel. Or another Brake Tech offering, their ceramic composite rotors, the highest-tech rotors you can buy for street use, with the feel of ductile cast iron and only

slightly more weight than MotoGP-type carbon rotors, but with much broader temperature range.

For calipers, AP and Nissin both offer superb kit, but the most desirable is Brembo's radial-mount Monobloc four-piston/four-pad caliper, again as close as you can get to real-deal MotoGP hardware. These are machined from a solid billet of aluminum and feature vented titanium pistons. Brembo's radial 19x18 billet folding-brake master cylinder—not just a MotoGP look-alike, but the real thing—is the only choice to accompany those calipers.

You should be getting the idea.

What are the advantages of such a wild spending spree? The usual reasons we've explored so far: more stopping power, better control, and superior feel at the lever. Mind you, even if you can't step to the *ne plus ultra* equipment name-dropped here, be assured you can approach it for a fraction of the absurd prices these kingly pieces command.

ABS AND LBS

How quickly can you stop your motorcycle?

Be honest. If a car turned left in front of you—the classic car vs. motorcycle accident scenario—could you apply the brakes hard enough, quickly enough, to keep from fetching up against the nearside fender? Just to make it more interesting, let's assume the pavement is wet, too. How about then?

That's the kind of situation when an anti-lock brake system (ABS) comes in mighty handy. ABS can be a lifesaver, literally.

To optimize your motorcycle's stopping power in an emergency situation, the tires need to be rotating right at the threshold of lockup, about 10 percent slower than

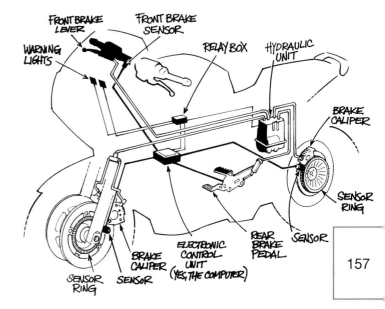

road speed. This optimizes the traction of the tires, allowing maximum braking action and stopping power.

Now, if you're an exceptionally good rider, you can achieve that by modulating pressure on the brake lever and pedal a bit. Incrementally reducing pressure until the wheels unlock will help you regain grip so you can stop efficiently or steer around the threat.

But unless you practice this on a regular basis—which wouldn't make you particularly popular with your neighbors—such a feat of braking is difficult, particularly in the heat of battle when you *really* need to stop before you hit a solid object. If you could threshold brake perfectly—applying *exactly* the right amount of pressure on the lever and pedal to keep the tires at the very edge of optimum traction—you could bring your bike to a stop as quickly as it was capable of stopping.

Enter ABS. In the simplest of terms, ABS is an electronic add-on to standard hydraulic brake systems. By monitoring the rotational speed of both wheels through a wheel speed sensor and feeding that information into a small microprocessor, the ABS system can recognize when you've overapplied the brakes and your tires are in the process of locking up. How does it know this? No, not by your screams. The system identifies that the rotational speed of one wheel is slowing faster than the other; that's the moment of impending brake lockup.

The ABS computer signals a hydraulic assembly to rapidly cycle hydraulic valves open and closed to the individual brake or brakes that are locking. The cyclic and very rapid valve openings bleed off just enough hydraulic pressure to those brakes to keep them at the edge of optimum traction. Thus, ABS prevents you from overbraking—applying too much brake force, locking the wheels, losing steering control, and reducing brake efficiency. And, in the process, ABS makes you look like a hero.

Note that a few motorcycle manufacturers offer linked braking systems that use valving to apply braking effect to both wheels when you hit one lever. In other words, a slight amount of pressure is applied to the rear brake when you use the front lever, and vice versa.

Honda, in particular, uses this system on some of its motorcycles. Their first incarnation appeared on the CBR1000, and it was judged helpful for inexperienced riders, but not so much for seasoned riders. And that system was awkward for both at slow speeds. Honda refined the system, and on models built in 1998 or later, it works quite well. The advantage is that you get a bit more stopping power if you only use one lever.

Project 42

Caliper and Disc Service

TIME:	1 to 2 hours
TOOLS:	Wrenches, rags; 60- or 80-grit sandpaper, toothbrush or other small cleaning brush, a thin piece of wood, brake/contact cleaner, organic cleaner such as Simple Green, waterproof, high-temperature grease, bike lift (optional), Mity-Vac, some clear tubing, an old-fashioned oil can, sockets and Allens, screwdriver, jar to catch brake fluid
TALENT:	1
COST:	0 to $
PARTS:	New pads, brake fluid, brake banjo washers, and master cylinder gasket or diaphragm
TIP:	Gently snug (rather than heavily tighten) the bleeder screw
BENEFIT:	Maximizes brake performance

Fortunately, brakes are easy to work on—and much cheaper to maintain by yourself than pay to fix up once they've gone south. In this project, we'll disassemble and clean the calipers and disc(s). In Projects 43 and 44, we'll replace the pads and refresh the hydraulic system.

Cleaning the caliper removes the obvious stuff such as brake dust, but it also plays an important role in preventing the need for rebuilds. Most brake fluids absorb moisture through the piston seals. That moisture combines with the brake dust and grit and whatever else happens to be wedged into the calipers, forming a "shellac" that bonds to the surface of the pistons and keeps them from sliding smoothly through the rubber seals.

Remove the front caliper(s), slip out the brake pads, and support the caliper on something other than the brake line. Place a thin piece of wood between the opposing pistons and squeeze the brake lever to expose most of the pistons. Using a toothbrush and an organic cleaner like Simple Green, which won't hurt the caliper O-rings, carefully rub the shellac off the pistons. If your front brake has been sticking, you see leaking fluid, or the piston is rusted or pitted, buy a caliper rebuild kit and swap out the pistons and seals. Otherwise scrub off the shellac, rinse with

water to remove the cleanser, and then blow away all traces of moisture with an air hose.

To finish your caliper cleansing, on single-action calipers (those with pistons on only one side of the caliper), pull back the rubber cover protecting the pins upon which the caliper slides back and forth. Using the same organic cleaners, remove the old, tired grease and check for any notches or unseemly wear to the pins. Lube the clean pins with waterproof, high-temperature grease and slide them into position under their protective covers.

Now you need to prepare the disc. Brake pads can leave deposits in the rotor's surface. You want to remove these deposits and take the rotor back down to smooth, clean metal before reassembling your brakes. Use a piece of 60- or 80-grit sandpaper. With your bike on a lift or jack with the wheel off the ground, press the sandpaper against the disc and spin the wheel a few times. (Keep the caliper secure, not hanging from the brake line.) Repeat the process on the other side of the disc. Remember: You're not trying to score the disk, just remove the buildup. Finish the disc prep by spraying it with brake cleaner and wiping it down with a clean rag.

Now you can replace the pads.

Many a chromed caliper needs to have its bore honed slightly to get rid of the crud that's deposited inside during the chroming process. The caliper piston must be a light, sliding fit, but without any noticeable side-to-side slop once it's pushed home.

You may find it to your advantage to run a well-oiled tap down the threaded holes in the caliper, as well. This may be the only way to ensure no-problem installations on chrome pieces (not just brake pieces either). Once you've gone this far, it only follows that you should check that the internal passages are clear, and then meticulously clean the thing.

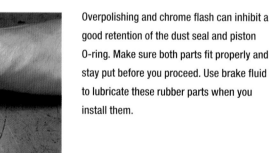

Overpolishing and chrome flash can inhibit a good retention of the dust seal and piston O-ring. Make sure both parts fit properly and stay put before you proceed. Use brake fluid to lubricate these rubber parts when you install them.

CALIPER AND DISC SERVICE

Project 43
Brake Pad Change

TIME: 1 hour

TOOLS: Wrenches, sockets, flathead screwdriver, Allen keys, torque wrench, anti-seize lubricant, bike lift (optional)

TALENT: 1

COST: $

PARTS: Brake pads

TIP: Don't forget to pump the brake lever a few times after you are done so you have immediate stopping power when you go for a test ride

BENEFIT: Better stopping power

Many bikes use single-piston sliding calipers that squeeze a rotor like a hydraulic C-clamp. The design principle of the front and rear brake calipers is the same, but the way they are mounted and their respective pads are different.

To install new front brake pads, unbolt the front caliper from the lower fork leg and slide the caliper up and off the rotor. Insert a large flat-bladed screwdriver between the pads in the caliper and use it as a lever against the outer pad to push the caliper piston back into the caliper body. Remove the outer pad carrier from the caliper body and remove the inner pad. It's rigidly mounted to the rear of the caliper body via a small bolt. The other pad is probably already on the floor. Inspect the caliper and replace anything that's damaged or worn beyond service limits. (Check the shop manual.)

When reassembling the caliper with new pads, make sure that the rivet head is inserted into the cutout in the sliding nut. The retaining spring keeps the pad from vibrating. Slide the caliper onto the rotor and insert the mounting bolts.

When reinstalling the caliper mounting bolts, give them a light coating of anti-seize lubricant, which will allow the caliper mounting bolts and outer pad carrier to move freely and align properly with the disc. Use a torque wrench and tighten the bolts to spec as outlined in your factory manual. If your bike has twin front brakes, repeat the process for the other brake.

The procedure for the rear is nearly identical to that used in replacing front brake pads, though it may involve different tools, such as a Torx bit.

BRAKE PAD BREAK-IN

The surfaces of both the pads and the discs aren't really as smooth as they look. In fact, they're made up of lots of hills and valleys. The break-in procedure wears down the pad so that the hills and valleys match each other, giving the maximum surface-area contact. Get too aggressive too soon, and the hills melt and glaze over, lowering the coefficient of friction for the pads and reducing braking performance.

Begin pad break-in by riding in a parking lot and lightly applying the brake, bringing the bike slowly to a stop. Do this a few times with slightly more pressure each time. Now, go for a ride.

Just like when you have new tires and you know not to immediately throw your bike into corners, allow yourself some extra room for braking around town. Begin to vary your braking pressure. Each stop should be more firm than the last. Allow for some cooling between applications (i.e., no maximum-braking exercises).

There is no magic number for how long it takes to break in a set of pads. If you vary the pressure and don't build it up too quickly, a short ride may be enough. However, if you're ever in doubt about how to break in a set of pads, simply look at the instructions that came with them—the manufacturers know.

Once you've freed the caliper from its mount, you may want to pry the pads apart with a screwdriver. Then they'll slip out of the center as shown here. Before you set them aside, inspect them closely. Did they wear evenly? If one pad is thinner than the other, take a look at the pistons to see if they may be sticking. Another symptom of a dragging caliper piston is having one end of the pad more worn than the other. These signal the need for a caliper rebuild.

After the caliper's interior is clean, press the pistons back into their bores. Otherwise, you won't be able to slip the new, thicker pads into place.

If you can't get the pistons back into their bores far enough to allow the disc to slide between the pads, you can use a pry bar to gently open up more space. Be careful not to mar the pads' surfaces. As you install the new pads, place the factory antisqueal plates or springs in the proper position. Check the other caliper if you can't remember how the pieces go together. If the pads are not held in place with a pin, pay attention to the way they fit in the caliper, and verify that they haven't shifted once you've remounted the caliper to its bracket. Torque the fasteners to the proper specification. Also, pump up the brake lever as soon as you finish remounting the caliper to build pressure and seat the pads against the discs. This way you won't experience the unfortunate surprise of having the lever come all the way back to the grip as you try to stop at the end of your driveway.

Project 44
Changing Hydraulic Fluid

TIME: 45 minutes

TOOLS: Wrenches, sockets, rags, torque wrench (16-in), Teflon tape, brake bleeding tool (optional), clear hose, glass jar for brake fluid, rags

TALENT: 1

COST: $

PARTS: Brake fluid

TIP: Only use fresh fluid from unopened containers, and never mix fluid brands

BENEFIT: Better lever feel, no nasty surprises

When wrapping the bleed screw's threads with Teflon tape, make sure you wind it so that screwing in the valve tightens the tape. Also, be careful not to cover the bleed holes.

This Mity-Vac is a handy tool for bleeding hydraulic systems—particularly bone-dry ones. Be prepared to empty the catch container at least once when freshening fluid. Since you'll be working by the caliper instead of the master cylinder, don't forget to keep an eye on the fluid level in the reservoir.

Bleeding the System

Brake fluid should be replaced every two years with the spec your manufacturer recommends. The easy way to change the brake fluid without getting air in the system is to bleed it clean.

Three different techniques can be used to do the actual bleeding. No matter which you choose, a few basics are the same. First adjust the handlebars so that the master cylinder sits flat, then clean and remove its cover. Fill the master cylinder to about 3/8 inch from the top; this gives the cover gasket-bladder some room.

Then bleed the brake fluid down to about 1 inch from the bottom of the reservoir before filling its cylinder with new fluid. Continue to bleed the fluid until it comes out clean at the caliper. Then refill the reservoir and bleed the other caliper, if there's another connected. When done, top up the reservoir and replace the cap.

The cheapest bleeding method is to use a piece of clear tubing and an old plastic soda bottle. The main drawbacks with this method are that it's a two-person

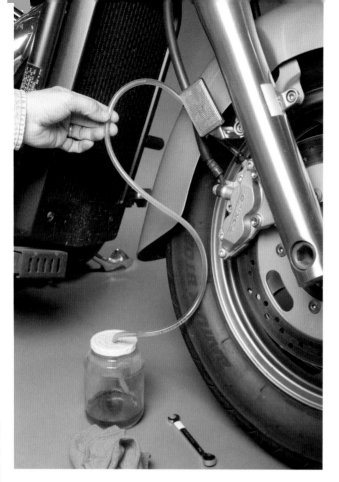

job and it takes what seems like forever (maybe an hour), unless you get lucky. Use a clear bottle so you can see the fluid. Connect the tubing to the caliper's bleed nipple and stick the other end in the bottle. With this setup, one person squeezes the brake handle and holds it back while another person opens the bleeder fitting at the caliper. When the flow stops, the second person closes the bleeder nipple. Repeat until the fluid flows clear, and then repeat for each caliper. Don't forget to keep filling the master cylinder.

There are also bleeder kits on the market to speed this process. They are faster and convenient; if you do brake work on many vehicles, buying a well-regarded one may be worth the effort. A quick Internet search or your local service station can tell you where to dispose of the used fluid safely and lawfully.

Keeping a big arch in the line will keep bubbles from being drawn back into the caliper. Don't be stingy with your fresh fluid. Keep pumping it through the system even after you think you're done. Some bubbles are tenacious.

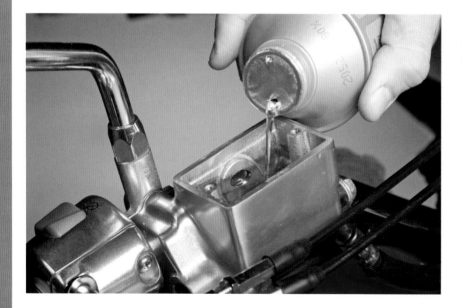

When topping off the reservoir, don't fill beyond the full mark. Be sure to clean the diaphragm that floats on top of the fluid before installing it. Always use name-brand hydraulic fluid.

Project 45
Drum Brake Maintenance

TIME:	30 seconds to 1 hour
TOOLS:	Wrenches, sockets, Allen keys, torque wrench, dial caliper, rags, brake/contact cleaner, high-temperature grease, bike lift (optional)
TALENT:	1
COST:	$
PARTS:	Brake shoes, brake shoe springs (if not included with shoes)
TIP:	To keep from breathing hazardous materials, don't blow off the brake panel with compressed air
BENEFIT:	Predictable rear brake performance

Drum brakes require a little regular maintenance that should take you all of 30 seconds every month or so. From the pedal's resting position, press it down with your hand and measure the distance the pedal is depressed until you feel the shoes contact the drum. If that measurement is greater than the factory spec, tighten the nut at the drum end of the brake rod. In many cases, you won't even need a wrench to do this. Simply press the cam lever (the lever attached to both the drum brake assembly—or brake panel—and the brake rod) slightly against the spring holding it into position against the adjuster. Since the adjuster usually has a machined curve to match the clevis pin in the lever, you'll be able to make changes in half-turn increments. Once the free play is back to spec, you're done.

Note the wear indicator when you take up the free play. Manufacturers build these indicators into the outside of the brake panel. Replace the shoes when they're about 80 percent used up to be sure that maximum power is available. (Pads/shoes can't dissipate heat properly when they get too thin, and they will not function properly.)

Every two years or 10,000 miles, disassemble the brake panel and lube the moving parts. Clean out the built-up brake dust, too, and give the assembly a close visual inspection.

To change the shoes, loosen the chain adjusters' locknuts to provide enough chain slack to remove the wheel. Then give each of the adjusters three full turns of slack and retighten the locknuts to maintain their adjustment relative to each other. (Once you get the wheel back on the bike, you'll just tighten the adjusters those three turns for a properly adjusted chain.) If you have shaft drive, check your factory service manual for rear wheel removal tips. Different bikes have different requirements. For example, the Yamaha V-Star 650 requires that you pull the shaft itself free with the rear wheel.

Remove the bolt connecting the torque arm to the drum brake assembly and the nut from the end of the brake rod. Now, loosen the axle nut and spin it off the axle. Jack up the bike so that the wheel is about an inch off the ground. While holding the wheel in position (use your foot to take the strain off the axle as you slide it free), remove the axle. Now, push the wheel forward to create some slack in the chain. Remove the chain from the sprocket and hang it on the swingarm. You may need to jack the bike up farther to help the wheel clear the fender. Disassemble everything according to the photos and captions.

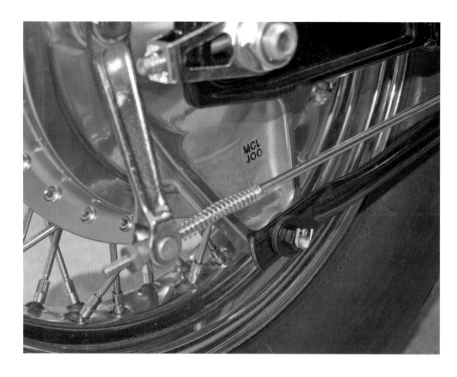

Don't forget to remove the bolt securing the drum to the torque arm. You'd be amazed how many people are momentarily surprised when the rear wheel won't come off after the axle is removed. Place the wheel on the floor with the drum brake side facing up and wiggle the brake panel free. You'll see lots of brake dust and grime on the inside of the panel, but resist the urge to blow it out with compressed air. Those particles can contain some pretty toxic stuff. Instead, clean the parts (in a well-ventilated area) with brake cleaner. It will flush the dust away without making it airborne. Don't worry that it'll also remove the grease from its rightful place; you're going to reapply it anyway. If you decide to clean the inside of the drum, take care not to get the cleaner in the wheel bearings.

With the brake panel exterior on a surface that won't scratch it, measure the thickness of the pads with a dial caliper to make sure they are within specification. As with disc brake pads, most brake shoe failure takes place on the last 20 percent of the shoe material. So, if the shoe thickness is less than 3 mm, replace the set. (The Vulcan 800 factory service manual, for example, specifies a service limit of 2.6 mm) You should also check the internal diameter of the drum itself with your dial caliper.

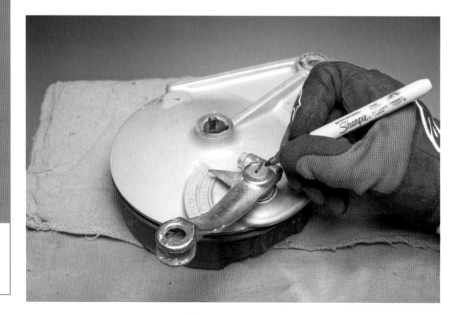

Turn the brake panel over and, using a Sharpie, mark the brake cam lever's position by drawing a line from the gap in the lever across the shaft to the other side of the lever. Unscrew the pinch bolt and remove the lever. Now, slide the camshaft out of the panel. Set the wear indicator aside. Clean the shaft and its associated hole in the panel and check for wear. If you notice any wear, consult your factory service manual for tolerances to make sure the parts are still within specification.

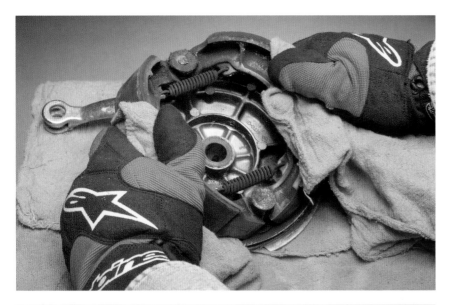

Grasp the brake shoes with a clean rag and lift them free of the assembly. The shoes will fold toward the center of the panel as they pivot around the anchor pin and the camshaft. Be careful, as the springs holding the shoes against the pin and cam are fairly strong. Set the shoes aside and wipe the panel clean of any crud. Protect your hands from the shoe material and the shoes from grease by gripping the two parts with a clean rag as you rotate them free of the retaining pin and cam.

Once everything is clean, lube the camshaft and the mounting hole in the brake panel with high-temperature grease. Slide the shaft into the panel and rotate it until the flats on the cam are pointing toward the center of the panel. Place the indicator on the shaft with its pointer at the right end of the useable range marker on the panel. Line up the Sharpie marks on the shaft and the lever and remount the lever. Tighten the bolt to spec. Apply high-temperature grease to the contact surfaces of the anchor pin and the cam. Add a little bit of grease to the brake shoes' spring-mounting holes.

Before replacing the brake panel, rotate the cam lever to make sure that everything works. Check that the wear indicator is pointing at the beginning of its range (or where it was pointing prior to disassembly if you just cleaned and lubed the unit). If not, remove the cam lever and adjust the indicator. When you're ready to put the wheel back in the swingarm, begin by cleaning and greasing the axle. Carefully slide the wheel into the swingarm and lift it up into the forward position you used to remove the chain. Take the chain from the swingarm and put it back on the sprocket. Pull the wheel backward until the hole in the hub lines up with the hole in the swingarm. Slide the axle into the hub far enough to support the wheel.

Move to the opposite side of the bike, where you can see through the swingarm to the hub. Lift the wheel until the hole lines up with the swingarm. Tap the axle through using your hand or a dead-blow hammer.

DRUM BRAKE MAINTENANCE

Snug down the axle nut, but not so tight that the chain adjusters can't move it. Make sure the wheel is all the way forward against the adjusters by giving the rear of the tire a couple of whacks with your dead-blow hammer. Reset the chain adjusters the three turns you loosened them. If you haven't adjusted your chain in awhile, now is a good time.

Verify that the marks on the chain adjusters match up on both sides. Coat the clevis with a light application of grease, slip it into the cam lever, and slide the brake rod into place. Set the adjuster into roughly the same position on the rod that it was in prior to disassembly. Loosely (finger tight) attach the torque arm to the brake drum assembly. Before torquing down the axle nut, spin the rear wheel and lock the rear brake by pressing quickly on the pedal. With the brake still applied, tighten down the bolt securing the torque arm.

Now, torque the axle to factory spec. Make sure that the chain adjusters are snugged up and their locknuts are tight. Verify that everything is in place and the wheel turns freely. Adjust the brake pedal free play to factory settings.

Project 46
Installing Stainless-Steel Brake Lines

TIME:	1–2 hours
TOOLS:	Wrenches, sockets, front and rear stands (optional), rags, torque wrench (lb-in), Teflon tape, brake bleeding tool (optional), clear hose, glass jar for brake fluid
TALENT:	2
COST:	$–$$
PARTS:	Brake lines, brake fluid
TIP:	If you've modified your bike by raising or lowering the bars or extending the swingarm, order a custom-length kit
BENEFIT:	A firmer squeeze at the lever and better feedback

Fitting a set of braided, stainless-steel brake lines can have a dramatic effect on your bike's stopping power. The initial onset of braking will be much quicker, since stainless lines don't expand at all. And since the lines are sheathed in metal (usually with a protective plastic outer coating), you don't have to worry about stainless lines cracking from age and exposure to the sun. Also, the Teflon interior is less prone to becoming brittle than rubber. So, a trip to the aftermarket will give you better braking and longer-lasting lines, to boot. Oh, yeah—they look cool.

Order a kit for your bike, specifying a custom length if you've changed your bars or swingarm. Check them again for length before you start installing them. The simplest way to do this is by zip-tying them to the existing lines. Although this takes a couple of extra minutes, you can tell right away if the lines will have the proper amount of slack in them. Having your brake lines go taut before the fork is fully extended would be a very bad thing.

Even in the best-case scenario, changing hydraulic lines is messy. Since brake fluid can damage paint and other shiny stuff on your bike, you should remove or

Quickly attaching the new line to the stocker will tell you if it is the right length. This will also help you to prepare for any idiosyncrasies of your bike's brake line routing.

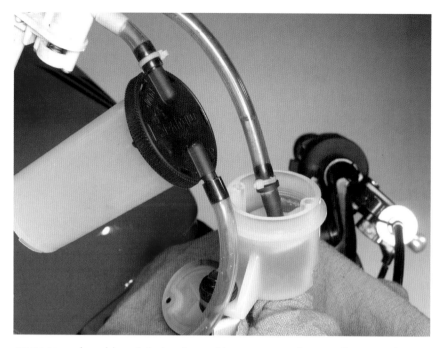

Sucking the fluid out of the reservoir will speed up the task of draining the system. Place the cap back on the system—but don't screw it down—to keep dust out of it while you're changing the lines.

cover any vulnerable painted surfaces. Unscrew or unclasp all of the fasteners holding the hydraulic line in place. Using a ratchet, remove the banjo bolt from the caliper. To keep fluid leakage to a minimum, wrap the banjo with a rag and secure it with a zip-tie or piece of tape. Remove the master cylinder banjo and feed the line out of the chassis. Now, feed the new line into place, following the exact same route as the stock line. Usually, aftermarket front brake kits will use two lines from the master cylinder instead of a T-junction further down the line. Be sure you run the correct line to each caliper. (One is usually longer than the other.)

Once you've torqued the banjo bolts down, make sure you attach the lines to the chassis at all the original points. Sometimes you'll need to use zip-ties to hold the thinner, stainless lines to the OE clips. Although most stainless lines are sold in protective sheaths, bare, braided stainless-steel lines can cut through metal like a hacksaw. If your lines are uncoated, make sure you wrap the lines with tape or spiral wrap specifically designed for the purpose at all potential points of contact with the chassis. Then follow the procedures outlined in the photo captions.

Using a vacuum bleeder is much more effective at draining the brake system than trying to pump it dry with the master cylinder. Begin by sucking the extra fluid out of the reservoir. Then attach the hose to a caliper's bleeder valve. Give the bleeder a couple of pumps to build up the suction, and crack the valve until fluid starts to be drawn into the catch tank. Keep pumping until the system is dry. Do this for both front calipers.

Notice the gentle curve of the stainless line as it leaves the caliper. If things don't line up right, you may have the banjos at the wrong mounting point. Hydraulic line manufacturers spend a lot of time making sure that the fittings have the same bend as the OE lines they replace—if something doesn't look right, it probably isn't.

The OE system only used a single line at the master cylinder, so the second aftermarket line needs to be held in place while the banjo is torqued. Always replace the crush washers when the banjo bolts have been removed. The soft copper (for steel banjos) or aluminum (for aluminum banjos) is designed to conform to any irregularities on the fitting or mounting surface. A washer should be used on both sides of the banjo. If two banjos are being bolted together (as on the front brake master cylinder), be sure to use a crush washer between the two banjos, as well. Screw the banjo bolts in finger tight and check your hose routing for bends or kinks before you torque things down.

Chapter 11
Exhaust

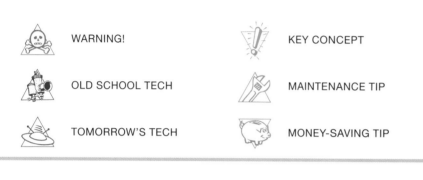

WARNING!

OLD SCHOOL TECH

TOMORROW'S TECH

KEY CONCEPT

MAINTENANCE TIP

MONEY-SAVING TIP

Motorcyclists often choose to modify or replace their bike's exhaust pipes to improve performance and give the bike a throatier sound. Riders typically seem to believe they have an inherent, intuitive knowledge of how exhausts work, even if they don't really know any more about them then a sea cucumber knows about a Russian Oscar-class nuclear submarine. If motorcyclists really did know that much about exhaust systems, they might be a little more circumspect before bolting on the first shiny pipe that caught their eye.

A well-designed exhaust pipe is a fairly sophisticated piece of equipment, as evidenced by how well a stock exhaust copes with the many pressure pulses that travel up and down its length. On a multi-cylinder engine, for example, as an exhaust valve opens, a positive pulse of exhaust gas starts streaming down the exhaust pipe. As that pulse hits a significant change in cross-section in the pipe, such as the collector, part of the pulse's energy bounces back toward the engine, but as negative pressure this time. If everything has been designed properly, that returning pulse arrives back at the exhaust valve during overlap, when both the intake and exhaust valves are slightly open and the piston is near top dead center. The pulse's negative pressure evacuates the remainder of the burnt gases from the combustion chamber. It also sneaks past the intake valve and starts sucking air into the combustion chamber even before the intake stroke has begun.

A well-designed exhaust pipe directs these exhausts pulses and precisely evacuates the combustion chamber of the incoming air/fuel charge, resulting in a bigger bang for a nice bump in torque and good acceleration. (That is a frightfully oversimplified explanation of exhaust flow.)

At some rpm, however, a returning *positive* pulse hits the exhaust valve, pushing the spent gases in the combustion chamber back out to the air box, resulting in a diluted air/fuel charge that gets sucked back into the engine. Such behavior causes torque to dip, which the rider feels as a flat spot in throttle response and weak acceleration. A stock exhaust is designed to take advantage of the former happy state of affairs over as broad an rpm range as is possible, while isolating the latter, less desirable situation over as narrow an rpm range as possible.

What's this mean to you? Your stock exhaust probably gives you close to ideal performance. They are carefully designed pieces of equipment that have been rigorously built for that machine. The days when bolting on an open pipe was guaranteed to give you more horsepower are long gone.

OXYGEN SENSOR

Increasingly restrictive emissions laws around the world (such as the Euro III regs) have caused modern motorcycles to sprout more and more sophisticated electronic

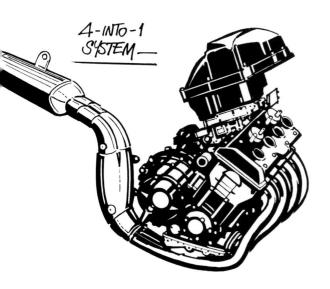

4-INTO-1 SYSTEM —

trim fuel delivery for optimum performance and efficiency and minimum emissions.

Mufflers

Motorcycles these days tend to have extremely quiet exhaust notes. That's because all motorcycles sold for street use have to meet ever-tighter noise restrictions. With power going up every year almost across the board, how do manufacturers do it?

The same way Wal-Mart makes a profit—through volume. Stock motorcycle exhaust mufflers, or silencers, need ample room in order to baffle combustion racket and to let the engine breathe freely.

devices to ensure they run as green—and lean—as possible. One particular component lives in the exhaust system: an oxygen sensor, plumbed into the collector just downstream of the head pipes, and just upstream of the catalytic converter. This little electronic gizmo compares the percentage of oxygen in the exhaust with the percentage of oxygen in the atmosphere, then generates a low-voltage signal representing that ratio, and feeds the signal to the electronic control unit (ECU), or engine management computer hundreds of times per second. The signal from the oxygen sensor allows the ECU to

Still, there will always be unreconstructed, old school motorcyclists who insist engines run and sound best with less-restrictive exhaust systems. And it's true that MotoGP bikes run such exhausts. However, if you look at a MotoGP bike's pipe, you can easily see that vast amounts of effort went into its design and construction. The likelihood of that being the case with typical aftermarket blooey pipes is around slim and none. Riders who favor such exhausts are just fooling themselves, if they're not just outright fools to begin with. Their engines often make less power so equipped, and their infernal exhaust racket makes all of us look bad.

AFTERMARKET EXHAUSTS

As mentioned at the beginning of this chapter, aftermarket exhausts have been the number one choice for motorcycle modifications. And their appeal is easy to ascertain. They're not prohibitively expensive, and an aftermarket pipe tends to announce its presence, both visually and sonically. Consequently, your riding buddies can quickly see the difference, and the rest of the world can hear it.

Riders have two choices with aftermarket pipes: slip-on mufflers, or silencers, and full systems with silencer and head pipes. Slip-ons are the least expensive route, and, at one time, were the easiest way to get a substantial weight savings over stock. OE silencers used to be real porkers, largely because they were made sufficiently sturdy to last for most of the bike's life. These days, though, manufacturers have started making them out of titanium, and aftermarket silencers no longer pay the weight-savings dividend they once did.

To get the full benefits of an aftermarket exhaust company's engineering, buyers are encouraged to pop for the firm's full exhaust system. The thing is, with few exceptions, OE manufacturers actually do a remarkable job of creating broad, easy-to-use powerbands with stock exhaust systems. In fact, what a lot of accessory exhausts do is simply rearrange the engine's powerband. They might make eye-opening peak power numbers, but at the expense of robbing power from the midrange and low end. Admittedly, back in the day, when motorcycle exhaust design was less well known, an aftermarket

company could indeed build better systems than the manufacturers. But that's far less true today. Yes, there are some instances where aftermarket exhausts can make a genuine, large-scale improvement over stock, but they're becoming increasingly rare.

Plus, just as it was back in the day, such improvements are all but impossible without recalibrating the bike's fueling. Then it involved rejetting the carburetors, but these days the preferred method is to have a Dynojet Tuning Center fit one of the firm's Power Commanders and whip up a custom map for the fuel injection. What many riders don't seem to realize, though, is that a Power Commander with a custom map on an otherwise stock bike can make huge differences in rideability. Emissions regulations have forced manufacturers to make certain compromises in the fuel injection mapping that can show up as abrupt off-idle response and dips in the torque curve. A well-mapped Power Commander can ensure the owner gets all the horsepower and performance he paid for, and that the bike's designers intended. And that's money far better spent than on someone's imaginative collection of tubing meant to serve as an aftermarket exhaust system.

Project 47
Installing a Slip-On Exhaust

TIME:	1 hour
TOOLS:	Wrenches, sockets, torque wrench, rear stand, rubber mallet or dead-blow hammer, spring puller, WD-40, soft cloth or work mat
TALENT:	1
COST:	$$$–$$$$
PARTS:	Aftermarket slip-on exhaust
TIP:	Stuck or ornery components can be loosened with penetrating oil and careful applications of heat
BENEFIT:	Power increase in portions of rpm range—possibly

Slip-on exhaust systems deliver the racy look of an aftermarket system and (possibly) some of the performance benefits at a significantly lower price than a complete system. Installation is much simpler for novice mechanics, too. One real benefit of a slip-on system is that it can retain auxiliary valves that improve low-end power in factory exhausts.

Although you could install a slip-on with your bike on its side stand, use a rear stand to stabilize it. Before you begin wrenching, take a look at the fasteners securing the stock components you will be removing. With some bikes, such as this R1, you don't even need to remove bodywork. While some bikes will need a little more work, installing this Two Brothers Racing silencer required removing only two parts—the clamp securing the connector pipe to the header, and the bolt attaching the muffler to the passenger footpeg bracket. A quick tap with a rubber mallet, and the OE canister and connector pipe slipped free. Once again, stuck components can be benefit from some WD-40.

Mount the S-bend and any necessary clamps, leaving the clamps loose initially. If the manufacturer requires it, squeeze a bead of high-temperature sealant around the exterior of the pipe approximately a quarter-inch below the lip. Slide the canister over the pipe until it is fully seated on the S-bend. Wipe away any sealant that

When you remove the stock pieces, loosen the clamp securing the connecting pipe first. Then unbolt the muffler and slide it free.

oozes out of the forward edge of the canister. Wrap the muffler clamp around the canister and slip it into position. You may need to rotate oblong mufflers on the S-bend or rotate the connector pipe itself to get the clamp's holes to line up with the footpeg bracket. Tighten the muffler clamp bolt finger tight and check all exhaust parts for proper alignment. When you're satisfied that everything is correct, install any springs and tighten the clamps and bolts.

This R1 didn't require the bodywork to be removed. There is just enough space inside the fairing to tighten the pipe clamp.

The high-temp sealant will keep exhaust gases from leaking forward out of the muffler and possibly discoloring the pipe.

Some systems require that the muffler clamp be secured to the outside of the footpeg bracket. Others need it on the inside. Make sure you follow the instructions, or the pipe may interfere with the swingarm travel.

If you don't have a spring puller, you can easily make one out of a combination wrench and some safety wire.

Cleaning the exterior of the muffler—especially a titanium one—and S-bend is vital before you run the engine. You risk burning any marks into the finish if you don't.

Project 48
Installing a Full Exhaust System

TIME:	1–2 hours
TOOLS:	Wrenches, sockets, universal joint sockets or universal joint socket adapter, 3- to 4-inch extension, Allen keys or Allen sockets, torque wrench, rubber mallet or dead-blow hammer, spring puller, flashlight, high-temperature grease, WD-40, soft cloth or work mat
TALENT:	2
COST:	$$$$$$
PARTS:	Aftermarket exhaust system, exhaust manifold gaskets
TIP:	Tighten fasteners from front to back to ensure you aren't pinching the system cockeyed against the chassis
BENEFIT:	Increased engine performance (possibly)

An exhaust system's primary, historic purpose is to direct stinky, toxic fumes to the back of the vehicle so the operator doesn't have to breathe them. But an exhaust system serves other purposes, too: it quiets the internal combustion engine, it can play a role in the way a vehicle looks, and it also affects performance. The system that came on your bike is your manufacturer's take on what its typical buyer will want in terms of sound, appearance, and performance. Bikers switch pipes to alter any or all of these criteria.

Note that pipes are not purely a restriction on engine power. How gases flow through the system can affect power in different ranges. While straight pipes may be best for full-out drag racing, they actually reduce performance for all-around riding because they provide little exhaust-gas scavenging—the process by which a negative pressure wave travels backward through the system and helps draw out the expended air/fuel charge and draw in a fresh one.

Aftermarket manufacturers can tell you what each of its systems is designed to accomplish. Research carefully—and ideally listen to and try out the system you're considering—before you plunk down your hard-earned greenbacks.

Screw both bolts in finger tight. You want the bolts to pull in evenly on both sides of the manifold. Before reaching for your ratchet, make sure the entire system is installed and in proper position.

Begin by placing your bike in first gear on its side stand. Next, remove any bodywork that will prevent access to the exhaust manifolds. Unbolt the stock muffler from its mounting bracket. If necessary, unbolt the muffler from the collector outlet. You may also find clamps pinching pipe connections. If you have trouble pulling pipe sections apart, try spraying some WD-40

Space can be tight behind the radiator or the rear cylinder. Accessing the manifold nut can be just about impossible if not for a universal joint socket.

Don't forget to wipe down the system completely before you fire it up for the first time. Otherwise, you may get to look at your fingerprints every time you go for a ride.

into the seams and letting it soak a bit. Tapping the offending part in the direction you want it to move with a rubber mallet can also help. You may find expansion chambers tucked away under the bike that need some additional mounts loosened before they'll slide free.

Work your way to the front of the engine. On some bikes you may need to loosen and tilt the radiator or oil cooler up out of the way to give you access to the exhaust manifold nuts (or bolts). You may need a socket with a universal joint to reach the fasteners. Loosen all the manifold nuts before removing them. This will keep the header from falling off while you're unscrewing the rest of the nuts. Once all the nuts are removed, wiggle the header loose from the studs. Make sure to remove all the exhaust manifold gaskets. Sometimes they're hard to see. Use a flashlight to check.

Installing the new system is the reverse of the removal process. Start at the engine and work your way back. Don't secure any fastener more than finger tight until you have the entire system installed and adjusted into its final position. Otherwise, you risk torquing the system in a way that places unwanted forces on it. This could transfer annoying vibrations to the chassis and lead to premature wear (metal fatigue) and failure of your expensive new exhaust system.

Before you mount the headers, secure the manifold gaskets with a dollop of grease. Otherwise, you'll need three hands to hold the gaskets in place while jockeying the header and its assorted flanges into position. When you start the engine, you probably won't even notice the grease burning off, since new exhaust systems smoke

Working your way front to back, install the headers into the muffler. You might not believe it, but it can take some finesse to get everything lined up.

Sometimes just changing the exhaust tip or buying a pipe of a different length will dramatically alter the look of a bike. *Photo courtesy Cobra Engineering*

So many cruiser owners buy drag-style pipes that you might forget that there are a multitude of styles out there. This 2-into-1 megaphone looks good, and you won't see it on every other cruiser you pass. *Photo courtesy Cobra Engineering*

Staggered dualies are another popular style of pipe. Many manufacturers offer a variety of tip styles other than just the slash cut shown here. *Photo courtesy Cobra Engineering*

Aftermarket pipes for some bikes, by virtue of their multiple cylinders, can be pretty pricey. Slip-on systems are a less expensive and just as stylish option. A well made slip-on can make almost as much power as a full system, too. *Photo courtesy Barons Custom Accessories*

Just because pipes usually come in just chrome or stainless steel doesn't mean your custom vision can't incorporate other heat-tolerant finishes. *Photo courtesy Barons Custom Accessories*

on their first run-in anyway. Screw the nuts or bolts so that they are finger tight evenly across the header tubes. You don't want the clamps cockeyed or you may develop exhaust leaks.

Depending on your exhaust system, you'll either install the mufflers individually or in pairs. If you mount both mufflers to a bracket before sliding them into position, keep the bolts loose so you have some wiggle room to attach the canisters to the headers. A spritz of WD-40 on the portion of the pipe that slips inside of the other will make the parts slide easier. Again, this will burn off without you noticing. Once you have the canister(s) attached to the header, you may need to do some jiggling or rotating of the components to get all the mounts to line up correctly. Tighten all nuts and bolts finger tight and check the alignment of the system. You don't want the entire exhaust system to have an unnecessary load on it once you tighten the bolts. Install any retaining springs. Beginning with the manifold nuts or bolts and moving rearward, torque the systems fasteners to spec. Install the header heat shields with their clamps rotated in such a way that they will be out of sight but still within reach of a screwdriver or socket.

Chapter 12
Keeping It Clean

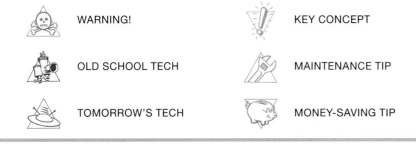

WARNING!

KEY CONCEPT

OLD SCHOOL TECH

MAINTENANCE TIP

TOMORROW'S TECH

MONEY-SAVING TIP

Having a clean, shiny motorcycle in your driveway isn't just a personal feel-good and a fun way to keep other riders envious. It's the best way to preserve the appearance and value of your bike. Ask any motorcycle dealer, new or used, and they'll tell you initial appearance and impression are the number one assets when selling a motor vehicle. Even if you plan on keeping your bike forever, keep it clean, top and bottom, and not only will it look better, it'll last longer too.

BIKE WASH 101
Plan on washing your motorcycle at least once per month or so—more often if you drive on dirt/salty/sandy roads, in winter, near the ocean, or any other highly corrosive environment.

Connect your hose to the hot water outlet in the mud/laundry room if possible. Make sure you're using a motorcycle- or automotive-specific wash product, and not laundry or dish detergent. These household products are too strong for the paint on your bike. If they can remove last night's baked-on lasagna from the dishes and that nasty grease stain from your work shirt, recognize that they will strip the oils and life right out of the paint.

A good bucket, wash mitt or big sponge, and the spray nozzle for your hose are all you need for the job. Oh, yeah, and an armload of clean, dry towels. Thoroughly presoak the entire bike from top to bottom, then it's time to wash. Simple enough, just make sure the painted surfaces are

thoroughly wet, use lots of your bike wash, and rinse your sponge/glove frequently to remove any solid debris. Wash in sections from the top down, rinse frequently, and keep finished sections wet until you've completed the entire job.

Once clean, put those nice dry, fluffy towels to work. Dry thoroughly, including all the trim and bright work.

POLISH AND WAX
After the wash, you might want to polish and wax your bike. All it takes is a shady spot and an hour or so of your time.

First, let's differentiate between polish and wax. Polish is a cleaner designed to remove stubborn dirt and light oxidation. (Oxidation happens when the air dulls the paint.) Wax is a protective coating applied to the paint to repel dirt, grime, and ultraviolet light and to prevent oxidation.

So, if your bike is new, or at least newer, and the paint is still in shiny, like-new condition, just use wax. Modern automotive waxes, whether liquid or paste, are much easier to apply than they were in the past. No longer do you have to rub it on, wait until it dries to a white powder, and then virtually scrub it off with a towel. Now, just wipe the wax on, wait 30 to 60 seconds, and buff it off.

Applying the wax with an electrically powered orbital polisher not only makes the job much easier, but you'll also be the envy of your entire neighborhood. Expect to have to retrieve the polisher from a neighbor every time you want to use it.

Again, you don't have to wait until modern wax is fully dry before buffing it off. The key is a perfectly clean surface and a modern wax or sealant. Sealants tend to incorporate polymers for added protection and that wonderful wet look.

POLISHING YOUR BIKE

But what if your motorcycle's paint isn't quite new anymore? That's where polish comes into play. Polishes are cleaners that can help restore that new look by removing light oxidation that tends to dull the paint. Polishes can also remove buildup or film of road debris, dead bugs, tar, and other junk that sticks to the paint on our motorcycles.

For the enthusiast, it's a 1-2-3 process: wash, polish, wax. For those with somewhat less enthusiasm, shorten the task to a simple 1-2: wash, polish/wax. Products listed as a cleaner/wax are made for precisely this purpose, as they contain both a polish to clean the surface and a wax to protect it. They do an excellent job in both departments, so you don't have to feel guilty about skipping the polish step.

BEGINNERS' DETAILING TIPS

- All your washing and detailing work should be performed in the shade, out of direct sunlight. It should also be a relatively calm, still day. You don't want wind to whip up grit and dust onto the gas tank surface you're waxing, do you? What's more, surfaces on the bike should be cool before you apply cleaning solutions, waxes, or polishes.

- High-quality microfiber towels can be vastly superior to cotton ones. Microfiber towels can remove water spots and smudges with no assistance from cleaners whatsoever. What's more, microfiber towels can dry or buff out wet spots better than cotton or chamois. Microfiber gloves can get into tight spots and around corners easier than anything else.

- For fine scratches, oxidation, and *minor* surface rust on chrome, use a mildly abrasive polish that will remove the slightest amount of metal without breaking through the thin chrome plating. The best of the bunch are the old favorites: Simichrome, Wenol (blue tube), and Flitz. Just go slowly and don't start off using maximum pressure. All three are also excellent for scratches in aluminum.

- Wheels, fork sliders, and engine cases and covers might look like bare metal, but quite often they're coated with clear plastic. Using too harsh a

cleaner will begin to strip the plastic, leaving a leprous-looking finish. Instead, use cleaners/polishes appropriate for plastic or a painted surface.

- You say you're starting to like the results of this wash/wax/detailing gig, but not the amount of time it takes? Cut some corners then, starting with simply getting the bike dry after you wash it. Rather than use wheelbarrow-loads of the ubiquitous clean, dry towels, or even the superduper microfiber ones, get a vacuum blower such as the ones available from Metro. Yes, you *could* use a hair dryer, but it doesn't seem as if it would save you much time.

- Tire makers get all flinchy when you ask them about cleaners and dressings. "No!" they howl. "Soap and water only!" And that's just what their lawyers like to hear. But not everyone likes the dingy yellow-brown color tires can take on. And if you're one of those people, consider tire cleaners from 3M and Mothers. Both manufacturers say their products are quite safe for your tires—and probably for the tire makers' lawyers as well. For dressing, Vinyl and Rubber Dressing from Griot's Garage has no silicone oils or petroleum distillates to harm your tires, or leave a greasy finish.

Project 49

How to Touch Up Paint Scratches and Chips

TIME:	2–4 hours
TOOLS:	Rotary tool and bits; 80-, 120-, and 220-grit sandpaper; 400-grit wet/dry sandpaper; flexible sanding blocks and/or Craftsman 3D Sander; scissors; plastic spreaders, Popsicle sticks, disposable paintbrushes; disposable containers for mixing resins; respirator; latex gloves
TALENT:	1
COST:	$
PARTS:	Fiberglass cloth, fiberglass resin, Plas-Tech repair kit
TIP:	The key to a seamless repair is the final sanding
BENEFIT:	No busted-up seams gumming up aerodynamics

The swoopy aerodynamic bodywork on sportbikes comes at a cost. As anyone who has had to stand by and watch his or her bike tip over can attest, ABS plastic is not very tough. Other easy ways to wreck ABS are over-tightening fasteners or bending or pulling ABS pins out of rubber grommets too quickly. Similarly, the lightweight fiberglass replacement fairings racers use often suffer from pavement abuse. Ruining your expensive bodywork is ridiculously easy.

If you're lucky, cracked or shattered plastic can be easily repaired with minimal visual reminders. In the case of sliding crashes, you're going to have to perform some reconstructive surgery to recapture the fairing's sexy curves. To add insult to already-expensive injury, this type of damage will also require painting. With plastic-repair kits or fiberglass and body filler, the bodywork can look new again—at least from the outside.

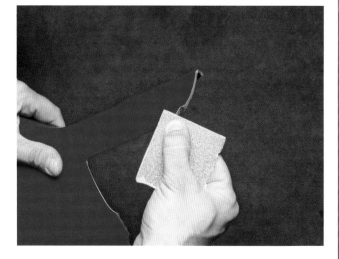

Sand both sides of the edge of the damage with 80-grit sandpaper. Make sure that there are no high points on the break. Do not make the gap wider with your sanding, though.

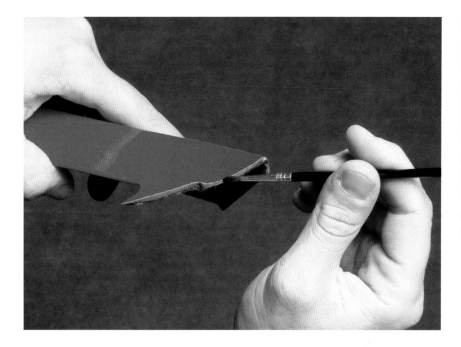

For this project, we'll be using a Plas-Tech repair kit. Before you attempt to repair cracks, wash and dry the bodywork to remove dirt and oils that could disrupt the bonding process. Then, using a small paint-brush, apply the Plastic Weld Accelerator to both sides of the crack. Let this dry for 15–20 seconds. Next, apply a healthy bead of the Plastic Weld Adhesive Gel to one side of the crack. Press the parts together firmly. Make sure they line up, because the adhesive bonds almost immediately.

After the gel solidifies, carefully sand away any excess on the outside of the bodywork with 220-grit sandpaper. Sand down any excess adhesive on the inside with 80-grit sandpaper. Scuff up both sides of the bodywork to prepare for the compound.

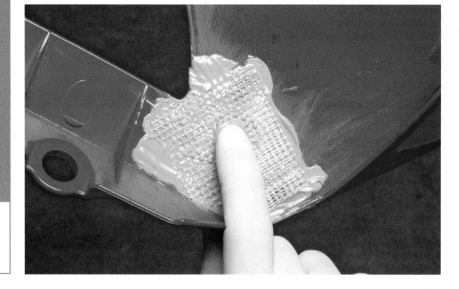

Press the reinforced tape into the repair compound on the back of the bodywork. Add an additional layer of compound over the tape.

Less straightforward breaks in ABS require a little more work. Using 80-grit sandpaper, rough up the back of the broken bodywork. On the seams, sand both sides of the break at an angle so that you expose approximately 1/16 inch of fresh plastic. Sand to a minimum of 1 inch around the opening. Make sure that the edges are lower than the surrounding material so that the filler will have someplace to grip. In other words, you want both sides of the fracture to touch, with the sanded angles creating a V as they taper up to the surface of the panel.

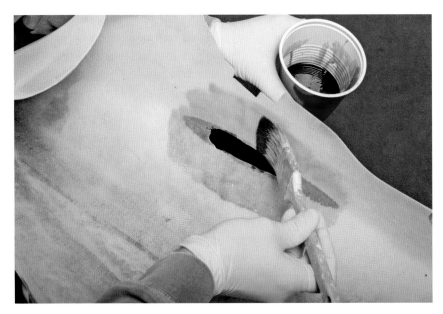

You're going to fill in the V you created on the crack. Without something tying both sides of the crack together, the bodywork would easily break at the same location. A coarse fabric tape combined with body filler will help to bind the two pieces together. Wash and dry the bodywork and glue the break together as described previously. Sand down any excess adhesive with 80-grit sandpaper until it is flush with the surface. Clean off the dust. Measure and cut the fiber tape to a length that allows approximately an inch overlap on all of the cracks. Damage with big holes to fill should be treated the same as with the fiberglass repairs described below. You'll bind the pieces together and then add a filler coat to fix the hole.

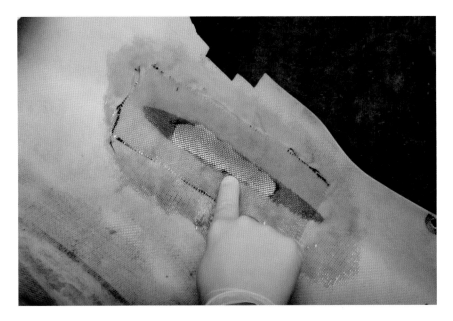

Mix equal parts of the two plastic repair compounds. When the color is uniform, spread it over both sides of the repair. A flexible, plastic spreader will make the job much easier. Smooth the fiberglass fabric until it is wrinkle-free. Make sure no air bubbles are visible between the bodywork and fabric and that the filler extends beyond the break on both sides of the bodywork. Press the fabric tape into the repair compound on the inside of the panel, and then let everything dry. Apply a second coat of plastic repair compound over the fiber tape. Make sure the compound extends at least 1 inch beyond the tape for additional strength.

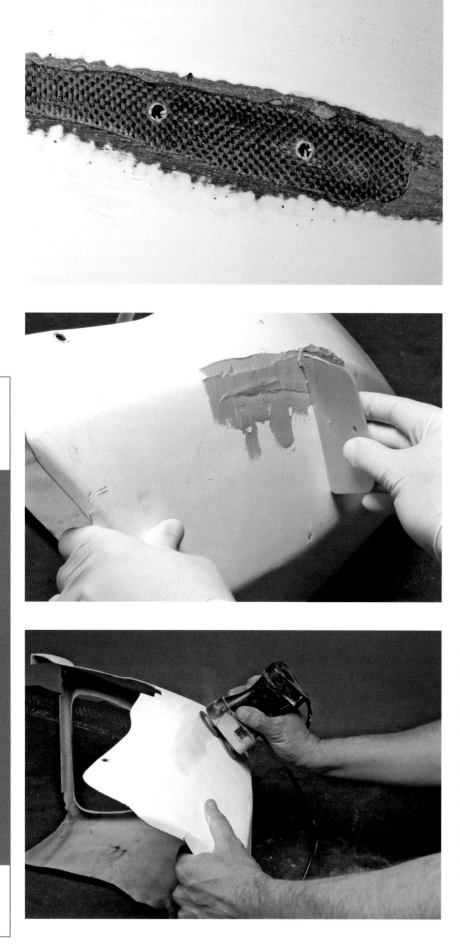

Drill a couple of small holes in the fabric for repairs of more than a couple of square inches. Note how the fabric pattern can still be seen, meaning it wasn't overly saturated with resin.

Move quickly, or the body filler will harden unused. Don't worry if you can see bumps and lines. You'll be sanding the surface down and applying more filler.

After one to two hours of drying time, the repair will be fully hardened. Begin sanding with 120-grit sandpaper. If you find any voids that still need to be filled after the compound has been sanded down, mix up another batch of the filler and spread it thinly over the indentation to fill it. Let it dry, and begin sanding again. Although flexible sanding blocks can give you a mirror-smooth surface, the Craftsman 3D Sander is worth its weight in gold when repairing or painting bodywork. Once you've painted the body panel, you shouldn't be able to tell that the plastic was ever damaged.

Project 50

How to Clean Your Bike

TIME:	4–5 hours
TOOLS:	Bucket, rags, towels, brushes, cleaners, waxes
TALENT:	1
COST:	$
PARTS:	Plastic bags and rubber bands to keep water out
TIP:	Rather than think front to back, think top to bottom
BENEFIT:	Increased compliments per mile

You can't keep your bike new forever. But you can keep it clean, and a suitable amount of attention to basic cosmetic upkeep can make your sled look as good as new, even decades down the road.

The place to start is with a standard hand wash. Avoid coin-operated cleaning, because the caustic chemicals in the detergent aren't good for most surfaces, and there's a real problem if the stuff sneaks into brakes, wheel bearings, carbs, and electrics. Don't go there! Stick with a bucket full of proper car/motorcycle wash, some sponges and rags, and good old elbow grease.

Speaking of grease, if your bike is especially dirty or greasy, you'll need degreaser to get rid of the heavy stuff. Try to find a good solvent that will not harm your paint; degreasers with bleach or reactive chemicals could cause hazing and bubbling of the paint. Be careful how and where you try these before you glop them all over the sled. Cosmoline remover dissolves just about everything and will not harm the paint. Gunk is an emulsifier that turns grease into water-soluble foam and works brilliantly, if you can get past the smell.

If your bike has been rolling around in the mud, try a soft bristle brush or toothbrush. Bugs are best removed with plain soap and water and gentle applications of one of those nylon sponge scrubber things you use on dishes—be careful to use mild abrasive versions; the coarse ones can scratch paint and plastic. By the way, good carnauba wax will help prevent bugs and stuff from sticking to your bike in the first place.

If you plan on applying anticorrosion or dressing products, do this before the final wash; it makes a mess! After shampooing and scrubbing your bike, dry it with clean towels or a chamois. Next, polish the frame. Protect All (a good spray-on polish) works well here. Be sure to let it haze over, then buff it out to avoid streaks. You can use S100 here, as well, or any spray polish you have faith in, for that matter, but frames are a bear to do with paste wax, so stick with something logical. It's the most tedious task of the bunch, but when the frame looks good, it makes everything else look better.

One reason chrome stays popular in the Harley world is that it's dead easy to keep clean. Any proprietary chrome polish will make good chrome look great in minutes. If your chrome has started to pit, (A) you waited too long to clean and seal it, (B) hard rubbing with a piece of tinfoil or the finest steel wool can clean it up surprisingly well.

Next, move onto the paint. For heavy scratches and oxidation, use an electric buffer and very little pressure; let the tool do the work. Routine waxing by hand with carnauba is the single best thing you can do for factory paintwork. Carnauba is a natural wax that can be cleaned off and stripped back to the paint without difficulty, so if you need to repair a blemish, you can get at it. Silicone-based waxes aren't so friendly.

Finish the job with a good leather (or vinyl) cleaner and conditioner on the seat, and properly dress the sides of the tires—avoiding getting anything slick on the tread.

The weekend project of choice for most proud owners is a thorough clean and shine. To do that takes as many special tools as anything mechanical. You need a variety of cleansers and polishes to go with that tube of elbow grease. Using all of them, you can have the bike sparkling from the chrome to the vinyl and everywhere in between in no time (OK, six to eight hours; it's a labor of love isn't it?). Oh, one word about wax. Fresh virginal paint with no blemishes whatsoever can be waxed with silicone-based products. It seals the surface so well, however, that it will trap anything under the wax like a fly in amber. That's why official Harley-Davidson wax is carnauba based without silicones. Carnauba can be buffed back to clean out those little imperfections, and then a rewax keeps the shine without keeping the dirt trapped.

INDEX

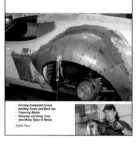
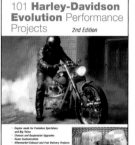

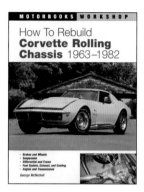
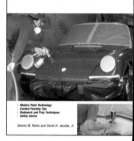